MINDS IN BATTLE

SHERIF BENHAWY

NOTEBOOK

PUBLISHING

This is not a novel. Life is already a live fiction.

First published in 2020 by Notebook Publishing,
20–22 Wenlock Road, London, N1 7GU.

www.notebookpublishing.com

ISBN: 9781913206338

A CIP catalogue record for this book is available
from the British Library.

Typeset by Notebook Publishing.

Doubtless, everyone is at war: every time you get out of bed, go in to work, engage with those you care about and love, interact with the society, or you're required to complete a task, it is a battle—countless battles every day. I came to believe that we are built to fight physically, mentally, and emotionally; *never* to relax.

And,

When what was once predictable becomes unpredictable;

When what you were certain of now appears to be smoke in the air;

When what you were holding that seemed solid now dissolves to dust in your hand;

When things seemed to blur you suddenly realize were so obvious all along;

Then you have arrived at a place on your journey whose name you need to know.

I warmly dedicate this book to the most wonderful woman I have ever met—my precious, darling wife—and my two children. I may be my own man, but I wouldn't be the man I am without you. You are the reason this is my life's work.

In loving memory of the precious souls that I lost during the early stages of my life:

My mother;

My father;

My brother;

My grandma.

Their loss dug a hole in my soul.

WHY THIS BOOK?

Some stories allow themselves to be told—and, when they decide to be told, they choose the storytellers.

I didn't choose the topic I am going to write about; it chose me.

It all started with a bizarre, hard-hitting dream, from which I awoke startled. It was after such an event that the characters and their events in this book compelled themselves to be written, shouting at me from my unconscious and thrusting their way into my conscious, exclaiming, "Here we are! Be attentive to everything we want to say, and write it down judiciously. You don't have to write a fiction, for we are the reality."

Minds in Battle is a book born from a powerful, persistent, and all-encompassing voice that screamed in my head—a voice that had been previously screaming in a void, but had now found its way to be heard. Its message is for me, for you, and for many of the people I know and I love. I write it as a self-guide and a tribute for all our paths of self-discovery in these shifting, stormy times. I deeply relate to the characters and their events, for they have emerged from an eventful journey of deep observation of myself and others, and it is thus real emotions that they struggle with behind closed doors.

Many of us have not had an easy life, riddled with disappointments and disillusionment; barraged by loss and betrayal; besieged with far too many occasions for sadness and despair. We have been forced to learn how to navigate through the unexpected—on our own and for long periods—, and many of us have not *yet* learnt the lessons that life has always tried to give to us. Unsurprisingly, life gives many of us these lessons for free through the mistakes of others, but, arrogantly and ignorantly, we refuse to observe and learn from them; we wrongly assume our experiences are different and better, in turn forming the assumption that we would be able to avoid repeating others' mistakes. Unsurprisingly, that rarely happens; our emotion-driven nature urges us to experience the drama ourselves!

What a piece of work is a man! How noble in reason! How infinite in faculty!
In form and moving, how express and admirable! In action, how like an
angel! In apprehension, how like a god! The beauty of the world, the paragon
of animals.

—From *Hamlet* (Act II, Scene 2)

Shakespeare is not alone in his appreciation for the human mind: in fact, we all think of ourselves along the lines of Shakespeare's depiction (although we quickly realize our neighbors, spouses, and bosses don't always live up to this standard). These assumptions concerning the human ability for perfect reasoning have found their way into most scientific domains. This very basic idea—*rationality*—provides the foundation for multiple scientific theories, predictions, and recommendations. Of course, Shakespeare's view is largely correct: our minds and bodies are capable of amazing acts, and so a feeling of awe at the capability of human is clearly justified; however, there is a large difference between a deep sense of admiration and the assumption that our reasoning abilities are perfect.

After thousands of years—since human existence on this planet—, even with the astonishing technological, social, and cultural evolutions we have witnessed, we still repeat the same mistakes. How could we be *so* wrong, considering the vastness of the human experience and the range of choices available to us? We cannot generalize and consider the behavior of all individuals as being due to maliciousness, stupidity, or neglect; rather, we are all most likely the victims of inherent biases in our perception of others, such as those of life, religion, and more—biases that apparently weren't altered even by our vast experience and premium education. Therefore, we tend to repeat mistakes without being able to learn much from our own experiences—or, indeed, others'.

The fact that we repeat the same mistakes we have been making for thousands of years with little learning drives us to think about the idea of us being irrational—and the fact of the matter is that we *are*. The fact that we repeat the same mistakes in almost the same ways drives us to think about the idea that our irrationality is *predictable*—it happens in the same way again and again. They are *systematic*, and, since we repeat them again and again, they are predictable. Therefore, we are *predictably irrational*.

Regardless of whether we are acting as independent social individuals, parents, students, consumers, businesspeople, or policymakers, we tend to behave with multiple forces simultaneously exerting their influences on us—and this complexity makes it difficult to figure out exactly how *each* of these forces individually shapes our behavior.

Unsurprisingly, when we are being asked about who or what has had the most meaningful influence on our transformational journey, we always give the same answer: "Painful experience."

Our life has been made "transformationally eventful" for a reason—and a good reason, indeed. Therefore, never think that it can't happen to you. Just assume that it will happen at some time.

MINDS IN BATTLE

Is there a soul that has not been battered,
Or a body that feels at ease?
Is there a dream that has not been shattered,
Or a pride not driven to its knees?
Is there a mind that has not been tattered,
Or a life to be lived in peace?
Is there a heart that has not been swallowed up by worry and pain,
Or not trying to heal their bitter and festering wounds?

A MILLION YEARS OR so ago, man roamed the earth much like any other beast: instinct moved him to seek food to remain alive, and to defend his life. As with other forms of animal life, he obeyed nature's voiceless command to procreate, and, thus, the human race went on in much the same way as that of other races. Slowly, man's mind found ample engrossment in pursuit of food and the evasion of danger, and, gradually, he achieved an easier pursuit and a more effective evasion. For the first time—perhaps unfortunately—, he had time to sit down and think.

It was this thinking—and not the fall of Adam from heaven—that started all the trouble in his life. Through the workings of his mind— which proved superbly better than the minds of his cousin beasts—, man created all sorts of evil: gender seduction; weapons of mass destruction; junk food; rude arts; genocide; racism; clumsy games; mind-controlling sciences (e.g., media; marketing; psychology; consumerism); and all forms of technology that proved to be valuable as well as wicked. His life grew apace, and it was still growing at a faster pace than he could catch up with.

PROLOGUE

GOD KNEW THAT HUMAN beings couldn't live alone. Before anything in the world had gone wrong—even in a place was as perfect as Paradise—, humans needed each other. God let Adam asleep and then sculpted a woman from his bone and flesh so that he would find a partner.

Why was this sculpted human being not another man like Adam? Why was it a woman? Isn't it logic to create the same gender so they can live happily together, with no potential conflict? Both would have the same physical shape, matching interests, close way of thinking, perfect understanding to the needs of each other, no power exploitation from one over the other, and, most importantly, no sexual relationship.

Reproduction of the human race would be the easiest answer to this question; however, I believe that there is another important answer to this question—one that you could perhaps discover alone, throughout your journey in this book.

We were created from the same source, and yet, in some ways, we spend our lives trying to work out how to achieve the oneness God originally planned for us. God's ideal plan was for the man and woman to live together, in synchronization—not in competition. Each of them was created with weaknesses that should have been balanced by the strengths of the other partner—and, to live in synchronization, men and women were supposed to consider the needs of one another in order to try to fulfill them as if they were his/her own needs. We were supposed to live with our individual differences and see them as assets—not problems that required solutions, or differences that need to be equalized. Indeed, modern society's culture of "me first" was not in the ideal plan; prioritizing self-desires and needs over the other party wasn't the pathway to the happiness of living together.

When considering the cruelest and most impactful of all wars, the war of sexes has, in varying degrees, disabled half of the world's population and impoverished the other half's sensitivities, emotions, feelings, and imagination.

Nothing is absolutely true of all women or all men: in some areas, men's behavior resembles that of most women, and vice versa; therefore, any discussion on gender differences in this book has the potential to bring howls of protest and rejection from feminists and gender equality activists as a result of it being perceived as undermining fair and equal gender opportunity. However, whilst the prejudices of society may reinforce and exacerbate stereotypical behavior in males and females, the stereotypes in and of themselves are not the sole cause of the behavior.

Thousands of years ago, power was mostly gained through physical violence and maintained with brute strength. There was little need for subtlety; only a select few had power. No one suffered under this state of mercilessness more than women: they had no means to compete, no weapon at their disposal that could force a man do what they wanted—politically, socially, or even in the home. However, men still possessed one weakness: their insatiable desire for sex.

A woman could always toy with this desire, but once she gave in to sex, the man was back in control; and if she withheld sex, he could simply look elsewhere—or, of course, exert force. Hence, a power so temporary and frail was the only weapon women wielded. However, there were some whose hunger for power was too great, and who, over the years—through much cleverness and creativity—invented a way of turning the dynamic around, creating a more lasting and effective form of power. Perhaps the greatest example of all of this is that of Cleopatra, who invented the art of seduction: she would first draw a man in with an alluring appearance, designing her makeup and adornment to fashion the image of a goddess materialized. Further, by showing only glimpses of her flesh, she would tease a man's imagination, stimulating the desire not just for sex, but also for something greater: the chance to possess a fantasy figure. Once she had her victim's interest, she would lure him away from the masculine world of war and politics and get them to spend time in the feminine world—a world of luxury, spectacle, and pleasure.

Men would grow hooked on these refined, sensual pleasures, and would quickly fall in love; but then, invariably, the women would turn cold and indifferent, confusing her victims: just when the men wanted more, they found their pleasures withdrawn. They would hence be forced into pursuit, trying anything to win back the favors they had once tasted, growing weak and emotional in the process. Men who possessed so much physical force and all the social power in the world would find themselves becoming the slave of a woman. Julius Caesar was one who was totally captured and enslaved by the seduction of Cleopatra.

In the face of violence and brutality, these women made seduction a sophisticated art—the ultimate form of power and persuasion they could use against men. They learned to work on the mind first, stimulating fantasies, keeping a man wanting more and creating patterns of hope and despair—the essence of seduction. Their power was not physical, but psychological; not forceful, but indirect and cunning. Women became expert seductresses, comparable to military generals planning the destruction of an enemy. Seduction was compared to battle, the feminine version of warfare. Cleopatra used seduction not for sexual gratification, but as a means of consolidating her empire and to gain more power. In seduction, the woman was no longer a passive sex object: she became an active agent, a figure of power.

Meanwhile, men didn't much concern themselves with such a frivolous art as seduction—that is, until the seventeenth century, when men grew interested in seduction as a way to overcome a young woman's resistance to sex. History's first great male seducers—namely the Duke de Lauzun, the different Spaniards who inspired the Don Juan legend—began to adopt the methods traditionally employed by women. They learned to dazzle with their appearance, to stimulate the imagination, and to play the coquette, also adding a new, masculine element to the game: seductive language. They had discovered a woman's weakness for soft words, as well as the weakness of a woman's ears. These two forms of seduction—the feminine use of physical appearance, and the masculine use of language—would often cross gender lines: Casanova would dazzle a woman with his clothes; Ninon de L'Enclos would charm a man with her words.

Therefore, oppression and scorn have generally been the share of women in emerging societies. This state lasted in all its force until centuries of experience taught women to substitute skill for force. Here, women at last sensed that, since they were weaker, their only resource was to seduce; they understood that if they were dependent on men through force, men could become dependent on them through pleasure.

With time, women learned to veil their charms in order to awaken curiosity, practicing the difficult art of refusing even when they wished to consent. From that moment on, women knew how to set men's imaginations alight: they knew how to arouse and direct desires as they pleased. It was here that beauty and love come into being. Now, a lot of women became less harsh—not because they had managed to liberate themselves entirely from the state of oppression to which their weakness condemned them, but because of the state of perpetual war that continues to exist between women and men.

The real and deadliest of wars is the one that involves minds fighting with beliefs. The atomic bomb is far less harmful.

MYTH

Every story has five sides: his perception, her perception, others' perception, the cultural myth feeding these perceptions, and the truth that is lost in-between.

THERE ARE TWO WAYS of looking at a fiction (myth): we can either consider it as a deviation from fact, or as an approximation to fact. Fact must always be the criterion, and, when the facts are under control, we can emphasize the degree of deviation. However, when we are out of touch with the facts, we utilize fiction to explain the unexplainable by some sort of approximation to it.

It is the interplay of fact and fiction that is so important to the discussions in this book: if there were not some truth in a cultural myth, it would quickly lose its power. The extent to which the facts are under control, however, is often unclear: when a logical base is clouded, a fear of the unknown often sets in to cement the myth.

Let us look at this phenomenon through a popular target of antimyth feminists. The myth here takes the form, "A child needs a mother's love." The element of truth in this myth is, of course, that a child needs nurturing—and, since the mother has traditionally been the person at home with the child, combined with the fact that mothers usually both nurture and love their children, the deviation from the fact became, "A child needs a mother's love." However, now that it has become more obvious that fathers and other caring adults certainly can nurture children on different levels, the logical base of this myth has been questioned—and yet a fear of the unknown has led to the continued cementation the myth for many mothers who do not want to risk breaking tradition with their own children. It is only as more women risk the consequences that the fictitious quality of this situation becomes more obvious.

The Cognitive Dissonance Concept: The unpleasant emotion generated by the simultaneous existence of mutually exclusive beliefs—whether they are facts or just mere myths. The human mind has an innate drive to maintain consistency between its pre-existing attitudes and beliefs and the new information it receives. It is the tendency to reject or downplay new information that contradicts other, more favorable views, about oneself or one's state of affairs. The mind filters out much information that is inconsistent with one's prior beliefs.

No wonder, then, that many of us still hang onto myths, convincing ourselves that they are, indeed, facts.

SOVEREIGNTY AND DERAILMENT

The sovereignty of one's self over one's self is called liberty. —Albert Pike

WHAT DO YOU DO when you wake up one morning to realize that all what you have done and achieved so far in your life is useless; unaccounted for; the majority turning out to be wrong; all ultimately leading you to a different place than that you planned to be in, or even wished to one day go to?

What do you do when you realize your old map has taken you in a direction you no longer wish to travel? What do you do if you come to a fork in the road and don't know which way to go? What do you do when life forces you to face the unexpected? What do you do when you find yourself forced to confront obstacles you did not expect to encounter, and feeling emotions you did not expect to feel?

Somehow, your plan for how you intended things to turn out seems to have been replaced by a set of circumstances you could never have imagined.

When you have no clue where to even begin, how do you map out the next part of your journey? What do you do when you have lost sight and don't know how to redesign the blueprint of your life? How do you begin again?

It is here that we reach a dead end—that is, when we realize how wrong we have been.

The Confirmation Bias Concept: It leads us to hunt for information that flatters our existing beliefs. Confirmation bias is stronger in emotion-laden domains such as religion, romance, politics, marriage, social interaction, or when people have a strong underlying motive to believe something.

From the Author's Diary:

Like many others, I always consider myself clever and capable.

Yesterday, in my dream, I had an early end-of-life interview with God.

I was in the middle of nowhere: the infinite and the emptiness. I was standing still, staring into the void, looking for cues to help me understand where I was—all I was able to see being the vast, desolate space lying before my eyes. Time seemed nonexistent as I sat alone in a light-dominated massive void, unable to determine whether I was in the present or the future. It was a struggle to adjust to my new environment whilst anxiously anticipating my upcoming interview, and, in this endless space, thousands of questions bubbled in my mind and paralyzed my thinking: just thinking about what could go wrong in this interview wouldn't help a damn bit in anything, except perhaps inflating my anxiety. Therefore, I promptly decided to direct my full focus on rehearsing the answers to the questions I was anticipating to be asked. However, because I had been captured by the space sightseeing, my organs all of sudden stopped functioning, my eyes my only functioning organ. I knew my time had come when I saw the light beginning to shimmer, dazzling my gaze and blinding my sight completely. Darkness and light became one interminable timespan of nothingness. I was thrown in a complete disconnect.

The interview had started.

"So, tell me, how do you think you did?" asked God.

I released an enormous, anxiety-filled sigh of relief to hear this question—the one question I was sure I could answer. Feeling confident, I began to speak.

"I have prepared a list of my accomplishments. I wanted to have my own business and become financially successful—well-off—, and I did that. I wanted to have a successful marriage, so I stayed married until now. I wanted to put my children through university, and so that's where I sent them. I wanted to own a luxurious home, and so I bought one. I wanted to travel to as many new places as I could, and so I went to as many places as I could. I wanted to play guitar and pursue all my hobbies, and I took steps to complete such a goal. I wanted to be liked and admired by as many people as possible, so I treated people well and with respect. I wanted to create a self-branding and be perceived as a smart, honest, tolerating, humble, firm, nurturing, and inspiring kind of person, and I do believe I have partially achieved that." A pause as I racked my brain. "Oh, and I donated to worthy causes and poor people on a regular basis."

I felt quite satisfied with myself, hearing my own weighted list. Certainly, God was going to be impressed: I was an achiever, no doubt.

"I would say, without intending to sound immodest, that I did very well, considering I accomplished most of the things I set out to do," I went on. "But, of course, since you are God, you knew all of this already; I'm not telling you anything new."

God smiled amiably at me. "Actually, you are mistaken."

"Mistaken?" I echoed quietly, surprised. "I don't understand."

"You are mistaken," God repeated gently. "Because what I wanted to know, and what mattered to me, is not the goals you have achieved."

The flare of panic in my eyes exposed my shock, but I pressed on. "You weren't? But I thought..."

"I know," God interjected. "Everyone thinks the better life goes, the more successful their life is—but it doesn't work that way up here. It doesn't matter to me that you've got what you expected and hoped for, for that wouldn't tell me much about what you were learning in your earthly existence. It wouldn't tell me much to what extent you would think of my presence during your difficult times. It wouldn't tell me much if you really believed in me—in my tolerance to forgive your sins, in my power, and in my awareness of every single detail of your life. I was watching you most closely during all those difficult times when you encountered the unexpected—the things you didn't plan on or wanted to happen—, and it is such difficult times that matter to me—not the good times. You see, it's how you dealt with the unplanned difficulties that reflects the growth and wisdom of your soul. That is the purpose of life. When you achieve what you had planned for, you fool yourself by believing in your power—but when the unexpected adversities shatter your soul and bring you to your knees, that's when I start counting your efforts to survive. I consider the how, not the how many or how much."

Stunned silence prevailed. I had gotten it all wrong; I had spent my whole life trying to do everything right. Had I been tricked into thinking achievement was the measurement of success when evaluating one's life? How could that even be possible? All the inspiring and motivational speeches, books, and seminars had educated me on the fact that achievement reflected my worth in life, but no one had taught me that my adversities and setbacks were the ones to be counted in the other life, rather than my successes and achievements.

"Well, to tell the truth, God, I was just being thankful and polite," I countered. "I didn't want to seem annoyed and tell you that I hated my life; it was hell! What hardships, what disappointments, what tests and trials! Let me tell you about the times when I lost my belief in you—my belief in your superpower that could have restored things to normality. When things went from bad to worse, I totally gave up on your existence. I lost hope! I'd been asking myself why it should all happen to me. What had I done wrong? Why had my sufferings been endless? The minute I thought one misery was over, the next took place. Why has always been the question rushing through my mind."

It was then that I awoke in complete shock: my breath had stopped in my throat, and it felt like my heart was shriveling up. The interview has remained stuck in my mind for more days than I can count as I have tried to mull it over from different perspectives.

In one way or another, many others are like me in my little fable: we do our best in life to get things right. We make lists, set goals, study, train, learn, commit to our relationships and our dreams, get organized, pray, affirm, and problem-solve—all in pursuit of experiencing the happiness and success we imagine for ourselves. Yet, inevitably, all of us arrive at times when, in spite of how steadfastly we have worked, how well we have prepared, how deeply we have loved, things still don't turn out the way we thought they would. No matter how hard we try, we cannot plan for the unexpected.

Whether these difficult surprises come in the form of small setbacks, horrible shocks, or gradual, painful awakenings, the result is the same: we end up face-to-face with moments of unwelcome revelation, when we realize, to our great dismay, that we are living a life that doesn't look like the one we wanted, often rendering us shaken, disoriented, and desperate for answers.

Some weeks before that interview, I had been struck by the idea of writing this book: I was going through some of my old notebooks in my safe, and I discovered a page where I had written a list of my personal goals and dreams. As I read the items on the wish list, I was astonished to find two things: the first was the fact that I had, indeed, accomplished a handful of the goals I had set for myself; and the second was my sudden awareness of the amount of unexpected things had happened to me since that certainly were not on my original wish list. Despite the fact that I couldn't recollect ever setting these events as goals, they had occurred just the same.

Then, it dawned on me: I had always believed my challenges would lie in overcoming the obstacles to my goals, but that wasn't true; my deepest turmoil and real-life tests had nothing to do with the things I didn't get, but, rather, with the things I didn't expect, and got anyway.

I have realized that so much of the pain, confusion, and unhappiness most of us struggle with derives from our encounters with the unexpected—in both our outer and inner worlds. Try as we might, these encounters are inescapable—an inevitable part of being human. This doesn't change the fact that we often feel we are the only one whose life is off-course or inexplicably unsatisfying, harboring the belief that everyone else's is deliriously happy. However, the truth is something quite different: all of us are lifetime warriors in a prolonged battle with change, all possessing reluctant endings and scary beginnings, featuring assessments and reassessments, with more moments of disappointment than we care to count.

One saying I have come to know by heart:

If you get rid of the pain before you have answered its questions, you get rid of the self along with it.

—Carl Jung

The dreams and wish list of my youth triggered me to go over all my old diaries, in which I had recorded my observations, stories, experiences, readings, and learnings. I realized that these old yellow pages held stories worth revealing, packed with lessons worth sharing, loaded with personal thoughts worth reevaluation. Hence, whilst doing so, I started to search for answers to the questions clamoring in my head.

I realized that my end-of-life dreams reflect, somehow, on Peter and Olivia's derailment—the heroes of this live story. However, the difference exists in the fact that their story is live, while mine is just a dream.

PETER NELSON

I AM IN A period of my life in which the saying "The mass of men leads lives of quiet desperation" is applicable: my mind is lost in a sea of negativity, and is overwhelmed at the position I find myself in. As I had started to share my story of personal failure and setbacks with the men closest to me, I began to realize a disturbing trend: the majority of men—although they are good at burying it— are also leading lives of desperation. The one metric that drew my attention was the alarming rate of suicide in the male gender; several studies suggest that suicide rates amongst men are up to three times higher than that amongst women.

Odds are that you or someone you know is experiencing anxiety, depression, and suicidal thoughts—and what makes matters worse is the fact that there is an unwritten rule stating that you and I, as men, are not supposed to talk about our weaknesses, struggles, and shortcomings—because we are men. When things go wrong, everyone looks to the man; when there's no money coming into the household, people look to the man; when there's an emergency or disaster, people look to the man. Makes sense, right? After all, men are supposed to have it all figured out—and if we don't have things under control, we'll be led to believe we're not as manly as we're supposed to be. So, instead, we walk around with a happy face, puffing out our chests and putting up an emotional wall. We pretend we don't have emotions, that nothing gets to us, until we die.

I have been dreading going to work for a while, and it was recently that I finally admitted the truth to myself: I have been miserable because I hate what I do for a living. I don't understand how this could be happening; I spent years in business school, did my masters, and own a really successful practice. I make a good living: I have excess money to save, travel, and enjoy my life—which is what I always planned to achieve. And yet I just don't want to do it anymore. I am really frightened; I can't start life over in my forties. How did I get here?

In March 2015, I gave away my sovereignty, the result being a broken man sobbing alone in a cold, dark room—a room in the house my wife and I had built together several years earlier. In that room, I was hanging onto a memory of the family I had driven away—a picture of a husband, wife, and their two children. Through my tears, I told the children in that picture that I would find a way to get them back.

Leading up to that event, I had spent several years giving away my sovereignty—as well as all the power that goes with it—to my wife, my employer, the economy, society, my peers, the government, and anyone and anything else that placed itself between what I wanted and where I am. The demise of my sovereignty manifested itself in the lies and excuses I fabricated to justify my lackluster business, my poor health, and my failing marriage.

I didn't believe it could possibly have anything to do with me; I'm a man. I'm the man. I'm supposed to have all this figured out. And yet here I am with my business, marriage, and world crumbling around me. I am alone in that dark room, shattered by the world I created for myself—or, more accurately, what I have given away to others.

Just a few months earlier, my wife—Olivia—and I got into a row: the many years of disagreements and discontent had come to a boiling point that evening, to the point where the words "I don't even want to be married to you anymore" slipped out of her mouth, and mine in response.

She agreed. And I was gone.

For some time, I blamed her; it had to be her fault, too. It couldn't possibly be mine alone; I'm the man, after all. I was bringing home an income. I was growing a career. I bought her a home.

From the outside, I was doing it all right; I had this all figured out. But it became apparent that I didn't. I don't remember why or how, but as I was on a drive one day, I came to the conclusion that would alter the course of my marriage, my career, and my life. For the first time during my separation with Olivia, I told myself the truth concerning the fact that our marriage may be over—and, if this were the case (as much as I hated to admit it), I resolved to be the greatest catch for the next woman to come into my life.

That's when it all clicked for me: I had been blaming her, but what I'd failed to realize was that my blaming her meant I was also giving her all the power I had once possessed to make something of myself. You see, if it was her fault, then all I could do was wait for her to do something about it—and that's why I felt so powerless. Because I was.

The moment I began to accept responsibility for my part in the demise of our relationship, the more I began to wrestle control back in my life; the more I faced the reality that I had been inadequate in our marriage, my career, and my life, the more I gave myself the power to do something about it.

Loss Aversion Concept: Peter found his losses more painful than his gains pleasant. People act as though losses are from two-to-four times more painful than gains are pleasurable: we set ourselves up for loss aversion almost instantly. Imagine that I offered you the chance to play a game: we'll flip a coin, and if it lands on heads, you'll win $100; and if it lands on tails, you owe me $50. Would you play?

Losing sovereignty leads to derailment—and derailment means I lose sight, and definitely my battle.

What is sovereignty? Perhaps it's better to start by illustrating what sovereignty is not. To do that, you don't have to look very far: take a walk around your neighborhood, or a stroll around your office. Have a conversation with your buddies. Everywhere you look, you'll find the signs of men and women who have neglected their responsibilities and, in turn, have given up their sovereignty—or, in other words, the power they inherently have to control the outcome of their lives.

Peter is no different: he's no longer in control of his heart and mind. He has traded his individual liberty and personal responsibility for a decent marriage, a steady paycheck, and a relatively painless life—and in doing so, he has unknowingly enslaved himself to his marriage, his job, and his government.

The shackles Peter willingly submitted himself to are hard to quantify; if they were easily spotted, he wouldn't have been so willing to give up his freedoms. These shackles come in the form of a marriage with potential, a skyrocketing salary, a huge retirement package, and the promise of safety and security, all in exchange for just a small percentage of their paycheck.

Because Peter gave up his sovereignty, he fabricated excuses; told himself stories. He fed himself lies, all to justify the reality—the reality that he had given away the one thing that had the potential to allow him to be the human he was meant to be. His sovereignty.

Unfortunately, it's easy to maintain the status quo; after all, the truth—that Peter was living in a cloud of delusion, magnified by a silent attack on the very traits that make him human—was hard to bear. This cloud of delusion made everything feel real: Peter felt as if he commanded his mind, followed his heart, and took control of his body. He felt as if he was in charge—but, ultimately, he was being controlled and manipulated by some outside forces he couldn't quite seem to see or understand.

However, if we look deeper—beyond the thick cloud of delusion—, we already know that, don't we? We can feel it lingering in the back of our consciousness, and, as much as we can't yet wrap our heads around it, we know it's there.

The first step toward sovereignty is to lift the cloud of delusion. This is not easy, nor is it pleasant—but it's a necessity if one has any chance of overcoming the nagging thought that their life is not their own, or that they know they are destined for more but don't know quite how to wrap their heart, mind, and hands around it. This is about control; about ownership. This is about facing the ugly reality that we aren't as good as we think we are, and that the life we live today is not the one we're meant to live.

It's painfully obvious that the sovereign human is becoming a rare breed. Take a look around society, and you'll see the results of a lack of sovereign people. The family unit is under attack; more and more young men and women are growing up without fathers or mothers; crime is running rampant; businesses are failing; leadership at every level—from the home to the boardroom to the city, state, and governments—is all but nonexistent. Nowadays, everybody is thinking on how to shrink their responsibilities for the path of the least resistance.

Blindness Concept: The masses have never thirsted after truth: they demand illusions, and cannot do without them. They constantly give unreal precedence over what is real; they are almost as strongly influenced by what is untrue as by what is true. And they have an evident tendency to not distinguish between the two.

OLIVIA MEADOWS

I ZIPPED UP MY skirt and turned to look at myself in the mirror. Six months ago, I wouldn't have been able to get the grey herringbone skirt over my hips, and now, I can slide into it with ease. Five months of severe diet protocol has worn my once-plump thighs and hips down a dress size. Five months ago, I divorced Peter.

I can't help feeling smug: when Peter comes to pick up the kids tomorrow, I'll go outside and talk to him—something I've avoided doing—just to show him how good I look now. Whenever he picks the kids up at lunchtime on Saturdays, they run out the front door with their overnight bags, and yet I never venture out to say hello. When he brings them home on Sunday evenings before seven, I sit in the sitting room, keeping an eye out for his car so I know when to open the front door for the kids. I haven't actually seen Peter for at least five weeks.

We've talked on the phone, of course—cool conversations, and sometimes rude, with lots of silences and plenty of "anyways".

I know I've sometimes been vicious during those calls—full of bitterness I thought I'd managed to conceal for so long. But I couldn't help myself; I wanted to hurt Peter, and I'd used the kids to do it. It hurt me so much that they were calling another place home—Jennifer's home, the bitch that hangs around with Peter.

In most of our phone calls, his voice is hollow and exhausted. He's still always managed to control his temper with me, though—as he always did during our marriage. He deserves a trophy for how much control he possesses over his emotions. "Emotionless! Rock-solid heart," I had always accused him.

Guilt at my bitterness is overwhelming me, all the time. I've been a nasty, manipulative bitch—everything I've hated in other people—, and Peter didn't deserve one bit of it. He didn't phone me for two weeks; he'd talk to the kids directly and ignore me. At least he had the chance to forget what I'd said before: I'm not proud of my shrieking.

Damn me. I never meant to let myself down so much.

Now, I've got the chance to show him how much I've changed, what I've achieved. He'll get a bit of a shock to see his ex-wife isn't the same old drudge anymore. The sight of Olivia Meadows, career woman, will certainly take him by surprise. Not that I'm exactly that—a career woman—, but let him admire my new figure, my increased self-confidence, and my air of calm. I certainly feel more confident about lots of things, but unfortunately my confidence wavers when I need it most—specifically, with Nick. Losing nearly three-quarters of a stone has given me more energy, as well as a smidgeon of my old self-assurance. Dealing with all kinds of problems with my clients and my boss has also given me a sense of job satisfaction—a kind that cleaning the oven in Peter's house never did.

But everything falls to pieces when it comes to Nick, my new date.

As part of an advanced scuba-diving certification, where Nick was the instructor of the program, the requirement of a night-dive loomed for me as the final and dreaded item on the checklist: although I'm very comfortable in and around water, night-diving initially deprives us of an essential sense-sight. Nick insisted that night-diving is a wonderful experience—"Seventy-five percent of sea life is nocturnal; tonight, you'll barely believe your eyes!"—, but I was uncertain.

At first, I was like a skydiver frozen in the doorway of a jump plane, holding the rails and refusing to leap from the gently rocking boat. There had intentionally been no light for the last twenty minutes in the hope that our eyes could adjust to the moonless, inky darkness. Nick tapped on my shoulder, signaling me to jump, giving no comfort to what seemed like a fool's errand in the making.

"Remember, no flashlights until I give you the okay!" Nick repeated. The descent into oblivion was unforgettable.

Eventually, I switched on my flashlights and the pageantry began. Bluish squids propelled themselves like ghosts across the expanse, and luminescent shrimp danced sideways on the ocean floor. Sea snakes weaved in and out of holes in the coral heads.

This scuba-diving night was an eye-opener for me: it was like I had been thunderstruck. In that moment, I reflected back on my life—with Peter, and even long before I married Peter. I realized that in order to see clearly, I must sometimes look into the darkness, and even distance myself from the picture. To see what was really there, I'd have to be willing to enter a space that appeared devoid of the light I so heavily relied on. The keenest insights into human behavior may emanate from our willingness to look not at what is light, but what is dark; not from what is seen but, what is unseen; not what is obvious, but what is covered. Paradoxically, looking into the darkness can be remarkably enlightening.

It happened to me.

Construal-level Concept: With more distance, we can see more clearly the most important dimensions of the issue we are facing; for instance, our advice to others tends to hinge on the single most important factor, whilst our own thinking flits amongst many variables. When we think of our friends, we see the forest. When we think of ourselves, we get stuck in the trees. That's why in helping us to break a decision logjam, the single most effective question that we should ask ourselves is, "What would I tell my best friend to do in this situation?"

OUR CULTURE'S OBSESSION WITH perfection made Olivia reluctant to look at her own duality—that some of her impulses are noble, whilst others aren't so benevolent—not that she's gone over to the dark side, but just that she has a dark side. We acknowledge our light and dark sides in a detached, abstract way, but really opening the door and look into the darkness isn't so easy; it's as though we have a quasi-dark side. Some may admit to having a "diet dark side" – just one calorie of dark side. Even in our most glaringly candid moments, we are reluctant to acknowledge that some of our inclinations are, at the very least, ineffective, if not dishonorable. Denial provides a safe way to sidestep our tension—or, at least, it seems that way.

The notion of a dark side needs a bit of calibration: Dr. Hannibal Lecter, the horrific antagonist in The Silence of the Lambs, defines the really dark side, while Sister Teresa reflects the really light side. We probably dwell somewhere in-between—the "Shadow Land". While many of our motives are altruistic and noble, others are less honorable.

Olivia and Peter, like most of us, lived in the Shadow Lands of conflicted motives: they missed the clarity of the noonday sun, and lost perspective about what was right. It's only when they had the will to shed some light on their own less-admirable qualities that it became painfully apparent they both had the latent potential to derail. The full expression of some of their dark qualities, meanwhile, got them off-track fast.

People who show off having great strengths also possess significant weaknesses that cannot be ignored. We all have the innate capacity for narcissism, arrogance, or disregard of others' opinions and interests in favor of our own—and it is only perceptive people who control these impulses and choose to manage their darker sides' intrusion on decisions and relationships. Others—either through blindness or foolish disregard—don't. Those who are more likely to stay out of trouble constantly remind themselves of their own vulnerability, whilst those most vulnerable live in denial. We should probably be honest about our duality. Indeed, in business management, the famous proverb is, "Build on your strengths to the point that your weaknesses become irrelevant."

It cannot be overstated how much stress influenced Peter and Olivia's behavior: they could only look good for so long before stress stripped away their façades and exposed their dark sides. It may take time—or a significant amount of stress—, but character weaknesses usually appear at some critical moment.

Insightful people monitor and manage their stress in order to mitigate its effect. Olivia and Peter derailed because they were more susceptible to stress and its sinister tendency to fuel their dark sides. We all carry around some level of stress, but some high performers seem to be missing the protective emotional insulation that mitigates the deleterious effects of it. Their chronically high stress level fosters a greater susceptibility to the dark side of their character.

We see numerous character flaws surface in well-known figures, their narcissism and bad judgment resulted in the stupendous suffering of their families, relatives, and friends—as well as the loss of the public's trust in them. Stress is one of those pressures that squeeze out what is really inside us, and, given sufficient time and stress, those character-rooted derailment factors will surface. Indeed, the majority of people who derail find themselves off-track long before they reach the deepest point inside the grave.

The derailment of Peter and Olivia resulted from a failure of character—something that forms our perspectives, guides our decisions, and influences how we treat others. All character-rooted qualities causing derailment are tied to a lack of/failure of one of the following four critical qualities: authenticity, self-management, humility, and courage.

The unmitigated expression of the dark side of these four qualities rendered Peter and Olivia—at any level of responsibility they may have been holding—ineffective, regardless of their other capabilities—when in fact, derailment is a process.

The majority of us can only imagine being in a train wreck—the concussion of impact, the wrenching sounds of twisting metal and shattering glass, the terrifying screams of passengers, the moans of the injured and dying—, and some experts believe as many as eight hundred passengers lost their lives in the worst train wreck in history. On June 6, 1981 (in Bihar, India), seven out of the nine cars plunged from a bridge into the Bagmati River. A cyclone in the area made the tracks excessively wet, causing flash flooding in and around the river. Such conditions made it impossible for rescue workers to reach the area in a timely manner, and, although the first responders found several hundred bodies, most were never recovered.

The real cause of this disaster was the fact that the engineer slammed on the train's brakes to avoid hitting a cow. We will never know exactly how this tragedy actually occurred, and can only speculate as to the real reasons: perhaps the hot, humid conditions made the engineer drowsy; or perhaps he wasn't exercising adequate caution under the worst imaginable conditions. Alternatively, he could have been preoccupied replaying a recent argument with his wife. Regardless, we know a sacred animal appeared in the watery haze and he overreacted, plunging the crowded rail cars into the river.

Derailments of leaders can be equally hard to sort out: certainly, each leader's downfall involves a complex set of reasons and circumstances. We see the headlines, watch the news coverage, and read the voyeuristic details of their demise. The smoldering piles of wreckage mark ruined companies, careers, reputations, and marriages, looking as if the crash took place in one cataclysmic instant—one wrong turn, followed by the screeching sound of twisting metal. But this isn't the whole story.

Derailment occurs over time, and, really, it initially occurs before the crash. Peter and Olivia ignored warning signals, inattention to feedback, and one wrong turn slowly but surely led to another. The force of momentum in the wrong direction was strong enough that they both left the two parallel steel rails—much like the train did; t's just that the consequences are more apparent after the crash, in the form of the damage and causalities.

Derailment occurs with a crescendo of intensity: if we saw it happening, it would perhaps be like seeing a train approaching a washed-out bridge in slow-motion. We would want to yell and wave at the engineer to hit the brakes before it was too late—but would he hear us? Perhaps he would simply ignore us.

Olivia and Peter's derailment occurred in a predictable progression—a process of five stages that those who derail seem to follow toward their demise. Perhaps there's hope for us to learn about these escalating stages of derailment and, thus, to stay on-track.

Whilst derailment is a progression, circumstances can also have an impact: in the Bihar train wreck, the cow happened to be standing precisely so that when the engineer slammed on the brakes, the passenger cars had nowhere to fall but into the river—not to mention the ill-timed cyclone, which had dumped a huge volume of water into the surrounding territory, making the river more treacherous. Whilst mitigating circumstances certainly played a role, the engineer was still at the epicenter of the tragedy: his decisions and reactions to the circumstances were what ultimately sent the train into the river.

Stage One: A Failure of Awareness

Being self-aware would have given Peter and Olivia insight into their own desires, hopes, motives, feelings, and moods. Both of them often manifested a lack of self-awareness—as though they viewed themselves through a foggy mirror—, and so self-awareness would be a prerequisite for managing themselves well.

Along these lines, they seemed to lack awareness of and concern for themselves and others. This type of insight would have informed them as to the needs, desires, hopes, and moods of the other(s) so that they may respond appropriately. This involves empathy, consideration, and general attentiveness to the interests of others.

Derailed people seem oblivious to the impact of their behavior on others, as well as of the resulting failure to build strong, aligned relationships. They also fail to see themselves as others do—i.e., to take into account the fact that others will relate to them on the basis of those perceptions. This type of interpersonal calibration requires understanding and humility.

Despite Peter and Olivia's stellar track records of success and popularity in their workplace and neighborhood, when the time had come to lead the giant engine of their marriage, they displayed an errant overconfidence in their abilities to run the train solos: each of them wanted to be in the driver's seat, none showing interest in the co-pilot seat—a role they both underestimated the importance of.

Each of them required the help of the other, but didn't appear to know it: they lacked insight and an overall awareness of themselves and the other person, both failing to see their own limitations—that they couldn't successfully lead their marriage without the support and alignment of one another. They also failed to successfully judge how their independence would alienate the very people they needed in order to succeed: each of them wanted complete control over the other, insisting all significant decisions were channeled through their own solo-thinking minds. They failed to see, within themselves, the rattling of their own demise.

Stage Two: Hubris—Pride Before the Fall

As kids, we didn't like the know-it-alls in our classrooms—and we don't like them in real-life, either. Hubris—extreme arrogance—manifests itself in two ways. You can see it in the partner who believes they are the epicenter of their marriage's success.

Here, instead of building and nurturing a fraternal culture in their relationship, Peter and Olivia presumed their controlling methodology was better—and, instead of using the positive momentum they had enjoyed at the early beginning of their relationship, they cut loose from the culture entirely.

Reality dictates that no matter how bright and capable a partner may be, the marriage's success must be accomplished through a trusted partner. A partner's inference that they are primarily responsible for the marriage's success demonstrates blatant hubris, such an attitude suggesting that the partner feels they are above everyone else and that they believe other people possess less value to them.

Stage Three: Missed Early Warning Signals

Like the train engineer who ignored blatant warning signals, the early warning signals of derailment had been there for Peter and Olivia from an early time, but had not been heeded. Signals had been yelling and waving their hands, and yet they were paid no attention to: in their arrogance, they didn't see the warning signals represented by the subtle but persistent feedback concerning their own inner states, others' diminishing confidence in them, or the wrong direction in which they were leading their marriage. If dealt with correctly, these early warning signals should have jarred their attention to avoid the danger ahead—but instead, Peter and Olivia barreled ahead toward the inevitable crash.

Stage Four: Rationalizing

When it became apparent to each partner that they were losing the confidence of the other partner, their defenses were heightened: a siege mentality took over and each partner began to rationalize their actions. This stage took them even further from considering the very information that could have either fended off disaster or greatly limited the damage.

In Stage three, each partner ignored the feedback being given to them; in Stage Four, each partner twisted data to fit their view of the world. In an attempt to maintain their psychological equilibrium, the derailing partner believed they were right in a desire to stay on-course, despite many warning signals suggesting the contrary.

Whilst a salvage operation may have still been possible, each partner focused solely on personal preservation, deflecting blame, denying responsibility, and accusing one another of jealousy, ambition... Anything to avoid accepting personal responsibility. Put differently, they assumed the role of the victim.

In this frame of mind, partners can do some very stupid things: they keep building defenses, and, in the end, the walls they erected inevitably caved in on them.

Stage Five: Derailment

The partners come to each other and say, "I'm sorry; it's over. I had high hopes for you, but I need to help you leave in a way that preserves our dignity as partners." This is the stage where we count the bodies and try to clean up the wreckage.

PART I:
TELL ME
SWEET LITTLE LIES

They believed their own lie until
it became their throttling truth.

OLIVIA

I WAS BORN IN April 1975, in Bronx—the North side of New York. I had always believed that my parents had done everything they could to make my older sister—Mia—and I live a comfortable life.

My dad, Harry, grew up with his mentality mirroring that of his dad's: work hard, educate your children well, buy a bigger house, and save. Dad was determined to be someone who would make his family proud. He and my mother wanted us to have the very best, so they sent Mia and I to a Catholic school. We got braces in middle school when no one else had them, and, after they saved all year, they took us on a family vacation to Disneyworld.

My mother, Nancy, always wanted more: "enough" wasn't in her dictionary. She sold furs at famous outlets so she could get discounts on designer furniture, and she filled our house with it. Our home was small, but Mom was a great decorator, so I felt like we had money. She was also super smart: she was very driven and determined, and so strong and powerful that she usually got whatever she wanted. She had a gorgeous body and held her head high: when she walked into a room, everybody knew she was there. She was always glamorous and well-dressed— makeup, heels, and great jewelry. Most importantly, though, she had a great heart to match. She always wanted something different from our neighborhood, and she dreamed of her family having a better life, in a bigger house.

At home, I was very shy and somewhat unable to be myself. Mia was my best friend and my biggest teacher: she started going over multiplication tables with me when I was in Kindergarten and she was in Second Grade. She took care of me, and I followed her around like her little shadow. I was also a Daddy's girl: I clung to my dad and would only show my mother what she wanted to see and tell her what she wanted to hear. She was a firecracker and very controlling: if I crossed her, I would never hear the end of it. However, outside the house, I was the complete opposite: I mimicked my mom—loud, impressive, and in charge—, and was the cool girl in school. I had my shit together.

I met my first boyfriend in middle school, and, even though he was eighteen, he didn't mind that I was only fourteen. I had a great body and was confident, always trying to be as mature and sophisticated as my mother.

Even though Mom pushed for open communication with her girls, I was too scared and embarrassed to open up to her. Mia always told her everything, but I was so shy that I would cover my ears every time Mom tried to talk about sex with Mia. It was because of this that it took me forever to work up the courage to tell her I'd had sex with my first boyfriend—and, when I finally did, she was hurt and disappointed.

"What do you mean?" she said. "You're only fifteen! I put you through private school! I gave you everything! How dare you do that to our family—and yourself!"

When my dad found out, he hugged me tight while the tears streamed down his face. An overwhelming pain seemed to have flooded through him, but, as always, he was the kindest father I had ever seen.

"Olivia, your mom told me about it," he said. "I love you, and I'd do anything for you. I want you to take care of yourself."

Deep inside, I loved Dad more than Mom. He was the complete opposite of my mom. I had also never seen him fighting with her: he knew how to control his temper, speak gently, and wisely end any potential fights. I believe he was avoiding clashes with her because of how stormy she had been, and why he was always so strategic with his decisions. However, it was always Mom who had the final say: it was her that had insisted Mia and I must move from public school to a private one; it was her who made us move to a new, high-class neighborhood. My dad wasn't dominated by Mom: he was just a peaceful soul, wanting to keep his family together under one roof. It was because of this that he avoided going head-to-head with Mom.

It was because of this that I felt an overwhelming amount of guilt for his current reaction—but, in the back of my mind, having a boyfriend and private life was going to make me a woman; I was finally going to be my own person. My mom wasn't going to be able to run my life anymore, and I was going to have to follow less rules. I had my boyfriend and could finish school and spend the rest of my life with him. I was in love and mature, and my mom couldn't tell me a damn thing.

Of course, that didn't happen: I hated how strict Mom was, making me follow the same rules and giving me the same curfew. My boyfriend would come over to see me, leading to my Mom screaming at me, "You can't sit on his lap in my house! You can't be in the same room together alone!" Not one damn thing had changed.

This lack of change actually wound up being a good thing: I still had the stability of a home, and it was this that pulled me through when my boyfriend started to cheat on me—and, when I told him I wanted to break up, he punched me in the face—the first time anyone had ever put their hands on me. I lied to my parents and told them I'd gotten hit in the eye with a snowball, and then stayed with him for two more years; I thought I was doing the best thing by saving our love. Here I had been, this supposedly strong, mature young woman, and I was letting this man control me.

The person who finally saved me was my dad, who had always been beside me. I couldn't let him see me falling part, so I broke up with my boyfriend and never looked back. I felt nothing but animosity toward my ex, and I instead started to focus on my studies. I even had a part time job at Dunkin' Donuts, earning a wage and trying hard to be responsible.

Whether you're fifteen or forty, every mother and father wants what is best for their kids—but, again, none are perfect. We all have our breaking points, and, toward the middle of high school, I had mine.

Trying to tell a teenager that their perception or judgment is wrong or biased is like telling grass that it shouldn't be green.

Peter and I met during my final year in high school. Ours had been the fairytale relationship: Peter had been the captain of the football team—a large, attractive specimen with the personality of an extrovert, much like his father. He was the son of the president of a multinational financial institution, a man who had started out as a salesman and worked his way up to president of the business. His family was fairly well-known in town, were upper-middle class, and thoroughly involved in social and community activities.

Before dating, Peter had always been an attractive target to me, but he was also a hard-to-reach target. In addition to being well-off—at least more than me—, his social status, charming looks, and extroverted personality lent the way to a self-confident attitude and behavior. He was the type of person I called the "Anti-Seducer".

I had always been observing him: a man devoted to his sports, his academic success, and his inner circle of close friends. I also knew from our mutual friends that every summer, he'd work in order to gain experience, as well as to make some money to finance his trips.

He is a man of impeccable manners. He doesn't waste his time, I thought to myself. This moment of awe was short-lived, however, as I remembered I wasn't one of his privileged friends; he'd rarely even spoken to me directly, even though he was always funny and talkative to the other girls—even those I knew were less beautiful than me.

Peter was both amiable and hostile. Whilst his gaze would sometimes be warm and comforting, it could also be arid as the desert. He was tough and tender—both spiritual and earthly, both innocent and cunning. He had mastered the role of the seducer with me. These mixed signals and contradicting qualities suggested to me a certain depth to his personality—one that left me both fascinated and perplexed.

"He's one hell of a mysterious man," I once said to Mia. "He's not shallow."

Peter never gave me any clear signal that he really liked me any more than anyone else; my compelling beauty appeared to be meaningless to him. In hopeless moments, I would feel desperate and want to completely eradicate him from my mind, but always failed—miserably at that. The confusing personality he had mastered made me eager to discover more; to fall under his spell. This elusive, enigmatic aura constantly drew me into Peter's circle. I had become determined to become his sole center of attention.

In response to the desperate mood Peter's inattention and mixed signals were constantly putting me into, my female instinct started to awaken: deep inside, I was sure there must be a key to his personality—a way to seduce him and bring him to his knees. I knew that females should never push back and easily surrender to a male; it should be the man who surrenders. Thus, nothing was more infuriating to me than being paid no attention—especially by the person I liked the most. It slowly began to take a toll on my self-esteem—his complete inattention—, and, in the dead of my boundlessness nights whilst laying on my bed and staring up at the ceiling, thoughts would creep like shadows to the back of my mind.

With Peter, I understood that depending solely on my beauty would get me nowhere, and continuing to rely solely on that would be a complete waste of time. Why not to play it the other way around? I wondered to myself one day. Deflect the attention from myself and focus it on Peter! Yes, that's perfect. Getting closer to his inner circle.

It was then that I realized that this was exactly what Peter's intimate friends had been doing with him. He was the center of their universe, but I was much smarter than my female competitors had been. I decided to take my mission several steps further and begin to penetrate Peter's spirit: to understand his pains, moods, dreams, ups and downs, and insecurities. I reached a level where he completely opened up to me, and, in return, I opened myself up to him. I had never been so impulsive, but I knew that seduction implied opening oneself up; in fact, I consider myself to have been brave to adapt myself to his moods and needs. I would talk about my adversities so he could feel comfortable around me, and I would always note a spark of warmth flashing in his eyes when I did. I learnt to cast my spell by targeting Peter's primary weaknesses: vanity, and faked self-esteem.

I wasn't a particularly excellent student: I was pretty average, and never caused problems in my classes. My teachers essentially ignored me: to them—as to me—, my academic performance wasn't particularly important. I was satisfied at the prospect of a mediocre job, but I would probably prioritize getting married and starting a family first. I needed only a fair education to survive in the world.

"You should be grateful that you were gifted with such a natural beauty that instantly attracts men to you," my mother used to say to me. "In just a few years, you'll make a fortune with that."

I enjoyed hearing my friends' love stories full of freedom, romance, and sex, but they predominantly made me map out how I could go about living the same experiences with Peter. Little discussion revolved around improving my academic performance or after-university work ambitions; instead, I ordered my priorities in terms of what my mom, girlfriends, and society said. This stereotype shaped my mind and way of thinking: from a young age, I was accustomed to the fact that a female's physical beauty and sex appeal is of the highest importance, everything else coming second.

After graduation from university, I got a job as an office manager for the CEO of a trading company—a job that I considered fair to my ambitions. I was predominantly hired because I was pretty and friendly rather than for my education, and I knew it. I was good with clients and on the telephone, but I knew that was a dead-end job—something for me to do temporarily until marriage, which was my real ambition. Back then, in my society, the image was that any woman who wasn't married by the time she was thirty was destined to a life as an old maid—perhaps the worst thing that could happen to a girl, and certainly worse than having an unhappy marriage, getting a divorce, or being widowed. As I stood then, I knew I could at least attract a man and get him to propose; an old maid, however, was an automatic complete failure of a woman. Of course, this wasn't a concern for me: if Peter hadn't made a commitment to me fairly soon, I could have moved on to someone else. Peter, however, had potential: his family had money, he was well-educated, he seemed to have a promising future in terms of his career, and he was cute and fun. Hence, I decided I would be better off waiting a while.

The sexual relationship with Peter quickly heated up, and I found myself allowing him to take more liberties, sip by sip.

"In this phase of our relationship, I have to loosen the robe to get him more attached—enough to tie the knot," I explained to Mia at the time. "Now, he's the one asking to meet."

My girlfriends praised me on the progress I was making in my relationship with Peter—the advancement in my seduction plan.

Through regular consultations with my girlfriends, combined with what I read on female groups on social media, I had come to the conclusion that the one thing that had really motivated Peter to get to see me more frequently than before was the fact that I had sexually opened up to him; all the other details of our relationship had stayed the same, and so came second. With the exception of my shallow sexual relations with my first boyfriend, I wasn't particularly sexually experienced: I had gained most of my sexual knowledge through romance novels, movies, social media, and from my "experienced" girlfriends—all these sources informing me that if I could keep Peter interested sexually, I may be able to get him to marry me.

I was careful to stay distanced from my own passions so that I could keep him "hot", but never satisfied—as a Siren would behave. I abided by the plan. I often told him—when he was begging for me to "go all the way"—that I couldn't do that unless I was sure he really loved me—by which I meant, but never stated, that he should marry me.

The Social Proof Concept: When people are uncertain about their actions, they tend to look outside themselves and to other people around them to guide their decisions and actions.

FEMINISM TAUGHT OLIVIA TO accept her body: to not be ashamed of her natural body shape, and to be generally proud of her natural overall look (body, skin, color, and face)—and yet women all over the world are still desperately out of balance, obsessed with weight, dieting, food types, and calorie control. Have we not gotten anywhere?

"Such beauty!" and "That is a beaut!" are compliments often uttered about objects of sleek or elegant design (e.g., a new car; furniture; antiques), and yet women are also referred to as these things. Generally, the word "beauty" describes attractive female bodies, whereas attractive male bodies are described as "handsome"—a word derived from "hand", which refers as much what one does—"He is handy"—as much as how one looks. Aspects of strength, ability, and achievement are connoted by the word handsome, but not by the word beauty—a decorative aspect. This suggests that whilst men are instrumental, women are ornamental—and it is these connotations that undergird gender role expectations for embodiment. Furthermore, the tendency of females to define themselves by their bodies or their faces, as well as to describe themselves with language also used to describe admired objects or things, is the essence of objectification.

Not only do women themselves contribute to their own objectification, but advertising techniques used by pro-consumerism companies also contribute greatly to this: advertisers intentionally show women's naked bodies, exposing particular legs, torsos, thighs, and hips, morphing a woman's body into a product. These advertising techniques are a confirmation that women are merely all about beauty of the body.

Cosmetics and fashion have been used by females to change the look and shape of their bodies and faces since the beginning of society: cosmetics add color to, or enhance the pallor of, the face, and hide blemishes of the skin. They are used to make some facial features look smaller (noses; wrinkles) and others larger (eyes; eyelashes; lips). Cosmetic procedures (Botox injections; dermabrasion) temporarily alter the appearance of the face, breasts, and hips, and many treatments (e.g., bleaches, and dyes) are available to change hair color, relax curly hair, and curl straight hair. Garments (e.g., corsets; brassieres; bustles; girdles; Spanx) have been used for centuries to change the shape of the body by cinching the waist and flattening the abdomen, making breasts appear smaller and flatter or larger and rounder, and simulating large buttocks.

High-heeled shoes change the shape of the legs and accentuate the sway of the hips.

Today's beauty ideal is tall, with long legs, a thin body, small hips and waist, large breasts, well-toned muscles, no obvious body fat, and wrinkle- and blemish-free skin. This ideal—much like others before it— is nearly impossible to achieve: one cannot be tall if one is short, and one cannot have European hair and facial features if one's ancestors are Asian. It is quite difficult to be both muscular and very thin, and very thin women with large breasts are a rarity. One cannot have both no obvious body fat and large breasts, which are composed almost entirely of fat. Therefore, women who desire to approximate the beauty ideal would have to make use of some of these techniques—plus restricted eating, frequent exercise, and cosmetic surgery—in order to do so.

Beauty is more than attractiveness: it is an idea of perfection, and this ideal varies across cultures and historical time periods. Perfection is nearly impossible to attain, and thus ideals can be matched by only a minority of women—and only at a specific point in time, when that specific ideal they adhere to is still held in high regard. If too many women approach the beauty ideal, then the ideal must change in order to maintain its extraordinary status—and, when the ideal changes, women are expected to change their bodies, too. The size and shape of women's bodies are important parts of the beauty ideal, and women have for a long time made use of the technology available to them to make changes that bring them closer to the ideal; in fact, they are lured to spend fortunes and suffer physically and emotionally in order to reach such an ideal.

And, unsurprisingly, they fail!

PETER

OLIVIA MEADOWS WAS A cute, perky, blonde girl who had been popular in high school. She had been on the cheerleading squad and choir, and was well-liked due to her friendliness and outgoing temperament. Olivia's father was a banker, and her family may be considered as middle-class. When we had begun to date, everyone thought we were perfect for each other: we were a popular couple with our fairytale. Our love story was an example to be followed by our colleagues.

Olivia was one of the prettiest girls I knew, but I was too stubborn to approach her: I knew she was depending on her beauty and natural ideal body shape. Watching that beautiful body move with her natural grace, her creamy skin glowing, was like my daily drug fix.

These are your weapons, Olivia, but you cannot use them against me, I would think to myself. The advice of my father was engraved on my mind: "If you let women lead you by that hard thing between your legs, they'll take advantage; that's why they should be controlled." I knew that Olivia liked me: I was talented at reading people. Her eyes had always been fixed on me wherever I went. In several instances, I had noticed her lascivious stare. I also noticed she was always present at the places I preferred to go to. I was seamlessly playing the role of the seducer who paid no attention to his prospective victim: I knew Olivia was my perfect chase, and so I kept sending mixed signals.

It couldn't be denied that in her presence, I felt better about myself.

"I feel like I don't recognize who I once was when I'm with Olivia," I told my brother, John.

OLIVIA

WHEN I CONSIDERED THE advice of my girlfriends of changing my looks in order to attract Peter, I started with simple changes: I began to smile more, wore a full face of makeup, and dressed differently—mostly tight blouses, tight jeans, or shorts and tight T-shirts. Previously ignored and even ridiculed for my masculine looks, I quickly noticed something shifting without me having to say or do anything: males fell passionately in love with me. My admirers would all say the same thing in different ways: it was my fault they wanted to kiss and hug me; it was the way I looked at them, with eyes full of passion; it was my voice that lured them on; I gave off vibrations that floored them. I sensed a way to gain attention—perhaps even power—, for I was wildly ambitious to garner control over Peter.

One day, Peter stunned me by saying, "You're a bombshell; you drive me crazy." That day, I felt I was flying, the skies at my fingertips. I couldn't sleep all night long. My underwear was the only piece of clothing covering my skin, and frankly, I didn't want to put anything else on: I wanted to feel the sensations of my body. So I lay on my bed, stared up at the ceiling, and thought of his words and how he would make love to me. I dreamt of all the touches and sounds that would issue from him, arousing myself in the process. I was delighted.

Over the next few months, I taught myself through trial and error how to heighten the effect I had on Peter. My voice had always been attractive, but it was a young voice, and so my girlfriends taught me to lower it, giving it the deep, breathy tones that became my seductive trademark—a mix of the little girl and the vixen.

Before hanging out with Peter—or even at a party with my girlfriends—, I would spend hours before the mirror. Most people assumed this was vanity—that I was in love with my image—, but the truth was that the image had taken hours to create, and so I would spend months on end studying and practicing the art of makeup. The voice, the walk, the face and look were all constructions, an act. I loved the devouring look I had been seeing in Peter's eyes, and how others appreciated my image. At the height of my ecstasy, I would get a thrill by going into a place without my makeup or fancies, passing unnoticed.

One day, Peter stunned me once again. "Do you think of sex with me?" he'd said innocently. I felt paralyzed, and, unconsciously, found myself saying no. He continued, "All through the time we spend together, I keep receiving sex vibrations from you—as if you were a woman in the grip of passion. I see it in your eyes, Liv: you're a woman of sexual magnetism, no matter what you're doing or thinking. My body automatically responds to you."

I loved the effect my body had on Peter—on the male libido. I tuned my physical presence like an instrument, forcing myself to reek of sex, painting myself so I appeared larger-than-life. Other women knew just as many tricks for heightening their sexual appeal, but what separated me from them was an unconscious element—the one that brought Peter to his knees before me.

My deepest need was to feel loved and desired by Peter; it made me seem constantly vulnerable, like a little girl craving protection. I emanated this need for love before him; it was effortless, coming from somewhere real and deep inside. A look or gesture that I didn't intend to arouse his desire would do so doubly powerfully, all because it was unintended. My innocence was precisely what excited Peter.

I think it was this touch of innocence and vulnerability that separated me from a courtesan or whore. The mix was perversely satisfying: it gave Peter the illusion that he was a protector, or a father figure to me.

I wasn't born with these attributes; I don't think any woman was. The majority of them were a construction, the key being the air of schoolgirl innocence. Whilst one part of me seemed to scream sex, the other was coy and naïve, as if I were incapable of understanding the effect I was having. My walk, my voice, and my manner were delightfully ambiguous; I was both the experienced, desiring woman and the innocent gamine.

It took me two years of hard work to wear Peter down, and it was after such a period that he finally gave me an engagement ring, promising to marry me. In return, I began to have sex with him—as often as he asked. Now he is committed, I will reward him to get him even more attached.

The Seduction Concept: A psychological process that transcends gender. Men are vulnerable to the visual; women are vulnerable to the language and words. Each use their technique to attract the other.

SINCE THE BEGINNING OF time until now, little has changed: the most valuable commodity a woman has with regard to attracting a desirable male is her beauty and sexuality. Feminism struggles getting society to value other attributes of a woman (e.g., competence; critical thinking; independence; career orientation; self-satisfaction), sexuality still being largely regarded as a woman's most important commodity. Women are still preoccupied with the accoutrements of beauty, including everything from makeup, revealing clothes, body shape, dieting, face-lifts, haircuts, cosmetic surgeries, skincare, haircare, colored eye contacts... The list goes on.

Unsurprisingly, a large percentage of women worry constantly about men finding other women more attractive than them, tending to scan the competition to try to keep up. They spend a fortune just trying to maintain their beauty, or simply to look just as (or more) beautiful than their female friends. No matter what other qualities a woman may have, she feels she must maintain a certain level of attractiveness if she expects to keep her spouse interested. Male emphasis and appreciation of the female's beauty inflates her passion concerning maintaining her beauty and using it as her first method to attract males.

Olivia, like many women, believed that through marriage, she would have secured the relationship with Peter. Women often believe marriage will result in their men being tied to them and their families indefinitely—and, for men, marriage often connotes a security in the fact that they own a readily available, safe sexual partner. However, the majority of women fear that the passionate sex that comes with courtship will disappear after marriage. Hence, the loss of physical attractiveness in a sexual partner is often one of the main causes of a reduced sex drive in men.

In fact, the media typically showcases rather narrow and stereotypical portraits of women and femininity: for female characters, the focus is typically on their physical appearance, sex appeal, and romantic success. Women are, essentially, objects of desire—and this leads to the women of the public following suit and presenting their bodies in the same way—as objects for others' viewing pleasure, others' praise and evaluation, competition with other females, and a means of gender and social confirmation and seduction. When women are almost always presenting themselves—with the help of media channels—as sexual objects, this normalizes the objectification and creates a narrowed perspective on women.

The concern is that if females present themselves with only a limited range of attributes, skills, and abilities, viewers will develop equally limited assumptions about the sexes; therefore, the relationship between the media and females is mutual, as females willingly present themselves on the media as objects of beauty and sex, the media abusing them by doing the same.

The media have bombarded both genders with the unrealistic fantasy of the perfectly shaped young male and female body: hungry for sex, always ready, always responsive, always ready to experiment other partners, and easily satisfied. To make matters worse, one partner may not be enough, and could be easily abandoned: if one partner isn't satisfied with his current partner, this is not seen as a problem, since there are an abundance of other beauties waiting to be invited and ready to engage.

The overwhelming bias toward thinness as the female beauty ideal on commercial television, social media, and fitness magazines has led to the majority of females being overly concerned with their weight and body shape. Whether it was led by multinational consumer goods companies or not, such enterprises have only benefited from them as opportunities to market weight loss products, skincare products, body care, etc. have only grown. The media's emphasis on physical appearance and the unrealistically thin ideal body shape has also led female audiences to become dissatisfied with their own bodies, creating depression, reduced self-esteem, increased anger, and negative moods.

This increased exposure to thin-ideal media is also associated with higher levels of dieting, exercising, and disordered eating symptomatology—and, again, companies that market for cosmetics, diet food, and fitness products are the main beneficiaries from this thin-body obsession trend. I call this the industry of Beauty-Myth, and beauticians, plastic surgery doctors, and dieticians are the new leaders of this female obsession.

The result is generations of confused women: should they be seductive to attract their desired male, or should they stay pure? The majority of women are aware of this contradiction, and so feel the need to be both seductive and pure at the same time. Most also fear abandonment if they cannot fulfill both roles simultaneously—almost always a difficult task. The media has taught women that keeping her spouse sexually happy is a measure of her femininity, and that she should thus take responsibility if her partner goes elsewhere. Therefore, they try to be both—and fail most of the time. Gender socialization plays a major role in these often-contradictory expectations.

The Social Comparison Concept: The way in which women come to know how much beauty work they need to complete. Women may compare themselves with celebrities, including models and actresses, that they would like to emulate.

Unfortunately, these role-models are unrealistic standards for comparison: they are typically unusually attractive, and spend a great deal of their time on beauty work with the help of experts unavailable to the average woman. In addition, it is rare for the average woman to see her favorite celebrities in person, so she doesn't know what they actually look like: she knows what they look like in movies and on social media, but those images are often enhanced through technology designed to hide flaws, or even reshape the body.

Women also compare themselves with other women they know in order to judge how attractive they themselves are, as well as to gauge how much beauty work those other women do. Beauty represents a form of competition between women: if their comparisons are upward (other women are prettier or thinner), rather than downward (they themselves are the prettiest or thinnest), they are typically ashamed and spurred on to work harder to approach the beauty ideal.

The Social Identity Concept: Individuals identify with a group (their in-group) on the basis of their perceived degree of similarity with others—which, in turn, depends on their social categorization of the self and others. They then do what they can to maintain that identity.

The Social Identity Principle is another reason why women adhere to the social norms of beauty work: they want to reassure themselves that they are feminine, that they are beautiful, that they are sexy, that they are attractive, that they are sophisticated, that they are chic. Women may also send signals or mixed signals concerning their age: for instance, girls engage in beauty work to appear older than they are, and middle-aged and older women often aim to appear younger than they are. The age window of peak beauty is narrow—from a woman's late teens to her mid-30s—, which evolutionary theorists may note are also the typical years of reproduction. The narrowness of the peak age means that girls and women will be out of range for most of their lives, and so their desire to pass as younger or older than they are intensifies.

Women derive their self-esteem, in part, from meeting social norms or ideals that are important to them—as well as from valued social identities—, and so beauty work may also boost a woman's self-esteem: it moves them closer to the beauty ideal, or at least shows that they are trying to move closer to it. From there, they feel validated in thinking that they are a "good" woman. However, some women refuse to adhere to the social norms of beauty work, and instead adopt different social norms in order to signal their identity, such as "I am butch", "I am Goth", "I am a feminist".

OLIVIA

I WAS ABOUT TO make a suggestion I sincerely hoped I wouldn't regret, and there were several reasons behind my thinking that it was a good idea: my mother kept asking me to invite Peter—mother's instinct to check her girl's boyfriend—, and I thought it could be another perfect opportunity to open up to Peter. We had promised to share more details about our previous lives with one another, and, secretly, my libido was involved in the decision-making: I had been craving sex with him. So I took the plunge.

With a suddenness that startled Peter, I asked him, "I'd like to go see my mom. Would you come with me?"

Peter shot me an incredulous look. "Are you serious? I booked the usual table in our favorite restaurant; we're supposed to be leaving now."

"So what? You call the restaurant, cancel the booking, and we redirect ourselves to my house. Easy, right?" My eyes locked with his, gleaming with warmth. Regardless of the fact that he was still surprised by my decision and unable to understand the reason behind it, Peter nodded stiffly and began to call the restaurant, turning his face to the taxi's window.

The taxi pulled up to the front entrance of my house, and, after he had got out, Peter held out his hand to me. It was this small act that stopped me cold as something flickered in my mind: the hand, almost twice as large as mine, darkly tanned, with a sprinkling of yellow hair and blue veins, looked so strong, so capable—lethal when necessary; and yet it had only ever been infinitely tender with me, providing me with incredible pleasure.

The night had been warm, the stars glittering in a sky that resembled an inverted black bowl. Dawn was creeping through the windows, casting the living room in a grayish tint. Whilst I was pouring our two glasses of wine, Peter's gaze swept over my body, and, with a suddenness that startled me, he stood, pulled me into his arms, and slammed his mouth against mine. His hands cupped my butt, pressing my softness to his hardening body. My body was soft and fitted into his, something he'd always adored. Wrapping my arms around this man had always been the best moments of life, and now, I shivered as every erogenous zone in my body stood to attention. We then fell into hours of lovemaking.

It was at one point that I had to pull back to catch my breath that Peter smiled sexily, and, my eyes gleaming with need, I took his hands. He pulled me back into his arms and claimed my mouth again, and, that easily, climax zoomed, fierce and sweet, carrying me away on a wave of pleasure and searing, burning heat. As our bodies shook with satisfaction and exhaustion, we collapsed onto the bed, exhausted. Staring up at the ceiling, my body was in a cool-down state. A few minutes later, I started to talk with a palpable sense of relief.

"When I was a little girl, I grew up in a neighborhood that was mostly populated by boys. I was physically strong and athletically inclined, and the boys accepted me as an equal: I played baseball with them, swam in the bay, went exploring the cemetery in dark nights, rode my bike with no hands, played with cars and trucks in the dirt piles. I also got into a few fistfights, started by someone else, which I usually won. On the playground at school, when the boys and girls segregated themselves, I still played sports with the athletic girls and totally ignored the girls who liked to stand around and talk—sissies, as I used to call them. I found them extremely boring." My voice was thick with nostalgia.

"Since the start of junior high school, my experience became traumatic—not because I was unprepared academically, but because of the reactions of my peers—especially the boys. In fact, I did very well in my courses, and maintained the A averages I had gotten in elementary school. I kept my high athletic and academic superiority, and yet found that the boys were openly hostile to me, at the same time constantly looking at and trying to impress the girls who wore lipstick, curled their hair, and giggled incessantly about stupid things and jokes. Even the girls who had once studied hard with me to get good grades spent much of their time now talking about how cute the boys were and which movie stars or social media influencers they thought were real hunks. I was in total shock at this new world unfolding before my eyes: they spent all their time worrying about what they should wear, making sure they all dressed alike. However, all of that seemed like a boring waste of time to me. For several years, I was isolated. The boys who had once been my friends were spending their time in sports activities with a much larger group of boys, and didn't want to associate with me anymore. 'What did I do wrong? Why have they changed?' I would ask myself. The girls were almost all 'sissies' now, except for the nerds and the jocks—both being groups I fit into but did not want to join.

"One day, when he was far away from the other guys at school and safe from discovery, Groucho—the boy who had been my best neighborhood friend since we were seven—had a serious talk with me. 'Olivia, you have to know that boys my age are interested in sex, and so they want sexy girls, with boobs and makeup and flattering outfits. Boys want to feel strong and tough so that they can attract the sexy girls, and so when someone like you beats them at playing pool or ping-pong or running, it's embarrassing, and so they start to hate you. You're are competing with them in something that is seen as a boy-related. It's bad enough not to be the strongest, tallest, fastest guy in the group—never mind to be beaten by a girl.'

"He told me that if I wanted guys to like me, I should lose in games with them, pretend I didn't know the answers to questions and ask for their help, wear makeup, shave my hairy legs, and try to make myself look a little more like a real woman; that way, they would feel good around me and want me.

"I was outraged—not because he'd told me all this, as I understand he'd done so to help me and was taking a terrible chance of being ostracized, too."

Peter lifted his cool gaze and gently caressed my hair. A rare glimmer of vulnerability flickered in my eyes. "I was furious that the rules were so unfair," I pressed on. "Why should boys have to feel stronger, smarter, better? Why couldn't they like me, as they once seemed to have, without my having to play dumb and helpless? And why did the girls place so much importance on looks, dating, sex, and boys when there was so much more to life than that?

"I felt so isolated, hated, and like my normal life was over. I felt helpless. In a moment of crisis that afternoon, I sat behind an attractive-looking new boy in my class and I laughed hard at his jokes, asked him for help in many courses, and praised him for his ability on the basketball court. Eventually, I started wearing makeup, showing an interest in dressing in revealing clothes, and showcasing my barely developed chest out whenever I could. Sure enough, he asked me to a dinner gathering at his home, and from then on, I became part of the in-crowd again. I abided by the rules. Simply, I started the well-known female seduction game."

I signaled the end of my talk by throwing my head back to Peter's chest and drew in a couple of ragged breaths. In response, Peter leaned forward and kissed my lips softly, tasting himself on my mouth. We remained silent for a while, talking as our thoughts strayed through our minds.

I never stopped playing the game, really; I still played the same seduction game, and it was working perfectly with Peter. I dieted constantly and dressed in a revealing way—the same as the models my age. I'd had breast and butt surgery to make them larger. I was still tentative when talking to a man I didn't know, nervous of accidentally crossing the male ego. I would always side with Peter's opinion, even when I thought he was wrong, rather than argue him down. I just couldn't stand losing him. To tell you the truth, I was even feeling better than I had during my young days: I felt like a real woman, not a boy in a woman's body. I felt authentic.

The After-Play Concept: Whatever a couple does immediately following lovemaking, most often cuddling, caressing, and sharing intimate thoughts or secrets. The insight is that people are more vulnerable to each other after sex than they are at other times. Tender and affectionate after-play drives lovemakers' vulnerability.

ADOLESCENCE IS A PARTICULARLY vulnerable period of development, and most people mature beyond the years when "belonging" is the most important thing and everyone is so easily molded by the messages of parents, public figures, culture—especially the subculture of the adolescents—social media, influencers, movie stars, etc.

Olivia is a real example of how males and society can influence the perceived value of females, simply by rejecting or accepting them—or, best of all, rewarding what they see. Olivia's gender expectations and the ways in which her female peers acted also played a great role in influencing her behavior. When faced with this situation, she started to awaken her innate seductive abilities, finding it very easy to seduce Peter—something she was uninterested in doing in her younger days. Her feminine nature began to take over at this time, and she felt better when she was praised and appreciated for her body shape, breast size, and clothing. She had totally changed her way of thinking, and was convinced the female shape was more important than her personal capabilities. She focused her energy not on what were once meaningful activities to her, but on her appearance and behavior: she learned how to deal with men and how to be accepted by other women to avoid being dubbed a "nerd" or somebody to not be taken seriously.

It's too much to expect an adolescent girl to resist the indoctrination she received from parents, extended family, media, teachers, movie stars, and religious leaders—much less the peer pressure of the moment. The point is not that the males in question were fully to blame, but they certainly did participate in the formation of Olivia's self-perceptions. These same characteristics would later become irritating and unfathomable to them, thus blocking the development of true intimacy.

Once a man or woman becomes aware of the detrimental effect of gender socialization on the quality of life they experienced, it is natural to want to find someone to blame—and the automatic tendency is usually to attack the partner as the culprit—usually the ones who made up the rules that oppress, endanger, or otherwise adversely influence one's life. Finding someone at whom to direct anger is one of the many stages of dealing with trauma.

Some women engage in beauty work to avoid the stigmatizing mark of ugliness. In a superficial society that places much emphasis on the consumer-driven pursuit of the beauty ideal, there is a fine line between being unattractive (simply not beautiful) and being ugly—which fits the stigmatized condition "abominations of the body". The more visible the unattractive aspects are (e.g., uneven facial features; scars; body fat) and the more controllable others perceive those unattractive features to be (e.g., Why does she not go on a diet? Why does she not seek cosmetic surgery?), the more negative the reaction of others is likely to be: when women resist the cultural norms of engaging in beauty work, they may be seen as eccentric, weird, or, worse, a threat to feminine women and those who objectify them.

Women who resist social norms appear to be less objectified than those who do adhere to such norms. In social psychology studies, women tend to take a more objectified view of themselves, reporting a preference for "a less natural, more appearance-oriented standard for women's bodies". This is known as a form of reaction named "terror management", meaning women will vocalize a desire to avoid stigmatization.

Women engage in beauty work because of the punishment that those who deviate from the norms are likely to suffer: conformity occurs because they want to be liked and fit into their social group, believing others know what "should" be done, such things leading to social rewards. On the other hand, nonconformity leads to punishment. Punishment may take the form of mocking, teasing, cajoling, nudging, or sexual harassment—including "hogging", a form of harassment directed toward women and girls of a heavy weight, whereby they are targeted by men as an "amusing" sexual conquest.

Even well-intentioned comments by family and friends (nudging) can include body shaming, reminding the female in question that she deviates noticeably from the beauty ideal. Shame may motivate her to increase the amount of beauty work she does in an effort to avoid future embarrassment—or, alternatively, it may contribute to depression as she believes she is hopelessly distant from the ideal.

Punishment for deviation can be more severe than social marginalization: it may have economic implications, as some jobs primarily filled by women (e.g., receptionists) are advertised as requiring "front-office appeal" (high attractiveness). Women have also been fired from positions in various fields (e.g., fashion; media; business) for reasons that include an unappealing or dowdy appearance—a form of discrimination that women contribute to by doing the beauty work they insist on. Legal prohibitions against this form of discrimination based on appearance are weak, and don't extend to style of dress or grooming. As may be predicted at this point, very few companies also have policies against this sort of discrimination.

Women may also experience punishment indirectly: there is ample opportunity to observe other girls and women being rewarded for approaching the beauty ideal, and punished for the deviance from it. These observations can be made in everyday life, as well as in the media: content analysis of popular television programs demonstrates that these themes are prominent, cartoons for children, for example, frequently showing positive consequences for attractive female characters and negative consequences for unattractive female characters. General observations of movies and situational comedies also clearly show the thin and average female characters as receiving more compliments from male characters than heavier female characters; further, female characters that don't diet make more disparaging comments about themselves than those portrayed as dieting, and heavier female characters receive more negative comments from male characters about their bodies and weight than other female characters. These negative comments are also usually followed by laughter.

In an opposite study on male characters' weight, we can see that heavyweight male characters tend to make negative comments about themselves, such comments also usually being followed by laughter. However, it seems less cruel to invite others to laugh at oneself than to be mocked and laughed at by others.

Almost—if not all—of female-targeted commercials include messages about attractiveness—and, indeed, even male-targeted commercials (e.g., shaving creams; perfumes; deodorants) end with a scene showing an attractive female being attracted to the male character as a result of the product's use. Unsurprisingly, the bestselling genre of women's magazines and TV programs is Health/Beauty/Fashion—and yet even the Health magazines/programs concern themselves more with beauty than health. Going back in time to traditional women's magazines, diet and beauty advice is still prevalent in every issue, and is often advertised on the cover.

A study of women's magazine covers showed that messages about body weight and shape are often positioned next to messages about other topics in a way that suggests that changing one's appearances brings psychological or relational rewards: for instance, "Get the body you really want" next to "How to get your husband to really listen", "Tighten your butt" next to "Habits of confident women", and "Lose 10 pounds" next to "Ways to make your life easier and happier". As we can see here, the placement of text on magazine covers is carefully planned, these pairs of messages all fitting into a common cultural narrative: if women look better, they will be better, rewarded, and more lovable.

If you ask a woman to name a part of her body that she would most like to change, she will likely answer quickly and decisively; and if you ask her to name a part of her body that she particularly likes, she will probably demur. The sexualization and objectification of women, combined with the increasing popularity of cosmetic surgery and procedures, has encouraged the commodification of women's bodies, as well as the tendency to view women as a collection of parts, rather than as a whole person or body. Myriad products and services are marketed to women to "perfect" particular parts of the body, and advertising for those products and services reinforces the beauty ideal of perfection. Probably unsurprisingly, women are generally more dissatisfied with their body parts than men are, 98% of women in a recent study reporting that they had been subject to criticism and pressure to change at least one of the body parts (e.g., breasts; buttocks; hair; vaginal odor).

The upsurge in the number of cosmetic procedures and surgeries provides ample evidence of dissatisfaction with particular body parts. The most popular elective surgery is breast augmentation, and the most popular elective nonsurgical procedure is Botox injections. We can see from surgeries such as breast augmentation, breast reduction, breast lifts, buttocks augmentation, calf implants, ankle shaping, arm lifts, face lifts, collagen implants, chemical peels, dermabrasion, laser skin resurfacing, ear pinning, eyelid shaping, nose resizing, nose reshaping, lip enhancement, cheek augmentation, alterations to the vagina or labia, liposuction, and tummy tuck, that women are experiencing huge amounts of body dissatisfaction—and, unfortunately, many women undergo such cosmetic surgery under the impression that changing their bodies will bring automatic changes in their self-esteem, well-being, and relationships. However, research does not support those anticipated benefits; in fact, increases in self-esteem—if any occurred at all—has been documented not occur for an excess of 6-12 months post-surgery.

The fact that so many women go through multiple cosmetic surgeries is clear evidence that "improving" one body part creates dissatisfaction with other body parts, as they now appear to look worse in comparison with the altered body part. There is no evidence that cosmetic surgery improves women's social relationships, some suggesting that it may even have the opposite effect, given that some men, after they discover that the woman has had a cosmetic surgery, view her negatively (i.e., not naturally beautiful).

Unsurprisingly, women who undergo cosmetic surgery are found to have higher high rates of depression and suicide attempts than their peers do—perhaps because they were depressed pre-surgery and/or had erroneously anticipated that the surgery would improve their well-being and intimate relationships—a message often conveyed to women by the media. The high rate of complications (e.g., ruptures; deflation; scarring; pain) associated with cosmetic surgeries may also contribute to depression. Moreover, many surgeries (e.g., breast implants) do not last forever, and must be removed or replaced after some time. This may not be known to all women who opt for such cosmetic surgeries.

Breasts and buttocks are frequent parts of bodily dissatisfaction, these areas being erogenous zones signaling sexuality. They are frequent targets of sexual harassment, and studies of ethnic differences in body satisfaction showcase that women perceive their genetics as keeping them from approaching the beauty ideal. Asian-American women—who tend to be petite—, report more breast dissatisfaction than Latina, black, or white women. Meanwhile, Latinas report more dissatisfaction with their eyes and nose than black or white women, Latinas and white women reporting more dissatisfaction with their lower bodies (hips, buttocks, legs) than black women. Jewish and Arab women are frequent consumers of rhinoplasty (nose work), and Asian women often seek eyelid surgery— procedures that move them both closer to the beauty ideal and further from their ethnic identity. Frequent hairstyle changes, body hair removal, and skin color change are other examples of women who are clearly dissatisfied with their body parts.

The obvious fact here is that both men and women influence the socialization process of one another by rewarding certain attitudes and behaviors and punishing others. This process begins at birth and continues throughout a lifetime. These ways in which men and women mold one another can be either blatant or subtle, direct or indirect, person-to-person or societal. Either way, through avenues of parental modeling, peer pressure, and the messages absorbed through the all-powerful media, children learn which behaviors, attitudes, values, and personality characteristics are desirable in men and which ones are desirable in women.

If one were to live in a resort town during the summer months, he would observe 50- and 60-year-old men with tans and gold chains around their necks parading million-dollar yachts adorned with bikini-clad, beautiful young women through the harbor. Indeed, there are things we not only see before our own eyes, but also in movies and social media. One may wonder what kind of gender messages adolescents are receiving from these images; we can speculate that perhaps they are absorbing the idea that (a) If I am a female and I want the good life, I need to be beautiful and find a rich man, and (b) If I am male and I want beautiful women, I better make a lot of money.

There is a circular pattern of reward and punishment that perpetuates the socialization process, beginning at an early age and continuing throughout a lifetime.

PETER

OLIVIA OPENED HER ARMS and I flung myself into her embrace. She held me tightly to her, my heart overflowing with passion. A surge of arousal quickly followed, and she laughed softly as I rubbed against her soft body.

"Damn, babe, you look good enough to eat." Shivers of arousal coupled with outrage flooded through me. She opened her mouth, and, whilst I was sure she was about to come up with a stinging put-down, she instead only released a sighing moan.

Answering her moan in the best way possible, my mouth moved softly along her jawline. I could feel her entire body, now a throbbing, melting mass of want. She almost sobbed as my mouth finally settled softly on hers, and, when she tried to take the kiss deeper, I wouldn't let her, continuing those tender, whispering kisses that triggered a chain reaction to every nerve ending in me. After some time, I finally let my lips cover hers firmly, drawing her tongue deep into my mouth where I lashed at it with mine, sucking hard.

Moments later, she drew back and rasped gruffly, "We'd better talk first." Ignoring the vehement protest of our over-aroused bodies, she pulled away. "We'll continue this later, my angel, I promise," she whispered. "For now, tell me what's weighing on you."

I didn't answer, but the hot gleam of promise in her eyes provided me with the response I needed. Settling me onto her lap, I looked her straight in the eye. She knew something serious was about to unfold.

"One time when I was really little, some girls threw snowballs at me and beat me up." My voice caught. "I knew I couldn't hit back, and so didn't: my father told me that boys should never hit girls. In that moment, though, it sure didn't seem fair: I hated the fact that they were allowed to hit me and I wasn't. I hated them. When you're a teenager, your hormones take over, and you need to do something about getting your sexual urges satisfied; it's just a matter of trial-and-error, really. You try various things, you watch other people, and then you figure out what works, and you do it. There are always the ones who are football stars and class presidents; who letter in all sports and belong to an honors society; who go to elite hangout spots; but most of us are just regular guys, and we do the best we can with what we have. No matter how big you are in any sport or activity, no matter how good you get, there is always someone bigger, someone more talented, someone superior. So, I had to find another way.

"To attract girls, you have to start somewhere: you have to be funny and make them laugh. They all went for the football stars, the guy with the great car, the one who frequented the most popular hangout spots, the guy with expensive style. Well, I was not any of these; I was not as rich as them, anyway. So, instead, I tried to position myself differently to be around girls: I played guitar and started to write songs and sing in nightclubs with small local bands. I tried out, but again, I never was the lead. I felt depressed because I hadn't reached the standard I'd wanted to. I wasn't a coward, you know: I had been indoctrinated enough to know that I was supposed to take care of girls.

"One day, a really pretty girl in my class was in a car accident. I was present at the time, and did what I was always taught to do: I took her to the hospital in a taxi, called her parents, and stayed beside her until they showed up. I went the following day to make sure she was getting better, and I called her almost every day after she was back home. It took several weeks until she was fine and came back to school, but I felt so good protecting her. She was so grateful; I wouldn't hesitate to do the same thing again. It felt good to finally be the hero."

Olivia didn't say a word, signaling me to continue.

"Of course, the girls I hung out with never thought of me as a hero, or as boyfriend—just a friend. They always asked me to fix them up with my friends—the ones with the cars. It was after another one of these incidents that I decided to watch Leonardo Hayes: He knew how to do cute and how to talk to girls in the way they like. The rest of us had no idea what to say to a girl, but Leonardo would just go up to them and start talking, inviting them to his luxurious house on the beach and driving them in his father's Mustang. And it all worked. So, again, I went to school and started trying out things I saw him do—or anything I could do—, and then if they worked, I would do them again.

"But I really didn't start dating until recently—when girls started to change. I don't really think guys change; I think they go on playing by the same macho, tough-guy rules. But at that age, girls start to stand back and watch, starting to notice that this guy is smart, this guy is careless, this guy is a prospective boyfriend, this guy have a bright future. And I realized that they had started going after the guys they thought were going to make money in the future. So, suddenly, as a senior in high school, I turned into someone who had potential. That's when I started dating."

Olivia gazed adoringly at me, as if I were her god. Her expression gently understanding and consoling, she couldn't help but grab me and hug me tight. There was something pure and bright about her, an untouchable goodness. Her deep blue eyes locked with mine and I felt my hands drift to her butt, pulling her closer so her breasts squeezed against my chest. My mouth hovered so close to her that I felt her breath on my face.

She whispered, "I want you more than my next breath."

OLIVIA

I THOUGHT OF PETER as clever, witty, good-looking, a talented employee, and an inveterate charmer of women. Of all the words I could use to describe him bearing in mind the last few of years of our dating, "paternal" would have been last on the list.

At the mention of the word commitment, Peter's eyes would glaze over and he'd pick up the remote control and switch channels rapidly, searching for something involving a muddy field, a football, or a newscast with in-depth sports coverage.

Of course, when you're an athlete and sports maniac, you have to keep up with current sporting events—but a tiny part of my mind was beginning to think that the manic channel-hoping that had ensued the last time I spoke to him about buying a place together was a ploy to avoid talking about settling down and getting married.

I had known what Peter was like when he'd given up the secure and pensionable first job to work at a private financial institution where his father was working. "It's driving me out of my mind," he'd told me. "Working for a big financial institution is one step up; this way, I have a better opportunity to move up faster in the career ladder and grow my income."

"Absolutely," I breathed, fascinated by his ambition and his aspiring future plans for us both—or so I thought. "I can't stand people who just sit still and let life happen to them. I want to make it happen; I want that excitement and that energy," Peter said passionately. "It's what keeps me going."

Gazing deeply into his eyes, I felt myself falling for him even deeper—low boredom threshold and all. I should have wondered what kind of man would dump a perfectly safe job and switch to a risky one, but I didn't; I was the sort of person who woke in the morning with my guts spasming with nerves if I had a difficult interview ahead of me. I found Peter's adventurous spirit intriguing—and, frankly, very sexy. There was something macho about it.

That wasn't enough for Peter, though: once he made some money, he was eager for the next challenge, longing for adventure. I began to yearn for quiet domesticity; he wanted to take up parachuting. I was scared of heights. He signed up for an ice-skating course and gave me some of it for my birthday, even though I hated the cold. But how could I now complain about the very traits I'd found exciting in him in the first place?

"Interest rates and conveyancing fees are probably responsible for more heart attacks than five bucks of Guinness a day, darling," he'd said only the week before, when the most gorgeous cottage in the mountains had jumped out of the property pages at me. The picture showed it bathed in sunlight, and I found myself longing for a house with twelve-inch-thick stone walls and a box-tree herb garden.

"Darling, you know I love living in the city," he said, throwing the property pages onto the floor and nuzzling into my neck as he breathed in the scent of the vanilla perfume he loved me to wear. "Anyway, the rent is swallowing up most of my salary, and I don't want to take on a mortgage when I can keep renting my flat in Manhattan for well under the market rate. You'd be mad to sell your apartment so soon after buying it," he added. "Let's leave things the way they are." And with that, we went up to bed.

Peter's arms were wrapped around me, making me more turned on than any man had been able to before. I hadn't been able to think about anything—never mind buying a house together. All I had wanted was this lean body wrapped around mine, his fingers tangled in my hair and his lips gently kissing my skin. And when he murmured exactly what he was going to do to me just before he did it, I melted in a puddle of anticipation.

His voice did the most amazing things to me—both in my mind and my body—, and, when we finally came together in a surge of passion, the intensity of my orgasm caused me to shudder. In that moment, I wondered how either pf us had ever enjoyed lovemaking with anyone else.

"We're wonderful in bed together," he said afterwards. It was true: we were perfectly in-tune in bed—even though we weren't so in-tune out of it.

"Look, Liv, this is an awful mess," he said abruptly. "Can't you see? I don't want to settle down now; I'm not ready for all that stuff yet. You know that. What made you think differently?"

I stepped away from him. For the second time that day, my pulse was racing and I could feel the blood racing in my veins. All I wanted to do was sink into my bed and close my eyes, or start reading my latest book, curled up under the duvet, immune to his harsh words.

"Let me get this straight: you don't want to settle down with me?" I said quietly. I was close to tears and terrified of his answer, but had to know. "Talk to me, Peter. What do you want to do?"

"Oh God, Liv, I didn't say that I don't want to settle down with you; I said just not now. I'm not ready yet. Don't you get it?" He ran a hand through his hair and, for a brief moment, I remembered lying in the cotton sheets on his bed, running my fingers through his hair while he lay in my arms. We were so close—so close that I never would have expected this answer. "Why now?" he pressed on. "In a few years, yes, but not now." He looked at me beseechingly.

"Commitment-phobic," Mia had called him the first time she saw him. Perhaps my sister was right.

Peter gently stroked my palm, tracing delicate circles and kneading the fleshy base of my thumb. People with lots of soft flesh in that precise spot were supposed to be very sensual, he had always said, joking that I must be the sexiest woman in the world because of my soft, caressing hands. Before, when he'd murmured endearments into my ear and stroked my skin, my heart leapt with love for this funny and talented man. But not tonight.

"Darling, don't be upset, please." He was all charm again. He'd always been able to charm his way out of any trouble: he just smiled that boyish smile and wheedled until I gave in and forgave him. "We can settle down later, my darling," he said pleadingly. "We aren't ready for this yet, are we?" He reached out to stroke my cheek, waiting for me to give in. I always gave in. But this time, I wouldn't.

"What are you suggesting?" I asked, my voice dangerously low.

"Well, you know, get rid of that idea—at least for now."

I snatched my hand away as though his fingers were burning me, staring him in the face angrily.

"And if I don't 'get rid of it', what then?"

"Olivia, you're being unreasonable," he chided. "All I'm saying is that this is the wrong time in my life for settling down." Peter's face was fast losing its engaging smile. "I'm not ready for it. We're not ready for it."

"No, you're not ready. You're so bloody selfish," I hissed. "You just couldn't bear having to think about someone else besides yourself. You can't have a defenseless marriage interrupting your plans, or getting in the way of your life, can you?"

"There's no need to be insulting." Peter gave me one of his firm looks. "We should talk about this tomorrow, when you're less hysterical."

"Hysterical!" I hadn't felt so close to hitting anyone in years. "That's typical! Just because I want to marry you and settle down, I've suddenly turned into a neurotic, moody brood mare with no brain whatsoever!"

"Be quiet. Someone will hear," Peter hissed.

"Oh, we can't have that, can we?" I snarled. "I don't care who hears me. In fact, I want everyone to hear me so I can find out what they think about the wonderful finance guy everyone adores, begging his girlfriend to postpone her plans because it's 'not the right time'. When will it be the right time, Peter? Because you're running out of time; you're nearly thirty, don't forget."

If someone had told me that my feelings for him could be reversed in a matter of moments, I'd have laughed at the idea: nothing could have wiped out the love I felt for Peter, the bond that had tied us to each other. But that was before he had looked me in the eye and suggested that we shouldn't talk about settling down now.

As I was about to throw a bundle of old papers in the bin a few days later, I looked longingly at the property section and wondered whether I was mad to think about settling down now: Peter was happy the way things were, so why wasn't I? His bachelor pad in the city center was perfect for a man who liked nothing better than to sway the few short yards from New York's trendy hostelries to his front door on a Saturday night. Trips to soccer stadiums before dancing the night away in a nightclub was Peter's idea of fun—not getting up at 3am for a feed.

For the third time, I felt as though I'd been punched in the face: I'd worked hard for that moment. Is it really that all what I planned for was wrong? How could that all my judgments be nonsense? the voice in my mind echoed fearfully.

On my way back home, surrendering my mind to the discussion was inevitable: reality was blurred. I couldn't swallow the fact that I was totally ignorant when it came to understanding men's psyche: I had always been convinced that females can—naturally, and by little learning—understand men, more than men could understand themselves. But for the first time, I'd realized I knew next to nothing: men were on a different planet. Although confused, I became hungry to know more to understand how I had messed up.

The Attribution Error Concept: The tendency to ascribe the actions of others to internal motives and attributes, rather than external situational factors. Olivia believed Peter didn't want to settle down because he had hidden motives of playing around; meanwhile, she ignored the probability that his inability to settle down now could have been related to many other situational reasons.

PETER

THE RELATIONSHIP WITH OLIVIA had heated up sexually, and she was allowing me to take more liberties, bit by bit. Essentially, all was right in my world.

"Yes, of course, babe, I love you so much. I cannot live without you, Olivia. You know that, don't you?" are the things I would find myself telling her whenever she, occasionally, agreed to have sex.

"Yes, Peter, I know, and I love you too, but I think of our future. We should seriously consider it," would always be her response.

Deep inside, I knew what Olivia had planned for: she wanted me to propose to her as soon as possible.

"I've started to hate having sex with her," I told John at the time. "Every time, she keeps pushing for marriage. She doesn't stop nagging." I felt like I was being pushed over my limits: money was part of the barrier, but I was also afraid of marriage—terrified of commitment. Marriage meant to me that I would be promising to spend the rest of my life working like a cash-cow to support a family, wrapped up in a long list of marital restrictions—and, most importantly, all the fun of my personal life would come to an end. Marriage meant to be chained forever: I'd need to give up motorcycle and hunting trips with my buddies, instead spending my weekends mowing the grass—or, in the best case scenario, spend the weekend in a boring gathering in my mother-in-law's house. Marriage meant the obligation of making enough money to buy a house; marriage meant having kids, and I didn't know how to take care of kids; marriage meant giving up the potential of having other women—although sometimes, I thought that having readily available sex was better than always having to seduce women. However, because men aren't supposed to be afraid or unsecure, I never shared these concerns with Olivia: I was worried she would take my concerns personally—and I was probably right in that fear.

Feelings of obligation may ruin friendships,
but they kill romance.

The Opportunity Cost Concept: A married man or one in a long-term relationship is always worried that single men are fully enjoying their worriless life: singles have a lot more things to do with their hard- earned money than spending it on marriage. He imagines wild singles parties, adventurous, commitment-free couplings, and beaches full of naked supermodels. He fears opportunity is passing him by. It doesn't matter that, when he had been single, such opportunities never presented themselves anyway: he just cannot help worrying that commitment means missing out.

WHEN PETER TOLD OLIVIA he wasn't ready to commit, she should have believed him the first time: he was being real, and Olivia shouldn't have pushed Peter to marry her. She couldn't convince him that he was ready; she only tried to fool herself. If a woman ever finds herself in a similar situation, it's better for her to stop for a minute and think: you're dating a man, and you want things to move to the next level (i.e., commitment); however, he says that he isn't ready yet. You tell him if he cannot commit, you're moving on. If he comes right back and says, "Okay, I am ready to commit," this simply means you have pushed him—even though he is still not ready to commit to you. He just doesn't want to lose you, or see you committed to someone else. That's why Peter always accused Olivia of rushing their marriage while he wasn't yet ready to commit—although afterwards, he agreed and appeared to be genuinely happy.

At the beginning of time, with the birth of man, Adam wasn't conscious that he was alone: God's statement was predicated on His own observation of the situation—on His own wisdom. The implication is that Adam was so totally unique and so whole that he hadn't been missing anybody! He was so "together", so separate, and so complete in himself, that he didn't even know he needed anyone else. Having a companion wasn't Adam's idea, but God's.

Adam didn't need a wife; that's another misconception we have gotten from traditional thinking. God didn't say, "Adam isn't a whole being, so I will make him a wife to complete him." In essence, God said, "I am going to make him another being who will complement him and be complemented by him."

The marriage came later on. God made a second human being—not just for Adam to marry, but also so he wouldn't be alone—and you don't have to marry in order to not be alone: all you need for that is to have some other humans as your companions. Have you been able to resolve your feeling alone by the addition of good companions in your life? Or do you feel that you must be married in order to fill that void?

There is a myth surrounding being single in terms of it being a "problem", when this is certainly not the case—and so sadness surrounding being single is actually the result of an entirely different problem. Let's consider the concept of that ever-abiding concern which seems to control and influence so many lives: singleness.

Any dictionary definition will have these words, or synonyms, for singleness: "To be separate, unique, and whole." Would you like to stop being a whole or a unique person? Would you like to lose your identity? Of course not. So, what's the problem with singleness? The problem is with our definition, which has been given to us by a cultural socio-economic system. We have confused singleness with being alone.

Will there ever be a time—and has there ever been a time—when you will cease to be "separate, unique, and whole"? Should there ever be time when you cease to be a single being who is unique and whole?

If your answer is "no", then the next question would be, does getting married do away with this definition of being "single"? When you marry, do you stop being a single individual who is unique and whole?

If a state of singleness means "to be unique and whole", then to be totally single should be your primary goal; in fact, I want to impress upon you that no one should marry until they are totally single—until you are a separate single, unique, and whole person.

Family research will tell you that 99% of marital problems arise because a husband or wife (or both) haven't seen themselves as unique, worthy individuals (i.e., they have a negative self-image, or are "not whole" or "not separate" in some way). Thus, until you are truly single, marriage will be a difficult—and perhaps negative—experience.

Simply stated, the marriage myth promises life Happily Ever After—when the factual core of this myth stems from those people who are happily married, and tend to reinforce the myth. The important fictional element is the subtly operating assumption that the institution of marriage itself has inordinate powers to make people happy—regardless of the personal maturity or mental health of those involved. Until recently, this particular combination of fact and fiction has comprised the majority of information given to young people about marriage.

The fictional element of the marriage myth has led to there being many rules and assumptions formed about marriage—and, paradoxically, these rules and assumptions inhibit the couple from attaining a more realistic view of a good marriage. The following is a partial list of these assumptions and rules:
- Things will work out if we love each other.
- Always consider the other person first.

- Keep criticism to oneself and focus on the positive.
- If things aren't going well, focus on the future.
- See oneself as part of the couple first, as an individual second.
- What's mine is yours.
- Marriage makes people significantly happier.
- What is best for the children will be best for us.

Although there are many minor rules, these eight are amongst the most basic, and are usually firmly implanted in the lifestyles of the couple by the end of the first mythical year.

To females: During your ovulation, do not
look for a long-term relationship.

Across cultures, many women believe that a good romantic partner is someone who is reliable, dependable, and will make a good father—and yet many women pursue, and are ultimately heartbroken by, men who are charismatic, adventurous, and physically attractive, but hopelessly unreliable.

You may find popular dating guides that teach bachelors how to be the "bad boy" women cannot resist; and, on the contrary, dating guides for women implore them to avoid commitment-phobic men and instead choose the reliable "Mr. Good Enough". However, despite the continuous warnings and recurring heartbreaks, many women keep pursuing the wrong guy. Do we ever learn from mistakes?

One reason for this concerns the female psychological mechanism during the ovulation period: past studies on the female ovulation period have concluded that the woman's psyche during this time motivates her to believe that it is a good idea to pursue men who are sexy, dominant, and charismatic, but also likely unreliable partners.

Male dating guides have played on this psychological mechanism deficiency, providing men with guides on how to attract women by being the bad guy that women will consider attractive.

Such a period may lead women to wrongly perceive that attractive men will become devoted parents and faithful partners, when in fact, the hormonal changes associated with fertility produce specific perceptual shifts, strategically altering a given female's perceptions of some traits (but not others) in some men but not all. Ovulation can mean "Mr. Wrong" appears to be "Mr. Right".

For those who are married, it'll be no secret that a woman has a greater passion and desire to make love after her menstruation.

Men have two mating strategies: Some men adopt a short-term mating strategy associated with having multiple, less committed sexual partners; other men adopt a long-term mating strategy associated with having more committed relationship partners. Although men may, at times, adopt a combination of these two strategies, the majority of men generally pursue either a short-term or a long-term mating strategy—the selection of which depending on many different traits.

Men adopting the short-term strategy are found to be more physically attractive and more socially dominant and rebellious; they tend to engage in flashy and ostentatious behavior, and possess an exploitative social nature. This type of man not only adopts a "love them-and-leave-them" attitude towards mating, but he also possesses traits associated with subclinical psychopathy and subclinical narcissism. Therefore, this type of man tends to display lower levels of stability, agreeableness, warmth, and faithfulness.

In contrast, men who adopt a long-term mating strategy possess the opposite features, tending to be less physically attractive, less charismatic and less socially dominant. However, they are more stable, agreeable, warm, and faithful than men who adopt the short-term mating strategy. These traits are associated with being a good long-term partner and an investing father. Such men are often referred to as "good dads".

Women, ideally, want the best parts of both types of men in a romantic partner, and so many women seek men who are attractive, charismatic, and dominant whilst also being faithful, reliable, and good fathers. However, because it's difficult to find and secure such an ideal mate, the majority of women must make a trade-off between pursuing long-term relationships with men who are good dads versus short-term relationships with men who are more attractive but less committed. As we have seen, this choice is often impacted by their menstrual cycle.

Women are especially attracted to "sexy", charismatic, and dominant men at a particular time each month: many empirical studies have documented that women's mating preferences are influenced by the hormonal fluctuations associated with their monthly menstrual cycle. During the days of the month when a woman is most fertile, she will tend to be more attracted to men who have more symmetrical and masculine faces, who showcase more socially dominance and have deeper voices. This type of man is the kind to adopt the short-term mating strategy, and are purported to be makers of male genetic fitness—something that unconsciously attracts the woman as features suggest such men can provide genetic benefits to potential offspring. Supporting this ovulation explanation, ovulating women show an increased desire for this type of man as sexual partners—especially if a woman's current partner lacks the indicators of genetic fitness.

Thus, generally speaking, ovulating women appear to over-perceive charismatic and adventurous men, inferring that they will be invested fathers and more committed and stable romantic partners—at least with respect to them. This ovulatory perceptual shift may motivate certain women to accept romantic offers from men who may be unfaithful and could ultimately desert them.

We should bear in mind that the ovulatory perceptual shift effect occurs only when women are evaluating certain types of males; thus, ovulation changes the perceptions of the "short-term" men, but not the reliable, good men. The ovulatory perceptual shift effect occurs only for the benefit of the female observer's offspring, as ovulating women believe that a charismatic and adventurous man will be a better father.

Notably, the ovulatory perceptual shift effect is driven by a specific subset of women—specifically, those who are pursuing a faster, more short-term reproductive strategy. This, however, does not apply for women following a slower, more long-term reproductive strategy. This finding supports those of previous studies', which show that positive illusions tend to be specific to one's own evaluations of the partner, and not outsider evaluations.

ABOUT THE MYTH
OF FEMINISM

The equality between males and females is a political or moral game; the factual, essential difference is a scientific one.

From Olivia's Diary:

YOU SEE THEM EVERYWHERE: they walk along busy highways in low-slung jeans and tank tops, peering into every car that passes. They sit with their friends in bars and restaurants, searching, their thoughts clearly on who is looking at them. They catch the eyes of the boys they pass, smiling and flipping their hair. They post selfies in bikinis on social media, seeking attention and praise; they produce porn content to gain money—although they sometimes even do it for free. They are just girls: they are your sister; your daughter; your friend; your niece. They are not remarkable, really, in any way: they are almost every girl you see. They believe in their hearts that they are worth nothing, that they have little to offer. They believe boys will pull them out of their ordinariness and finally—finally—transform them into someone better than who they are.

They have sex too early and for the wrong reasons; they get STDs, and they get pregnant too young. They have "friends with benefits," but with no benefit to themselves. They give oral sex like kisses and hope for love in return. They are ignored; they don't get called; they get dumped again and again; they lie alone in their beds and hate themselves for being so unlovable, for being so needy, for not being like every other girl, for not being able to just have fun. Contrary to popular belief, they aren't sex addicts, or even love addicts: what they crave is attention—that moment when a boy looks at them and they can believe that they are worth something to someone.

When these girls grow up, they find that in this way, they are still girls: they carry their pasts with boys into their futures, and they remain needy, desperate, and anxious for someone to prove their worth. The boys, though, become men.

For a lot of my life, I was close to that girl in many aspects—and when I became a married woman, I learned that there were many others like me, assuming they were the only ones who felt this way and that they suffered with this alone. But how could this be? How do we get so far into our lives and into these experiences without sharing them—and our feelings—with our friends and parents? Because we feel alone, carrying immense shame about our behavior and, more so, our desperation. Some came from divorce, like I did; others have lived through severe abuse. Still, others had untarnished childhoods, intact families, and the feeling that they had been loved. Some have had sex with only three men; others with fifty. The number of men, however, is not important: it's the feelings these young women experienced—feelings surrounding the belief that that if they got a man's attention, it would mean they were worth something in the world.

THE STRONG, INDEPENDENT WOMAN is a myth: a female cannot feel any of what she craves on her own. She always needs male affirmation that she is beautiful; that she is still desired. She wears makeup because she isn't certain that her natural beauty is attractive enough. She takes thousands of selfies trying to overcome the feeling that there are other women prettier than her. She's more confident about her professional success when she receives appreciation from her male co-worker, more than her female co-worker. She cannot bear her husband looking at prettier women than her. Still, the most rewarding job for any female is to become a mother.

Despite the sexual freedom women enjoy, many are still considering marriage—the normal evolution and logical objective of their relationship. She pays fortunes on cosmetics, clothing, and pills to become a mother, and plastic surgery to overcome her problems. Words still allow her to feel better about herself, and she is strong until she discovers she cannot become a mother. She is independent until she finds herself alone after her kids have grown up and her husband has died: then, you will hear her complaining that she cannot live in loneliness. She is proud that she is a woman, until she fails to complete a specific male-specialized job—in which case you should not be surprised by her envy. She is independent, and yet her primary point of pride is the fact that she is a wife and mother. She is strong and independent, but still craves care, understanding, love, kindness, protection, appreciation from her male—and if these qualities aren't found in her spouse, she'll complain. She is strong and independent, and yet, in this male-dominated world, finds herself still wanting to be treated like a female—and she will tell you, when she sees fit, "Because I am a female, I deserve to be treated like one."

How women came to be associated with physique and men with the mind is a subject for debate; however, anthropologists and sociologists have attributed the association of a female with her body to the female's capacity to give birth—which in ancient times appeared to be magical and mysterious. During the development of civilized societies, men placed a high value on control, competition, reason, power over others, hierarchy, domination, autonomy, instrumentality, and the use of abstract rules and principles to govern one's life—whilst women were associated with what (adhering to transcendence philosophy) came to be considered as lesser values (e.g., spontaneity; cooperation; compassion; emotion; affiliation;

submission; nurturance; expressivity; the pragmatic application of rules based on affiliative needs).

However, there is one major misbelief concerning these two concepts: the "mutually exclusive misbelief". Societies consider these two concepts to contrast one another—a man who is in control cannot be a man of cooperation, and a man in power cannot be a man of emotion and affiliation. Similarly, cooperative woman cannot be in control. Therefore, social stereotypes consider each concept as mutually exclusive to one gender.

Yet we've all experienced emotional men and logical women: there are nurturing and supportive male bosses, and aggressive female bosses. Again, I wish to stress that men and women have the capacity for a wide range of personality characteristics—and, indeed, I believe that the wider the range available to each individual, the healthier and fulfilling a life that individual will lead.

The wide spread of this stereotype and its real-life application by societies in the different aspects of life have motivated the feminists to embrace the idea of gender equality—and, again, this is because of the misbelief of the mutually exclusive man and woman concept. Two of the main factors that have aided in the spreading of this stereotype are—broadly speaking—the media, and the women themselves.

I always consider the quote, "There is no wholly masculine man, no purely feminine woman," Margaret Fuller (1810-1850). Indeed, it is quite noticeable to anyone that women feel proud when they are perceived as a creature of emotions, softness, nurturance, tenderness, and compassion; meanwhile, they don't like to be perceived as being aggressive, heartless, and emotionless, like men. Across all the different mediums of media, these "feminine" characteristics are reflected and reinforced: in movies, talk shows, and advertisements, the female body shape and face remain the key selling propositions. Women like to be treated like women, not like men—and yet they still fight to be equal to men, a point of great confusion to the public.

If women seek total equality to men, then they should accept to be treated like men—and yet in areas where they feel that they should be treated like a female, they tend to differentiate themselves from males. In other areas, where they find males dominate, they tend to equalize themselves to males and seek for equality, arguing that society is empowering men over women.

Women are caught up in the myth of feminism. When God created men and women, He designed them to be coheirs with a delicate balance of both power and submission to one another. In the centuries that followed, however, the balance of power swayed too far in favor of the male side, and women felt cheated of their basic human rights—particularly the rights to protect themselves from physically abusive husbands, to own property, and to vote. Today, however, some women are pushing in the opposite direction, resulting in women wanting power over men. Some men refer to the women of this bold movement as "feminazis"—women promote reproductive freedoms (abortion without the father's consent), alternative lifestyles (lesbianism), and a general hatred for the male gender. Now, many men are feeling the same way women did: somewhat cheated of their basic human rights to be respected in their homes and to be treated with dignity. Some even feel as if they are being emotionally abused by their wives, and that they have no right to speak out about it.

This self-centeredness cannot be denied if we look closely at our societies: in some circles, women are applauded for their courage to leave their husbands and children to discover "who they really are" and to pursue their own dreams (as if a successful marriage and strong family life aren't sufficient noble goals). When it comes to marital discord, society insinuates that it's primarily the fault of men.

Media have repeatedly taught us that men know nothing except how to use power tools, vegetate in front of a television, and complain that their wives don't give them enough sex. The decline of the masculine image in television and movies has created an undercurrent of disrespect and discord in many homes—and, even worse, some families cultivate sheer animosity toward one another.

What happened with Olivia is called the Cultivation Theory, which suggests that the more often women see images of ideal bodies and read or hear messages about the importance of beauty, the more influenced they are. High consumption of media that present the beauty ideal makes the ideal seem more important, and its pursuit more plausible. The parents and peers amplify messages from the media by directing others' attention to those messages, sharing strategies to become more beautiful (e.g., beauty tips; diets; cosmetics; fashion techniques) through complimentary weightism (e.g., "You look terrific; have you lost weight?"), through fat talk and sexual harassment, and by teasing others who don't seem to care enough or try hard enough to be beautiful.

The popularity of toys and costumes based on the Disney princesses, as well as sexualized dolls (e.g., Barbie' Bratz) and clothing (e.g., padded bras; thongs; high heels), which are purchased by parents and shared with peers, cementing girls' knowledge of the importance of beauty—and what the beauty ideals constitute—at early ages, strongly conveying the message that a female's primary value lies in their appearance. Nowadays, both girls and boys as young as six years old understand the importance of attractiveness and thinness, reporting that they prefer thin over heavyweight children as friends.

It is clear that girls learn early that beauty work is part of the feminine gender role—that is, something that girls and women are supposed to do. Thus, from a young age, girls learn that the female body is inadequate without the corrections that beauty work provides. They may also form the impression that beauty work provides fun—a type of creative play or a hobby—and, indeed, it may be that it is required. These beauty work activities are time-consuming and money draining, and form an important part of the transformation from "female" to "feminine"—and, as such, it is one of the norms to which girls and women are expected to conform.

And then you find women asking men to not consider them as sexual objects!

Although there are certainly men who are invested in their appearance, too much investment in appearance is suspected in men—whereas not enough investment is suspected in women. That statement is especially true for heterosexuals: appearance-related gender performance is a signal of social identity. Lesbians are expected to—or permitted to—invest less in their appearance than straight women are, and gay men are expected to—or permitted to—invest more in their appearance than straight men are. However, permission to avoid beauty norms may lead to stigmatization as a sexual minority—a choice that women may not want to make.

Ironically, women fight for more independence, gender indifferences, and gender equality, and yet still fall—either intentionally or unintentionally—under a state of insecurity about their appearances.

"Femvertising"—short for female empowerment advertising—is used as a label for contemporary advertising campaigns questioning traditional female stereotypes used in advertising. "Femvertising" moves away from using simplistic female stereotypes, toward more complex and varied female portrayals, placing less strain on a female audience to comply with a specific stereotype, thus leading to more possibilities relating to the female portrayals used. By being more open to the target audience, femvertising reduces the risk of ad reactance—and, by the same token, portrayals of women used in femvertising will be less likely to lead to ad reactance than that of typical advertising.

Female product industries and marketers have gained much from adapting to a more proactive and mindful approach to the female portrayals used in their ads: marketers historically worked reactively with stereotypes (waiting for societal norms change first), but now, marketers have started to work more proactively in order to challenge societal norms and stereotypes. By working on changing societal norms, marketers have found females to be an easy target audience in changing beliefs and behaviors. Challenging such stereotypes has been found to be beneficial—not only to a narrow set of products (e.g., household products), but also to a wide range of products categories, from cars to underwear, sportswear to shampoo. Over time, female audience perceived "femvertising" as liberal and increasingly reflecting their ambitions, being less stereotypical than traditional advertising. The positive reception of "femvertising" by their female audience has encouraged marketers to increase the feminine liberal tone in their advertisements.

When females are allowing advertisers, TV programs, and the media in general to use them as sex objects to sell or advertise a product and to grab the attention of the audience, then it is no wonder that women end up as still being considered as sex objects. Almost without fail, research shows a cross-sex bias: people rate the sexual images of the opposite sex more positively, ads featuring explicit sexual female content being positively rated by men and ads featuring explicit sexual male content being positively rated by women.

With more independence, freedom, and gender equality gained by women, it will become unfair to describe women as victims of an oppressive culture regarding her insecure state of her appearance, as women play a key role in their bodily preoccupation; in fact, anxieties surrounding the female appearance should be dealt with by the women in a culture stating that women are capable of resisting, subverting, or consciously and willingly accepting cultural demands.

ABOUT THE MYTH
OF LOVE

Lovers thrive on one another's broken dreams, which become lifelong fantasies.

From Peter's Diary:

LOVE IS A GREAT intangible: everyone admits that love is wonderful and necessary, yet no one can agree on what it is.

I don't know if there has ever been a time in history when the word love has been used quite so promiscuously as it is at present. We are told constantly that we must "love" everyone; leaders, media stars, official figures, etc. declare that they "love" followers they have never met. Nurtured by cultural and religious myths, social media's emotion-begging quotes and targeted media programs has led to the concept of love becoming a commodity—one that is widely spread and valueless. It has become an abstract word that nobody really knows the real meaning of. Just as a currency, through the process of becoming more and more inflated, has less and less purchasing power, words, through an analogous process of inflation and through being used less and less discriminately, are progressively emptied of meaning.

It is possible to feel benevolence and goodwill toward human beings one doesn't know or doesn't know very well, but it isn't possible to feel love: love, by its very nature, entails a process of selection, of discrimination, of targeting, and of the prey's seduction. Love is a response to distinctive characteristics possessed by some beings—"the prey"—, but not by all. Otherwise, what would the tribute of love be?

We use the word love in such a sloppy way that it can mean almost nothing, or absolutely everything. When the very meaning of the word love is cloaked in mystery, it should not come as a surprise that most people find it hard to define what they mean when they use, "I love you."

If love between adults doesn't imply admiration, nor an appreciation of the traits and qualities that the prey possesses, what meaning or significance would love have, and why would anyone consider it desirable? Why one would consider a particular prey more than others?

The kindest thing I can say about the current use of "love" is that such usages represent inexcusable intellectual sloppiness. My own impression is that people who talk of "loving" everyone, are, in fact, expressing the wish or plea that everyone should love them in return—but to take love seriously and to treat the concept of love with respect—as well as to distinguish it from generalized benevolence or goodwill—, is to appreciate that it is a unique experience and process possible between some people, but not between all.

Love is a feeling, and not a fact. One can change their feelings by changing their thinking

The Portrait Painter Concept: Under your seducer's eyes, all your inner and physical imperfections disappear. They paint you as a saint, bring out noble qualities in you, frame you in a myth, make you God-like, immortalize you. For their ability to create such fantasies in you, the seducer is rewarded with great power.

PETER AND OLIVIA HAD BEEN playing each other perfectly: their seduction plans had worked perfectly, her as the Siren and he as the Rake. As their relationship grew with intensity over time, they both unconsciously forgot about the preplans they had been following; the only idea that controlled their mind and feelings was, "So this is what they call love."

"Olivia, I love you to the moon and back," Peter would surrender.

"Peter, you're the only dream I want to live for, after all the bad I've been through," Olivia would concede.

Unconsciously, both fell under the spell of each other. They didn't recognize that, implicitly, they made false promises to each other by showing off a fake personality. It wasn't the real Olivia. It wasn't the real Peter.

Peter and Olivia renamed seduction love; they misinterpreted the natural gender attraction to be love; misunderstood opening up to each other to be love. They hadn't realized that they replaced their beliefs, altered their attitudes, and changed their behavior in order to attract each other; they didn't realize that they faked their personality to appeal to one another. In fact, Olivia and Peter are no different than the majority of us.

Successful seducers rarely begin with an obvious maneuver or strategic device: that is certain to arouse suspicion. Peter was a successful seducer: he began with his character—his ability to radiate qualities that attracted Olivia—and stirred her emotions in a way that was beyond her control. Hypnotized by his seductive character, Olivia didn't notice his subsequent manipulations—and from then, it was a case of child's play to mislead and seduce her.

Peter was often secretly oppressed by the role he had to play by always having to be responsible, in control, and rational. The Siren was his ultimate fantasy figure: she offered a total release from the limitations of his life, and because of this, Peter felt transported to a world of pure pleasure in Olivia's presence—an experience that had always been heightened and sexually charged. She was dangerous, and, in pursuing her energetically, Peter had lost control over himself—something he yearned to do. The Siren is a mirage: Olivia lured him by cultivating a particular appearance and manner. In a world where women are often too timid to project such an image, they learn to take control of the male libido by embodying his fantasy. However, it's important to bear in mind that it's not simply beauty that makes a woman a Siren, but rather a theatrical streak that allows a woman to embody a man's fantasies. If she had not embodied this, Peter would have grown bored with Olivia, no matter how beautiful she was; he would have yearned for different pleasures and for adventure. All Olivia needed to do in order to turn this around was to create the illusion that she offered such variety and adventure.

Olivia played such a game by creating the physical presence of a Siren (i.e., heightened sexual allure, mixed with a regal and theatrical manner) to trap Peter. He was not yet completely bored with her and hadn't yet considered discarding her, and we can confidently say that this was almost entirely down to Olivia's Siren persona; otherwise, she would have likely been deprived of affection—something that would have been detrimental to Olivia, since her deepest need was to feel loved and desired. This made her seem constantly vulnerable, like a little girl craving protection. She emanated this need for love before Peter, who falsely assumed it to be coming from somewhere real and deep inside her.

What differentiates the Sex Siren from the courtesan or whore is her touch of innocence and vulnerability. This mix is perversely satisfying, and it gave Peter the critical illusion that he was the protector, the father figure. The Siren operates on a man's most basic emotions, and, if she plays her role properly, she can transform an otherwise strong and responsible male into a childish slave. Olivia's effect was intense on the rigid, masculine type—the soldier or hero—, although the intellectual is often the most susceptible to the Siren's call of pure physical pleasure, since his life so often lacks it.

A woman never quite feels desired and appreciated enough: Olivia wanted attention, but Peter was too distracted and unresponsive. The Rake is a great female fantasy figure: when he desires a woman—no matter how brief the moment—, he will go to the ends of the earth for her. He may be disloyal, dishonest, and immoral, but that only adds to his appeal. Indeed, unlike the normal, cautious males, Peter reflected the image of being delightfully unrestrained, a slave to his love of women—and, as a result, there was an added sense of enticement to his reputation. Words are a woman's weakness, and Peter was a master of seductive language; he stirred Olivia's repressed longings by adapting the Rake's mix of danger and pleasure.

In seduction, there is often a dilemma: to seduce, you need planning and calculation—but if your victim suspects you to have ulterior motives, she will grow defensive. Furthermore, if you seem to be in control, you will inspire fear instead of desire. The Ardent Rake solves this dilemma in the most artful manner: of course, he must still calculate and plan—he has to find a way around any obstacles, after all—and, whilst this would usually be exhausting work for the average individual, the Ardent Rake has the advantage of an uncontrollable libido at its very nature. When he pursues a woman, he is aglow with desire, and, upon seeing this, the victim is inflamed, despite herself. How can she imagine him to be a heartless seducer, susceptible to abandoning his prey when satisfied, when he so ardently braves all dangers and obstacles to get to her? Even if she is aware of his rakish past—of his incorrigible amorality—it does not matter: she also sees his weaknesses—more specifically, the fact that he cannot control himself, and is a slave to all women. As such, he inspires no fear.

The Ardent Rake tells us a simple lesson: intense desire has a distracting power on a woman, just as the Siren's physical presence does on a man. A woman is often defensive and can sense insincerity or calculation, but if she feels consumed by your attentions and is confident you will do anything for her, she will notice nothing else about you—or will simply find a way to forgive your indiscretions. This is the perfect cover for a seducer, the key here being to show no hesitation, to abandon all restraint, to let yourself go, and to show that you cannot control yourself and are fundamentally weak. Don't worry about inspiring mistrust; as long as you are the slave to her charms, she will not think of the aftermath.

The Rake is as promiscuous with words as he is with women: he chooses words for their ability to suggest, insinuate, hypnotize, elevate, and infect. The words of the Rake are the equivalent of the bodily adornment of the Siren: a powerful sensual distraction; a narcotic. The Rake's use of language is demonic in the sense that it is designed not to communicate or convey information, but to persuade, to flatter, and to stir emotional turmoil. Adapt the character of the Rake, and you will find that the use of words as a subtle poison has infinite applications. Remember: it is the form that matters, not the content; the less your targets focus on what you say and more on how it makes them feel, the more seductive your effect.

It may seem strange that a man who is clearly dishonest, disloyal, and has no interest in marriage would have any appeal to a woman, but throughout all of history—and in all cultures—, this type has had a fatal effect. What the Rake offers is what society normally doesn't allow women: an affair of pure pleasure; an exciting brush with danger. A woman is often deeply oppressed by the role she is expected to play, being expected to be tender and to want commitment and lifelong loyalty. However, her marriages and relationships often fall short of the romance and devotion she craves, instead giving her a stringent routine and an endlessly distracted mate. It remains an abiding female fantasy to meet a man who will give all of himself freely; one who lives for her, even if only for a while. The great seducers don't offer the mild pleasures that society condones; they touch a person's unconscious—those repressed desires that cry out for liberation. Do not imagine that women are the tender creatures that some people would like them to be: like men, they are deeply attracted to the forbidden, the dangerous... Even the slightly evil.

To play the Rake, Peter had been able to let himself go; to draw Olivia into the kind of purely sensual moment in which the past and future lose meaning. He was able to abandon himself for the moment. An added benefit to this quality is that it made him appear as wholly unable to control himself—a display of weakness Olivia enjoyed. He completely opened up to her, appearing like a child. By abandoning himself to Olivia, he made her feel that he existed for her alone—a feeling reflecting a truth, though a temporary one.

PART II: GENDER POWER STRUGGLE

*If you understand a person's personality, their behavior won't be a surprise
to you; instead, it will begin to
make sense to you.*

OLIVIA

IN THE EARLY YEARS of our marriage—when I still had a job and Peter and I had succeeded in our careers, achieving fair positions—, our careers had been given the top priority: our objective was to earn an adequate amount of money in order to live the comfortable life we dreamt of.

Thus, our relationship was, to a large extent, based on equality concerning opportunities for achieving desirable career goals; however, our marriage reflected a more traditional pattern when it came to the organization of daily chores. I had the responsibility for the daily household chores during the weekdays—such as preparing dinner and taking care of the children in the afternoons—, and Peter would usually come home later than I. Saying this, he still had committed to helping me out with some duties—such as shopping for the daily necessities, dish-washing, and other house-cleaning duties that he was capable of.

My friend, Nicole, advised me to give more duties to Peter in regard to the household chores. To this, I responded, "I'm the mother; it's important for me to be in control of the household, and I want to remain as the primary parent." I gave Peter the duties that I knew he could do without difficulty, fitting his capabilities as a man; meanwhile, the ones I knew I could do better than him as a woman I did myself. This way, we were both satisfied and appreciative of the other's contributions. "Our life is going smoothly this way," I added.

I had made an active choice in relation to Peter's participation, attempting to strike a balance in order to make my marriage a successful one. I knew that Peter was concerned about my work at home, and for that, he did what I asked in terms of helping with chores; meanwhile, I retained the core duties as my own—the duties that keep me as the central figure of the family. Because I was maintaining such a balance in my relationship with Peter, I felt that our affection for one another had deepened over the years, and that our commitment and admiration for one another were growing.

Now, with our falling-apart marriage life, I believe I had been wrong: my larger amount of household chores represented a subordination to Peter's career demands—to his self-oriented ambitions. I believe that our relationship was skewed in terms of power in favor of Peter: I sacrificed; he didn't. If I had simply given him more household responsibilities, I would have been more emotionally fulfilled, this sharing of equal responsibilities potentially having formed stronger emotional ties between us.

Life sucks, and one must always remember that something will almost always be missing from their life; one can never expect to get what they want all the time.

My sister, Mia, and her husband, Paul, had been working full-time since their youngest daughter, Suzy, had turned one, working regular hours, neither ever doing overtime, so that both would come home at the same time. Both were satisfied with what they had achieved thus far in their career lives, and their marriage was entirely based on equality concerning the division of labor; meanwhile, the organization of daily chores was based on joint decisions. They shared the duties of parenting and housework almost equally, and so whilst Paul was practicing the model of the "New Father"—the man sharing the responsibilities for parenting with his wife—, he was automatically prioritizing developing a close relationship with his daughter. He didn't consider his participation at home as an adaptation to the demands of his wife, but rather a result of his own choice. Mia was satisfied with Paul's contributions at home, and she appreciated the close contact he had with their daughter.

Despite all this, Mia felt that Paul held a dominating position regarding their intimate life: he was the one who decided how much time they spent together, as well as how much intimacy occurred between them—and the depth of it. In fact, Paul pursued his own interests and hobbies, these being considered as a red line with no negotiations. He was active in different kinds of sports, and often went on weekend trips with his male friends. He always told Mia, "I need time of my own; I like to have things that I do alone." On the other hand, Mia found it difficult to accept that Paul insisted on a space of his own; she felt he was ignoring opportunities of developing their relationship. However, Mia's main problem was that she felt that her opinion had very little influence on the situation.

Despite the growing independence of Mia, she, as a female, still felt she was missing a more intimate relationship with Paul. She was very satisfied with his contribution to the household and the care he gave to Suzy, but she wasn't fulfilled emotionally. She always complained to Paul that they had differing views on many things, and that these differences, from her perspective, had been creating a rift between them. She complained she hadn't found time to speak to Paul about the things that were most important to her, and that he didn't understand her. "I miss having closeness and consideration from Paul. I wish we could have a more intimate relationship," Mia told me.

I think Mia wanted to have total control over Paul: she wanted to prohibit him from spending time of his own and enjoying his own interests. She thought that having time of his own created a rift of emotional distance between them.

The Marriage Expectation Concept: Men cling to old expectations, but every day, women create new expectations that are equally unrealistic. Unrealistic expectations make changing gender roles nearly impossible, and, as a result, a man loses interest in his marriage life when he senses that he can't continue to meet a woman's growing, ever-changing expectations.

I T IS OBVIOUS THAT Olivia regretted her decision—although at that time, it made a perfect sense to her. However, because the results weren't as expected and her marriage didn't work out despite the sacrifices she had made, she doubted the relationship as a whole. It is important to note, though, that Olivia's decisions were made on the basis of her wanting a central position in the family.

Olivia and Peter came close to an equality-based structure of power, in that both felt that they could equally influence their way of living according to their own individual values. Olivia knew Peter harbored concerns about her amount of housework, and so made it known that she could count on his participation, if needed.

Her choice concerning Peter's contribution to the household chores was the basis for the concept of the "woman's influence in the home": the archetype of male-dominated families is that the husband either refuses to participate or neglects his jobs altogether.

The satisfaction they both felt with this division of labor was an important factor in the close emotional ties between both of them: their fondness, affection,, and appreciation for one another deepened over the years, as had their admiration for, and commitment to, one another. The development of their closeness could be understood in terms of the concept of the "economy of gratitude," in which the partners involved receive more than they would normally expect, or "something extra." Olivia and Peter appreciated the contributions the other made as if they were constantly receiving gifts from one another. They developed their own value system—that is, the economy of gratitude.

Peter considered the responsibility Olivia had taken for the daily chores as a gift to him, feeling that she provided him with a wealth of freedom in relation to his duties at home. He always said that he felt "free to work long hours in the office without you being complaining that I didn't do my house chores on that day; I have much freedom in organizing my daily life." Peter felt grateful towards Olivia, since the freedom she provided him with was more than he would have expected. When asked about his marriage, Peter mentioned to his divorce lawyer that, "In the first years, our marriage had been all about collaboration; no competition."

Meanwhile, Olivia felt Peter thoroughly supported her choice to have a career before having their kids, considering this support, again, as a gift to her. "He was proud of me: he encouraged my career, and wished me to have the kind of position I would enjoy," she said to her divorce lawyer. "There would be many days I would come home very tired, and he would never complain about not having dinner."

In their case, a shared cultural baseline is crucial to the giving and receiving of gifts: when they shared beliefs about manhood and womanhood, they had a common basis for interpreting and appreciating the contributions each of them made in the marriage. What felt like a gift to Olivia also felt like one to Peter, and, in turn, they generally agreed upon the basic principles on which Olivia organized the relationship between work and home. The couple shared a shared basis for evaluation of each other's contributions, implying that each could appreciate what their partner had been doing.

The key insight, in Olivia's case, is that each partner confirmed the identity of the other: Olivia confirmed Peter's identity as a man whose life was rooted in work and who required a relatively high degree of freedom, and Peter confirmed Olivia's identity as a career woman, also supporting her aspiration to reach higher levels in her career and to remain as the central figure in the family.

Therefore, the freedom Olivia had given to Peter was motivated by two things: her concern for him; and her own desire for receiving his confirmation as to how her womanhood was being shaped. Meanwhile, Peter's support for her career was motivated both by his concern for her and by his desire for receiving confirmation on his way of shaping his manhood.

In the beginning of their marriage, Peter and Olivia had enjoyed close emotional ties: neither of them felt they were subordinate to their partner, a power structure being completely absent in their relationship. Thus, receiving confirmation of one's gender identity was an essential motive for the actions they both had perceived as gifts. This relation of gratification between them strengthened the intimacy of their relationship, since such confirmation implied reassurance and acceptance.

If Peter had refused to participate on the division of household chores with Olivia, their relationship would have been under major threat: a power conflict would have arisen at the very onset of their relationship if Peter's position of power—and, in turn, definition of masculinity—had been based on prioritizing his job over the sharing of household duties.

Similarly, if Olivia had insisted on his participation of household chores because she would otherwise feel her identity as a professional career woman was threatened, Olivia would have been the one to feel a power imbalance and lack of confirmation of her gender identity. Consequently, the emotional distance with Peter would have arisen, accompanied by frustrations.

Mia

In Mia's case, the power structure in her marriage is largely based on equality concerning the division of labor; meanwhile, the organization of daily home duties is based on joint decisions.

However, the problem Mia and Paul faced concerned the intimacy and closeness between them: Paul had a dominating position in their intimate life, being the one who defined the amount of time they could spend together, as well as the quality of intimacy between them.

Mia was lonelier in her marriage than she had expected and hoped for, and, when chatting to Olivia, she mentioned, "I miss having closeness and consideration from Paul. I wish we could have more time together; have a more intimate relationship." As time passed, Mia gradually began to accept that she couldn't have the intimacy with Paul she was longing for. Mia told Olivia, "I accept better now that there are many things I cannot speak with Paul about. I cannot share my thoughts and feelings with him; he doesn't have time. We don't have the closeness we used to, but the lack of intimacy doesn't hurt me as much anymore."

Because Mia had insisted on an equal division of labor with Paul— and because he wanted, in return, time of his own—, Mia had given up her most closely held hopes. This couple illustrates the gender gap in expectations of intimacy and closeness. The wife wants more intimacy than the husband, and the husband wants more time for himself than the wife.

Paul also felt that their relationship had been growing apart, but he didn't understand why; he performed his duties both outside and inside the home, which Mia felt satisfied with—at least, that's what she always told him. So, what was the problem with Mia? Why had she become so distant? In the early years of their marriage, he'd felt Mia had forged for intimacy and togetherness with him—something that made him feel wanted. Now, with everything being constant in terms of division of labor and the career progress of his wife, he felt that all these things hadn't made her happier. He was disappointed with Mia's emotional distance.

It should be understood that men and women generally possess different views of what living together means: whilst men tend to focus on the practical aspects of the marriage—that is, the duties and responsibilities—, women tend to focus more on the emotional side and need to share feelings.

The Expectancy Principle: Individuals change their behavior according to their anticipated satisfaction in achieving certain goals. One will not repeat a process that hasn't added significant value to their objectives.

Mia had given up in pursuing a sense of closeness with Paul, as she had come to consider Paul to be the type of man with little competence in speaking his emotions. Indeed, Mia had brought up this issue with Paul several times before, but had been disappointed with his reaction: he always perceived these complaints to be offensive in nature as she would accuse him of emotional incompetency, despite doing all of his duties. Hence, as a defensive reaction in one of their rows, Paul told Mia, "I know that you want me to be more romantic, but it's not my style; I don't do it."

It's obvious that this relationship experienced a skewed power dynamic, this being the key reason as to why there was a growing emotional distance between them: Paul had a dominating position concerning their intimate life, creating an imbalance in their economy of gratitude and the appearance of Paul seemingly exploiting Mia's love for him, expecting to receive more than he was willing to give. He demanded his own independence at the cost of Mia's emotional needs and wishes, but still expected her loving care of him; however, he was still the one most disappointed with their lack of intimacy. Meanwhile, Mia had surrendered to his power.

This couple applied the egalitarian model concerning the division of household chores, they were happy with this structure; however, they experienced a skewed power dynamic concerning love and intimacy. Paul's restriction on intimacy and his refusal to meet his wife's emotional needs reinforced his power. This wasn't helped by the fact that Paul defined his masculinity by being a man of power—and, by adhering to such a definition, he was distancing himself from what he thought was a typically "feminine" area of competence (i.e., meeting the needs of another person) so as to avoid a feeling of reduced power and feminine conduct.

Meanwhile, Mia hadn't had corresponding conditions for confirming her gender identity: Paul's lack of interest in her inner life meant that she wasn't being confirmed as to the thoughts and feelings she wanted to share with him.

Contrary to the feminism myth, women are more dependent on their spouses—or males in general—for confirmation of their gender identity than men are: men confirm their masculinity not only in relation to women, but also in relation to other men; however, a woman cannot confirm her gender identity in relation to another woman, or by depending on herself for confirmation.

The power imbalance between Mia and Paul limited the growth of intimacy within their relationship: the dominating partner defined the relationship on their terms, and the subordinate partner wasn't acting on the basis of care and consideration, because they didn't feel satisfied in terms of their needs own needs. The result was a dissatisfaction for both.

The Sacrifice Concept: A death-game to any marriage; the ongoing series of complementary ulterior transactions progressing to a well-defined, predictable outcome. Each partner plays the sacrifice game to satisfy some hidden motivation, and it always involves a payoff. The majority of the time, people aren't aware they are playing games; it's just a normal part of social interaction. Games are a lot like playing poker: you hide your real motivations as part of a strategy to achieve the payoff—to win something.

PETER

MY MOTHER, EMILY, AND my father, Steve, had practiced a relatively traditional model of organizing the relationship between work and household chores: my father was rooted in the traditional gender ideology, taking the role as the family bread-earner and protector. He believed it was essential that the mother was at home for the children, as well as the fact that it was the responsibility of the mother to raise her children properly. This was our experience of Mum growing up.

In the first years of their marriage, however, Mum worked full-time—and, with the birth of John, she changed to a position requiring fewer working hours. She hadn't been able to balance between her full-time job and the considerable amount of time and effort her two kids required from her.

At this time, Dad was also rapidly achieving a higher administrative position. When mum was still a full-time employee, my parents had shared the household chores almost equally; however, after she expressed her desire to change to part-time employee, Mum insisted Dad should still commit to the same amount of household chores as when she was full-time employee. She had subtle ways of carrying through her decisions: Dad didn't mind sharing his duties, but his problem was that he felt he had to adapt to Mum's desires in ways which seemed unfair to him. It had been her endless unexpected demands that represented a dilemma for him, and it didn't seem fair that he should have the same full duties as before when Mum already spent more time at home as she came home earlier than him. To add to this, Mum also insisted on having every fourth weekend off, where she would be free to meet her friends, travel, or practice her hobbies. She would leaving us with Dad during her weekend off, such an arrangement leaving Dad no time to practice his hobbies or to go out with friends: instead, he would come home late from work during the weekdays, and during the weekends, he had to spend the time with his wife and children as way of compensating for the little time he spent with them during the weekdays.

From Mum's point of view, their marriage was characterized by Dad's dominance: ironically, she believed she'd given up all power and control to Dad within the relationship, since his job took priority over hers, when hers directly benefitted the family. Therefore, she felt she should be rewarded for such a sacrifice—especially considering Dad insisted on dropping a few of his household duties because of his late nights at work. Mum felt she wasn't appreciated as much as she should have been for giving her husband's job priority over hers. On the other hand, Dad felt that Mum had been abusing the situation, wanting to take full advantage of the fact that she was a part-time employee. Mum couldn't even see that Dad was entitled to have some free time of his own (like she did), since he already spent little time with her and us.

I believe they made a mistake when they didn't review each party's commitments and responsibilities based on their new conditions.

THIS IS WHAT IS CALLED the hidden power between spouses: in this relationship, Steve perceived some restrictions on his life; meanwhile, he felt that Emily didn't experience corresponding restrictions. Steve overheard Emily telling her friend, "Steve doesn't dominate me; I have the freedom to pursue my interests. He is a compassionate man." Several times, Steve thought Emily may have wanted to go out for dinner with him, but she always had her weekend off, with friends. Both avoided open discussions concerning how they wished to spend their leisure time, although Steve knew Emily preferred to spend her weekend with friends. Meanwhile, Emily didn't want to skip her weekend for fear that Steve would have asked her each weekend to stay home or go out with him, which posed the risk of it becoming a habit in the future.

The result of this lack of open negotiation was that Emily took it for granted when Steve complied with her wants. This led to Emily feeling free to pursue her interests, leaving Steve to endure restrictions.

On the surface, their relationship was characterized by a traditional gender strategy, characterized by male dominance: Emily confirmed her husband's gender identity as the main family provider and the person in control of the family economy, and Steve confirmed his wife's gender identity as the organizer of the household and central figure in the family. He knew Emily considered the bearing of the responsibility for the household as the essence of femininity, so he confirmed that through his decisions. Each felt an appreciation for the contributions each had been making: Emily felt grateful for the freedom she had been given, and Steve appreciated the contributions she made at home and to their children.

However, deep inside, their relationship showed sign of emotional distance, despite their mutual affection. Such distance was the result of hidden processes of power in their marriage, the power imbalance in their daily life and leisure time seeming to outweigh the satisfaction they felt with the organization of their home and work. Emily didn't experience restrictions, whilst Steve experienced restrictions that he didn't quite understand. Not only that, but he also felt that he was being obliged to adapt to these restrictions.

The economy of gratitude in this marriage was relatively scarce: Steve didn't feel his contributions were appreciated, instead feeling that his wife was taking advantage of the situation and placing unwanted restrictions on him in favor of her own freedom.

Emily saw herself as a woman who, according to the traditional model, harbored the main responsibility of the household, although she was simultaneously practicing an egalitarian division of labor with her husband. Thus, her gender identity was being confirmed by the central position in the family, which implied control of her husband's participation and also his leisure time.

Emily was exercising power over her husband in hidden ways: Steve's gender identity at home was somehow shaky as a result of the hidden power relation with his wife, whilst at work, he was a leader and well-respected. Hence, at work, his gender identity had been confirmed, whilst at, home it very much so wasn't. He was confused and dissatisfied, feeling that at home, he was a subordinate to his wife, whilst he was dominant at work. This situation made him anxious once he stepped into the house every day after work, supporting the idea that men can confirm the gender identity and masculinity of one another, even when it is not confirmed by women. The workplace, for a man, represents an important arena for confirming gender identity in relation to other men—but being subordinate in relation to his wife's demands contributed to the emotional distance between Steve and Emily.

The opposite of this case is also true for women, and so women who don't find their gender identity confirmed from their husbands at home will seek it in the workplace, or somewhere else outside home. However, a woman tends to seek it from other men at the workplace or outside home—not from other women like her.

The importance of confirmation of gender identity for love is related to a need for recognition in close relationships. Thus, intimacy between the husband and wife is associated with validation of the gendered self: I am a woman, treat me like one; I am a man, treat me like one.

The relationship between gender, power, and attraction (seduction) is not a one-way road: the power of seduction can also be considered a motivating force, referring to the influence seduction can have on the relationship between spouses. A strong mutual attraction between spouses may mean that they are willing to accept and appreciate more from one another than when their attraction to each other is less strong from the beginning. Thus, the emotional bonding between partners is itself essential for how they shape their gender identity, as well as how it is confirmed by the other partner.

Attraction (seduction) as part of a given social interaction implies that gender, power, and attraction are interwoven in a complex relationship, each of these dimensions being essential in how the relationship between the partners develops, as well as when it comes to the degree of satisfaction felt within the marriage.

Women and men love as psychologically and culturally gendered selves, with gender identities and sexual desires that they consciously and unconsciously experience and act upon. Hence, the relationship between attraction and the confirmation of gender identity proves to be a challenging one within a culture where rigid and traditional gender roles are shaken off. In such cultures, men and women explore new ways of fulfilling their gender identity confirmation.

Therefore, the distant emotional ties between partners is, the majority of the time, related to/caused by a power imbalance and lack of confirmation of gender identity. Thus, the subordinating/dominating spouse directly relates to gender identity confirmation, and the power imbalance implies the subordinate person's self-worth is not heightened by the dominant partner.

The mythical feminist perspective emphasizes this same concept: women complain that their self-worth and gender identity confirmation is threatened because of the male dominance, and, because of that, the male power inhibits attraction and men exploit women's attraction.

ABOUT THE MYTH OF POWER BALANCE BETWEEN SPOUSES

THE POWER BALANCE BETWEEN the two genders—even in marriage—is a myth.

I see no logic behind people getting married when, nowadays, they can easily live together as couples/partners, have children, and have sex—plus, when a split occurs, it is a far easier process compared to the long-winded termination of a legal marriage contract. The contract of marriage is a legal exchange of freedom to the illusion of a stable family life and free sex—but, paradoxically, it turns out that marriage, still, doesn't guarantee a stable family life, nor does it offer a free sex; in fact, it is the most expensive sex people can get.

The cases of Olivia, Mia, and Peter's parents illustrate the gender power dilemma within the family context: the weapons women have used during their struggle with society have been largely those that men have used before them—forgetting that men have never won anything like the amount of liberty, equality, and fraternity they expected. All the feminist movements focus on the power of men, rather than on their vulnerabilities and their natural weaknesses; the main objective has always been to gain more power than that men possess, and what men and women can achieve together, in a mutually sustaining relationship, is always overlooked.

In reality, there is no such thing as an equal relationship: a so-called 50/50 relationship leads to constant arguments, as every decision must be discussed and debated—which inevitably leads to hurt feelings, critics, and fights surrounding every decision that has to be made. Hence, it should not come as a surprise to find that even within 50/50 relationships, the divorce rate is as high as that of relationships with a skewed power dynamic. In fact, there has to be a final authority in any relationship—whether that be in a career context with a boss/employee relationship, or in the family context, with the parent/child relationship. The same goes for the wife/husband relationship: there should be one person who has a final word, and for which they will hold full responsibility—otherwise, the responsibility of any critical decision will be lost and debated between the two parties, since each partner will negate having full responsibility for the consequences of a specific decision that they have not fully made by his/her own will.

A spouse that fears a surrendering of power to the other partner compromises to a 50/50 relationship in order to maintain some sort of control; however, after marriage, the partners realize that only one of them should be in charge—and, in the institution of marriage, wives have always been compared to mothers, both in a positive and a derogatory sense (e.g., male peers teasing a husband that he is "hen-pecked" and has lost his freedom to this "new mother"). Such comparisons are only natural, however: both a mother and a wife display the maternal instincts of the female nature. Saying this, both partners seem to forget that a woman is a wife before she ever becomes a mother to a child.

The matriarchal role of Olivia commenced with her marriage, long before children came into the picture. It didn't take her long before she began to exert her authority and influence over Peter: in order to bring alive the man of her dreams, she attempted to change the way he dressed, get him to treat her in the way she wanted, and would point out his many flaws in hopes of training him to become what she expected in a man. At the onset of their relationship, Peter would have yielded to Olivia the majority of the time—especially during the "courtship" phase, whilst he was under the spell of the woman's female sexual power. Once they had entered into the legally binding marriage contract, however, Olivia often attempted to exert more control and more power over the relationship. Indeed, some other women will act as if the man is in charge in order to massage his ego and to conform to the patriarchal society model of marriage. Therefore, women want to run the show—either openly or covertly, through her clever and manipulative ways.

Only knowledgeable men know these subtle ways of the female gender to take control and lead the relationship, and this type of men refuses to fall under the spell of a woman; they will always try to remain in full control, and the majority will probably face many problems with their dominance-craving wives. He refuses to be her child—tamed and controlled—, and he resists doing what she asks when he is in disagreement with her requests. He also refuses to let her having the final say in the matter.

On the other hand, other men fall into the trap of seductive women, and this type of man seeks—and, most probably, needs—the maternal and feminine authority of a woman in their life; in a way, they try to replicate what they grew up with during their childhood. This type of man has been taught that because he was born, raised, nurtured, and disciplined by a woman, he will need another woman to give him the love and care he has always been given by his mother when he is an adult. He often doesn't realize that what he was granted by his mother was for free, and that the woman of his adulthood will not give him the same for free. He always misses the fact that this female is a wife, not his mother, due to the fact that he has been taught he will always need a female authority in order to bring peace, order, and purpose to his life.

Usually, the male who lacks the loving female authority in his childhood—the mother—will seek it in his adulthood, whilst the male who has experienced the loving authority of his mother during childhood will realize early enough that his female partner uses her seductive power as a way to get him into her area of control and dominance.

For too long, both genders have bought into the lie that the wife could play the role of her partner's mother—or vice versa (that the male could play the role of his partner's father).

Women have always craved influence behind the closed doors of the marriage relationship, but now, we can see women expecting submission from their husbands in an ever-growing wide array of areas; we see women who begin to become comfortable being open about their dominance in the marriage relationship. Indeed, women crave dominance over their male partners for several reasons: they believe that the man who will yield to his wife's authority, who will submit to her will, will provide a productive, fulfilling husband. If a man fights against his wife's authority, for her, this means he tries to shirk responsibility and to run away from his marital obligations.

On the other hand, the husband who considers his wife as his authority figure and who will obey his wife is perceived as the husband that is more likely to complete household chores and spend time with his children and mother-in-law; he is also perceived to be more likely to be faithful to his job and to her. Therefore, women prefer the man who will revere his wife and honor her, just as he hopefully reveres and honors his mother—the woman who gave him life.

A wife isn't a mother, but a woman is a woman—and the nurturing and disciplinarian traits of the maternal nature of the female is present in all women. Therefore, a woman prefers the male who submits to her will—as he did to his mother.

The other reason for which women crave for dominance over their male partners is their desire to fight back and eliminate the male patriarchal system, believing that society is possessed by the demon of patriarchy and that this is a demon that women must exorcise. Patriarchy is defined as "the organization of society based on the supremacy of the father in the clan/family, and the legal dependence of the children and the wife". The patriarchy extends and spills over general society, beyond the family, by both the law, customs, and the supremacy of the father in the family—resulting in the oppression of women within society.

As mentioned previously, women's craving for dominance is resisted by the majority of the male gender, although is accepted by some others. Further, although women fight the legal and societal system of patriarchy, the psychological remnants of patriarchy have a dreadful hold on them, leaving the progress of the women's movement a slow and uneven progression. The frustration of women in such a system often results in a horizontal violence as women begin to attack one another; it is natural for a female to not trust other females, which results in a lack of self-confidence and also explains why some women continue to require male recognition and appreciation.

The Female Dominance Concept: The female dominant nature still lies dormant in many women, taking a male's submissiveness to draw it out. Knowledgeable men exclusively desire constant control, not giving in to the woman's desires for power—potentially leading the woman to take advantage and attempt to control them.

The suggestion that if only women ruled the world then gentleness and kindness would prevail neglects the fact of how inexorably power corrupts: the struggle for privilege and power has so far distracted attention from something much more elusive. The war between the sexes has been like a battle for territory, the only fruits being gaining or losing a few yards, with little chance it will end in the future. Mentalities don't change, and so the war will not end—although fortunately, this is not a war that can be won by battles.

THE FEMINIST PERSPECTIVE ON men's exploitation of women's love indicates the way in which the gender gap concerning expectations of intimacy and closeness can reflect power imbalances: feminists emphasize the fact that men use women's love for their own empowerment, and, as a consequence of this, men feel they have the right to receive love, without giving love and consideration in return. If men take women's love for granted, why should they make the effort to meet women's expectations for intimacy and closeness?

In the past, studies on gender have suggested a fear of closeness is associated with masculinity. Indeed, we can associate men's priority of physical closeness—rather than a broader intimacy—with a demand of power and control. However, the husband can remain in control by maintaining an emotional distance between himself and his wife, thereby confirming his masculinity.

However, in modern society, the concept of the "new man" has widely emerged, this being one associated with men who renegotiate and engage in domestic responsibilities. This idea reflects a dramatic shift in the power dynamic between a husband and wife.

THE GENDER STRATEGY

THE MASCULINITY AND FEMININITY present in marriages reflect the gender ideology of the spouses, as well as the power structure between them.

The term "gender strategy" refers to both the plan of action and the emotional preparations for pursuing it. By applying their gender ideology to household chores, spouses pursue the gender strategy—which also contains "power". As a for-instance of this, the tendency for a wife to insist on her husband's participation at home can be associated with a subordinate position, since she may consider his contributions as recognition—symbolic of equality. The husband's role as the bread-earner, meanwhile, entails power and thereby confirms his masculinity. Thus, the way in which different couples organize household chores is symbolic of culturally gender-based power relations between spouses. Therefore, conflict over the division of housework tends to also raise issues of power and of conditions for shaping gender.

Even when Peter helped with housework, Olivia took the executive responsibility: she was the one who assigned tasks, and decided what needed to be done by herself and what by Peter. Women become frustrated when men are more likely to take responsibilities for the yard, the cars, or outdoor maintenance, hence neglecting responsibilities such as cleaning, dusting, or cooking; in fact, the responsibilities assumed by men and women are almost always related to their childhood in terms of what they have been trained to do as a result of their traditional gender roles. Simply through their early training within their childhood home, women assume the inside-home responsibilities, whilst men assume the outside-home responsibilities. For instance, because Olivia had not been trained to fix her car, cut the grass, fix broken appliances, vacuum the swimming pool, trim the hedges, or change her own car tires, she always left these responsibilities to Peter; in fact, Olivia often expected Peter to know how to do these tasks, and would have felt disappointed if that hadn't been the case. Further, because Olivia had been trained on cooking, dusting, cleaning, or laundering, she preferred to take these responsibilities, since she knew Peter had not been trained to do these tasks as well as she. This meant that on the rare occasion that Peter did take the responsibility of tasks such as dusting, dishwashing, or laundering, he would face Olivia's painful criticism since he did not perform these tasks as efficiently as her. He was gradually perceived to be useless to her, though he performed other tasks with perfection.

The inequity of the workload became overwhelming when Peter had time to watch the television after work whilst Olivia had to cook dinner, do the dishes, put the children to bed, and finish the laundry—or, conversely, when Peter had to complete some household chores after work and take care of the children whilst Olivia hung out with her sister.

Over time, Peter became reluctant to complete even a few household chores inside the house, since he knew Olivia' standards of cleanliness and the fact they were too high for his skills. He then knew criticism would be an inevitability, in turn discouraging further efforts on his part and, ultimately, leading to his giving up on the whole thing.

Olivia frequently criticized the way Peter had completed some of the household chores due to the fact that, generally speaking, a wife often defines herself through her homemaking and multitasking skills, and so wonders why a man can't feel the same and showcase the same degree of proficiency.

On the other hand, there are men who, due to their childhood training, contribute in household chores with excellency, and so are not criticized by their wives. Though very few and far between, this type of man supports the notion that early training and socialization lies at the root of the problem when it comes to contributions to household chores.

Indeed, a wealth of research showcases that women who work tend to wield an increased degree of influence in their marriages, also possessing higher levels of self-esteem. Nevertheless, this isn't seen to improve the quality of marriages between the two genders: in fact, divorce rates increase proportionally in these relationships.

The fact that men expect the woman to be the homemaker due to their perceived natural proficiency in such work becomes even clearer when children are introduced to the equation: many fathers believe that women possess more patience and understanding in dealing with children, and seem unaware that she, too, may feel frustrated, bored, or stymied.

Olivia had faced difficulty in dealing with her daughter's behavior, and Peter's response had always been to lecture her rationally about what needed to be done. For Olivia, this lecturing implied that she had failed somehow as a mother as a result of her struggling to manage her daughter—and, in such cases, when Peter did not take over—or even when he did!—Olivia felt even worse, as though she were an inadequate mother; after all, most societies believe that a woman is supposed to know how to raise children automatically. Here, however, we can see that assumption proves to be wrong.

When some fathers take the role of caring for their children and they do a good job, they are often seen as heroes—someone with very special skills, since they are able to function outside their normal domain. This is because of the usual belief that the children's caring is a woman's territory, not a man's.

The new generation appears to be more proficient in sharing parenting than previous generations. When men age, they become more interested in developing close ties with their families, and become less concerned with their success in business; they have either already done well in this arena, or are simply looking outside of their careers for gratification. In general, middle-aged men and women grow to be more in touch with the aspects of their personality that are generally associated with the opposite gender.

Recent generations have become much more interested in building close relationships with their children and families, since they have learned their lessons early after seeing their own fathers' feelings of being cut off and lonely, or their feeling the loss of a present father during their childhood. As a result of this, young fathers now tend to participate in the birthing process, and are encouraged and supported by new socialization messages to take a major role in parenting, from infancy to childhood. Fathers have been encouraged to be in the delivery room, to hold the baby and to care for it immediately after birth, to be involved in taking the child to the pediatrician, to participate in school conferences, and to be active in the daily care of the child in order to enhance bonding.

Additionally, due to the high divorce rate in modern society, many single fathers have developed a new sort of relationship with their children totally unmediated by the mother.

Unfortunately, being an involved father is not as easy a task as it seems to be: businesses are often not understanding of a man or a woman who puts family first, and so interruptions to the workday, delays in completing tasks, and missing deadlines, all due to a child's illness or school problems, are frowned upon if the employee is a woman and intolerable if it is a man. Therefore, the pressure on men to devote their entire lives to earning money increases, leading to their reduced involvement in family care.

At the same time, the pressure on women to stay home and take care of their children is equally strong: society is not reluctant to condemn a woman who puts more effort into her career than she does childcare.

In a wealth of social research and political discussions concerning family values, the mother has experienced more calls to leave work in favor of childcare than the fathers—implying that much of the perceived deterioration in societal values is due to the mother's absence in the home. In the same way, many psychological theories have overemphasized the essentiality behind the maternal influence in a child's life, conventional social wisdom maintaining that if a family has problems, the mother's neglect as a result of her stay outside home are is the root of the issue. Here, we can see that it is assumed that a mother should stay with her children, a father providing for them financially.

However, it is somewhat amusing to observe how the opposite case works: occasionally, a man would prefer to reverse roles, staying home with the child whilst his wife is responsible for the financial support of the family. When a husband expresses this desire, he may run into major objections from his wife; indeed, many wives have cited that their husbands' higher income is the reason for her staying at home, although they still believe it is her prerogative to take care of the children. It becomes clear in cases in which a man takes initiative in disciplining/caring for his children that the woman feels that her territory has been threatened.

Although women and men attempt to be equally involved parents, they both are likely to "let Mom do it"; just as men have traditionally identified themselves through their work, women have identified themselves through their children, and that unconscious claim to the childcare territory does not die easily.

When a parent has to take time off work in order parent, socialization messages say that it is usually the mother who is expected to do so. This proves to be an area of conflict for couples, since the man feels the pressure to succeed as the primary provider most prominently, whilst the mother resents the implication that her career and work are less important. Many women ask for extended postpartum after feeling pressured to return to work prematurely, struggling against a strong urge to stay home while the child is still young. Indeed, the husband may resent it when women make this choice to stay home with a child—a resentment he may not even express due to society's pressures on him to provide for his family. The internal confusion this issue creates for both spouses can, as one would expect, place strains on the relationship.

The feminist movement has had a powerful impact on the mentality of millions of women across the globe, serving as a disruptive influence triggering a cognitive shift that brought a dramatic change in values, behaviors, goals, communication styles, and attitudes in one or both of the spouses. It appeared to men—as well as society as a whole—that women who had once been perfectly content as housewives, mothers, and housemakers, suddenly became dissatisfied with their roles, beginning to branch out by going to work and either putting off having children or not having them at all, preferring to cohabitate with a significant other rather than committing to marriage. They have also been seen to lash out at men whom they perceived to be sexist, competing with men for positions of power, and acting disruptively to society's status quo.

For the man and woman who married under the traditional contract during the earlier years of this century, these changes in female attitudes and behaviors often felt like a betrayal to the man; suddenly, all of the gender expectations they had both taken for granted at marriage were discarded by her, leaving them confused, hurt, angry, and unable to solve the sudden issues resulting from this sudden change.

As we can see, many men have resisted these new demands placed on them, struggling to restore the status quo. Since the change was so strong and unexpected, a major clash in gender expectations have lent the way to chaos within interpersonal relationships. In the generations following the feminist movement, many young women have absorbed these new feminist attitudes, whilst the many young men who have had confused and frustrated fathers as role models, have not caught up with this change in society. Till today, after this long period of feminism, many marriages have struggled with new perceptions of what constitutes a good woman.

The men's movement has risen up to fight back the women's movement. This was formed in response to the perceived injustices and inequities in the present structure of the society, and, before long, both groups started to shout, lock horns, and perceive the other group as the ultimate oppressor/abuser who needed to be changed/controlled. The inflammatory rhetoric, myths of the media, and the advice of same genders have often led to the escalation of this conflict in male/female relationships. In an effort to make sweeping sociological changes, both genders have encouraged aggressive—almost militant—stances on conflictual issues, rather than trying to understand and consort with the enemy. This becomes quite problematic when a man and woman wish to resolve issues revolving around gender in order to reduce the present conflict and build warmer, more intimate relationship. Instead, as a result of the fact that they are encouraged to do so by their same-sex friends, the media, and organized gendered political groups, some men and women find themselves in entrenched positions, a simple disagreement escalating into a major disruption of their relationship, rather than looking for common grounds. This is always tragic for the couple: all is done in an attempt to make their relationship work, but instead, they find they cannot see their way around the political stances they have taken in order to compromise.

The purpose of marriage is "shared meaning"—not shared souls. Each partner supports the other's dreams and hopes, and a marriage will quickly start heading in the wrong direction if one partner has to sacrifice what they want in order to make the other person happy. Genuine friendships are equal, and friendship kindles romance—but also protects against a relationship getting adversarial. As long as you can retain "fondness" and "admiration" for your partner, you can always salvage your relationship; without these, there is more chance of disgust being expressed in arguments—and disgust is poison to a relationship.

A follower, a leader, or a partnership? A long-lived debate that consumes the majority of marriages.

The woman who expects her husband to fulfill the protector/provider role, without taking on any of those responsibilities herself, must be aware that certain consequences accompany such a position. If she is unwilling to take the responsibility of providing for herself and taking care of her family, she is then in a dependent position—which is one that requires playing the role of the follower, deferring to the preferences and decisions of the leader. This is how the traditional marriage worked—often to the detriment of the mental health of the woman, who did not feel she was taken seriously. Many women believe they should be heard and their opinions considered, whilst also believing they should be supported and protected financially and emotionally. They are still somewhat operating under the old exchange of beauty and sex in return for financial security.

In modern society, men, meanwhile, expect the woman to carry her share of the financial burden, and may begin to feel resentful if her offering is only her beauty. The old balance may be restored with the birth of children if the wife completes all the housework and cares for the children, although she then may expect the patriarchal attitude of the traditional husband, who considers himself the head of the house, if she plays the traditional wife/mother role. Her contribution to the relationship is to meet the needs of her husband and children, in return for her husband's financial support.

On the other hand, the man who wishes his wife to be a major contributor to the financial security of the family must be aware that he then must shoulder a share of the housekeeping and childcare responsibilities, as well as consider her wishes in decision-making. They would both have to accept these balanced marriage-politics, and he must be ready to accept the fact that she may openly disagree with him, act in a unilateral manner, or may purchase expensive things he does not like without asking him his opinion. He must be ready to accept that she can assume a new position that takes her away from her family for longer periods, leaving him to provide the childcare that she cannot. Therefore, women who wish to share an equal responsibility in making decisions regarding the couple's life together must also be willing to assume full responsibility of her acts and decisions if they turn to be wrong, or to negatively affect her husband and children. She must accept the fact that she may be required to fix, solely, the problems caused by her decisions.

These marriage politics/balanced power relations within a given relationship may appear to be easy to follow during the beginning of the marriage contract, when the two partners have had close examples amongst their families, but this is not always the case: many partners feel lost and like they cannot establish a balanced/equal partnership as a result of their lack of previous models of flexible, cooperative, or equal relationships within their families during their childhood.

PART III: THE
ROTTEN INSTITUTION

Getting rid of your single status only exchanges one set of problems for multiple other (more complex!) problems.

OLIVIA

PETER WASN'T MEETING MY emotional and sexual needs anymore.

After fourteen years of marriage, I was seriously considering leaving Peter and my two children in pursuit of the love I felt entitled to and didn't feel I was getting from Peter. I had no idea where I would go or how I would make it on my own, but what I did know was that I couldn't survive a lifeless marriage: I felt like I was nothing more than a maid, cook, nanny, and occasional outlet for sexual tension—positions for which I had been severely underpaid. I frequently had thoughts about what my life could be like after Peter's death: I had a lengthy mental list of men I would date, all of which would meet different needs at different times. I then thought of how wonderful it would be to be single again, relieved of this stressful life.

I wish I knew what happened to people when they got married; why had my mother not told me?

When Peter and I met and began dating—and when we were first married—, I couldn't imagine ever wanting to be with anyone else: he made me feel special, cherished, and desirable. The flame of our passion for one another burned brightly. However, after we were blessed with our children, I didn't feel special anymore: our life together seemed to have lost its magic spark. Confused and somewhat exasperated, I thought our flame was dying; at the time of our marriage, he had been the finest, best-looking, and most intelligent in our crowd. We were terribly in love.

I ought to be elated: wasn't that the whole point? This was supposed to be the best time of my life; so how was I to know whether this was happiness? How were any of us? Father and Mother weren't that happy, but they could have been happier, if they wanted to. Their married friends hadn't been happy, either—and, come to think of it, my married friends weren't very happy once the first few years or so had elapsed. Thousands of people are in court every day due to their unhappy marriages; it gets them out of the jam they're in, and allows them to not have to live any longer with the man/the woman they can no longer stand.

I didn't want to think of divorce before I was even married; to me, it was as gruesome as getting measured for your coffin before you were dead. I wanted to get married with the idea that it was going to work in my case; I had expectations for married life that could not have differed more from this. I wanted to give myself to my husband with the feeling that I would always be his—yet I had the horrible feeling that all these divorced people around me must have had felt the same way when they were married, this feeling eventually fading.

During our engagement, I felt constantly inebriated: I was dizzy with anticipation, and the very sight of the man I was going to marry was enough to fill me with so much emotion I felt I could burst. The gowns I chose for our honeymoon trip made me ache for the time when I could put them on for just his eyes to admire. The more intimate details of my wardrobe were even more carefully chosen: I loved to lock myself in my room and gaze at them until I grew giddy with thoughts of what they represented.

Our wedding was what was called a "social event", and, whilst I don't believe I was fully aware of the sanctity and importance of the ceremony about to take place, there was no mistaking the longing that wrapped around my soul and body—omnipresent and all-consuming. We drove away in our new high-powered car after the reception, and, in just two hours, we'd reached our destination—the city where we were to spend two days before taking a steamer to Europe. Our hotel reservation was excellent: Peter had thought of everything—even down to the flowers in our room. Yes, he had thought of everything!

Everything went beautifully for four or five years; we were perfect lovers, and played up to each other in a way that we sometimes used to speak of and admire. We both felt truly blessed, a sense of pride radiating through us when we would hear of other people's envy of our happiness.

Then, like a slow poison, a change sat in. For a while, each of us secretly felt the other had been distracted by someone else, and, sure enough, we were slowly being consumed with jealousy. It was during a burst of angry discussion one night that we both began to see how foolishly wrong we were. We then thought we may be over-doing our sex life—so, for six months, we carefully regulated ourselves—a diet, so to speak. However, the experiment was destined to fail.

For the next ten years of our marriage, we seemed to be slipping further and further away from one another. We frantically tried to hold our happiness, but with no success: we had enough money, were perfectly healthy, our children were our pride and joy, and our friends, pastimes, occupations, and tastes were admirably suited—and yet we failed. We were both unhappy when we were both still supposed to be young and passionate. And yet here we were, the intimate side of our lives having lost all its joy and zest, rendering us barely lovers. It was when it was clear we could go on no longer that we decided it would be a mistake to ruin the rest of our lives by blindly pursuing a dead ideal.

Peter failed me, miserably: he dealt with me as briefly and casually as he did the evening paper. I think he took more trouble with cleaning his teeth than he did about making love to me. He wasn't rough or inconsiderate or stupid; simply, he just wasn't there when I agonizingly expected and needed him.

It was probably the umpteenth time we'd had this same argument: I didn't feel Peter was making any effort whatsoever to meet my emotional needs, yet again. It had been days since we'd had sex, and months since he'd taken me out for any quality time together. Rather than lovingly asking him, "Am I doing something wrong that's causing your heart to grow cold toward me?", I'm ashamed to say I went back to that lame old, "You're too passive!" accusation, angrily blaming him for the lack of passion in our relationship. "Why don't you pursue me anymore? Does it ever occur to you to just pick up the phone and ask me if I want to go to dinner? Or to bring me flowers? Or ask me to go on a walk? Anything! Anything to show me that you still care?"

As I lay in bed for what seemed like hours, awaiting a response to my barrage of demanding questions, I felt myself growing progressively angrier over what I felt was a major character flaw. Finally, I threw back the covers and dramatically exclaimed, "I'm so fed up with your passivity, I just can't sleep in the same bed with you tonight!"

I believed that yelling at him was going to be his wake-up call, pushing him to strive to do a better job of showing me how much he loved me. I was heartbroken, but comforted myself with the thought that the future would surely bring me what I felt I deserved.

But it didn't. And when I grew nervous and irritable and lost weight, Peter blamed it on every cause but the right one.

We've tried to adjust our lives to an impossible situation—and failed. It quickly became evident that divorce was the only answer, and we both voiced our desire to part amicably—though with a very thin shred of mutual respect; frankly, each of us thought the other had been terrible during the relationship.

The Reasoned Decision Concept: When we want something to be true, we tend to spotlight the things that support it, then drawing conclusions from those spotlighted scenes. We'll then congratulate ourselves on our reasoned decisions.

PETER

W E LIVED TOGETHER AS a very harmonious couple for a couple of years—but, when those perfect two years came to a close, it was time to do whatever Olivia thought to be the "right thing". We got married, and, fourteen years later, we were consulting a lawyer, having had enough of each other. We initially struggled to save our marriage—at least superficially—for the sake of our children.

With the legalizing of our status in 2001, Olivia changed drastically: she began to develop what I call the "nesting instinct", wanting to decorate our little rented apartment and cook exotic meals. She talked about having children someday and fantasized about the big house we would buy when I made enough money. She seemed to be in heaven during such musings.

"She doesn't know how things work in real life," I offloaded to my father at the time. "She doesn't know how hard it is to earn money. She lives on a different planet." It was during this time that I'd begun my application for a short-term loan.

Before our marriage, we had been comrades—and after marriage, she acted as if she owned me; as if I were one of her luxurious handbags or high-heels. If Olivia had given me a monthly report card, I would have been getting straight Fs. No matter what I did, it was never good enough for her: almost all the time I would make a great deal of effort to do everything she asked me to, or else I knew there would be hell to pay that night. Saying this, there were, admittedly, other times where I just thought, What's the use? She's not going to appreciate it anyway.

I always listened to her plans with a false but encouraging smile; I just didn't have it in my heart to dash her hopes, so I kept my mouth shut. Apparently, having a home and family was her dream come true—but all it did for me was bring about significant stress as I mentally calculated how many monetary pressures this would mean I'd be under. I knew she expected me to make the money to finance her wild dreams, and I have to admit that it scared me out of my mind.

Over time, I began to realize things had started to change: I didn't have a lot in common with Olivia, and I knew she didn't like the hobbies I'd had before our marriage (even though she used to praise me for them), and so had felt I'd had to give them all that up now I was married. I didn't enjoy shopping or decorating the apartment—that was woman stuff—, and yet I thought I should spend time with Olivia doing such boring married-couple duties. I began to feel trapped. What the hell have I done to myself? I want to get back my old self, I thought at the time. Despite my efforts to suppress such feelings, my resentment grew, and I became sullen and withdrawn.

Olivia was all-too aware of my moods, and knew instinctively it was her job to get me to talk about it so she could improve on our relationship better. She began to ask me why I was unhappy, but I would deny it, afraid to tell her in case I hurt her. Before long, her incessant questioning began to feel like nagging, so I would start avoiding coming home at the usual time, making excuses concerning having to work late or study in the library for my masters.

It hurt when Olivia began accusing me of being disinterested in her and the children whenever I rested for a few minutes when I got home from work; once, I was even accused of being an overall lazy person and lousy husband and father. She was certain that the very last thing I wanted to do was connect with her, and, from there, the rest of the evening was pretty much downhill: she continued to criticize my actions, despite the fact that the ones she had an issue with appeared to be perfectly normal and appreciated before our marriage. She complained of my staying out late, when she'd loved my friends and had always wanted me to have a good time when I was with them before our marriage. She insisted that I inform her of my every move on a daily basis.

Of course, this introduced me to a phase of married life that I hadn't realized would come into play before; I learned that married couples were supposed to be one—something I had never considered during our time dating, during which time we hadn't been one, but two. We'd both had full respect for the other's individuality and private choices; I valued her independency, as did she with me. The change in Olivia after our marriage had thus been strange to me.

Once the newness of love has passed, we gradually become vulnerable to the massive stress in our lives.

OLIVIA

I STARED AT THE crumpled-up receipt in my hand and tried desperately not to cry; a credit card counterfoil with smudged writing, it lay forlornly on the palm of my hand with the words "Lingerie de Paris" plainly printed on the left-hand side.

My hand trembled slightly as I pulled out a chair and sat down by the kitchen table, blind to the fact that my sleeve was resting on an island of marmalade and toast crumbs left by the children's usual breakfast commando raid. I closed my eyes and crunched the receipt into a ball, willing the words to have changed when I looked again.

Just moments before, Friday had stretched out in front of me in a comforting and familiar routine: a visit to the dry-cleaner's with Peter's suits; a quick detour to the hairdresser to get my hair blow-dried for the launch reception; and coffee with my friend Nicole in the shopping center for a thoroughly enjoyable gossip over a slightly-too-big slice of carrot cake smothered in cream.

Suddenly, my regular trip to the dry-cleaner's and bitching session with Nicole seemed a million miles away.

Peter never remembered to leave his suits out for dry-cleaning, and I had stopped reminding him a while ago, since it was easier to bring them downstairs myself than listen to him stomp around the bedroom, muttering about women with premenstrual tension and complaining about being late for work.

I had also given up telling the children to put their dirty football jerseys in the laundry basket: they copied their father slavishly in everything and, if he managed to escape from all things domestic, they followed suit. I was used to finding remnants of tissues and receipts glued to every wet item of clothing when I emptied the machine. I had realized that I was stuck with two teens fledging domestic incompetents along with a card-carrying, anti-housework husband. I simply cleaned out the pockets myself.

This morning had been no different.

I left the breakfast dishes on the table to go upstairs and collect the suits, trousers, and ties I was bringing to the cleaner's, scooping up my handbag and keys at the same time. I draped the dry-cleaning pile on the back of a kitchen chair, as I had dozens of times before, and reached absently into every pocket.

Amongst the bits of pocket fluff and unused matchbooks Peter always seemed to have stashed in his pockets, I found it: tucked into the inside pocket of the fine wool navy suit—the one that looked so good with his yellow Pierre Cardin tie—was an ordinary credit card receipt—the sort of thing I wouldn't have usually looked at. This day, however, was different; something made me smooth it out and look.

Two hundred bucks worth of goods from one of New York's most exclusive lingerie shops had been purchased with our joint credit card, but had somehow never made it into my underwear drawer.

Unbelievably, my loving husband had been lying through capped teeth when he muttered that expensive lunches with his clients and important contacts had sent his Visa card bill sky-high.

The receipt in my hand made me think that the hefty bill he'd complained about had nothing to do with lunch with clients; instead of buying bottles of pricey Rioja and the best-smoked salmon to lure his important clients, it appeared he had been splashing out on goodies of another kind—luxurious, silky goodies.

Two hundred bucks! I marveled. And in Victoria's Secret, at that. I had never even stood inside the door of the plushest underwear shop; I'd seen enough adverts for the shop's dainty silk knickers and bras to realize that they were ruinously expensive.

I felt a sliver of anger pierce the gloom in my heart. I'd been brought up to believe that spending money on expensive clothes was practically sinful, and so I'd never spent more than twenty bucks on a bra in my life. My lingerie collection consisted of the type of plain cotton knickers and sensible bras that wouldn't look out of place on a goddess. Safe to say that If I was knocked down by a bus, nobody was ever going to think I was a sexpot once they'd ripped off my sensible navy cardigan and long, full skirt: instead, they'd find underwear about as erotic as suet pudding. It would all match, of course: saggy off-white knickers, saggy off-white bra, and saggy off-white body.

No amount of Lycra underwear could conceal my spare-tire, cellulite-covered bum. Why waste money looking for sexy lingerie? After all, the sort of bras that could contain a well-endowed 38C generally looked as if they could also accommodate a few basketballs at a push—and were, therefore, passion-killers of the most effective kind.

Passion-killers. Ha! I imagined Peter walking into a lingerie shop to buy something for another woman. Had he given the salesgirl a blank look when she'd asked what size he wanted? Splaying out his hands as though cupping a couple of oranges to give an approximation for the bra measurements?

According to the magazines I had read, men never managed to check their wives' existing underwear before these shopping expeditions; instead, they muttered about small waists, "ordinary" hips, and blushed when they said "About your size" to shop assistants who'd seen it all before.

Had he asked for the best lingerie money could buy, keen to impress his mistress? Or had she been with him, smiling as he coughed up for knickers she knew he'd rip off later? I couldn't bear to think about it.

Peter wouldn't cheat on me: he barely had time to stay with us as a family, for God's sake. He spent every spare moment working—so much so that I was sick to the teeth of hearing about his work problems. Endless meetings resulted in cancelled evenings out and plenty of lonely weekends, only appearing for bed and breakfast, like a hotel guest who didn't fancy his room that much. Work had been taking over our lives for the past couple of years—particularly since we'd moved from the side-street small apartment we'd been living in to this new villa

Thinking about the children—two mirror images of their dark-haired father—, I began to feel better: Peter loved the children with all his heart; he wouldn't cheat on them. He wouldn't cheat on me. I just knew it.

There had to be an explanation for the Visa receipt. Yes, of course there was. I felt better then, on firmer ground when I thought about our family and what it meant to him; there was no way he'd risk losing his family for a fling with some floozie. Hell, I couldn't even imagine Peter in a bloody underwear shop; he hated shopping... Didn't he?

"You never wear anything like that anymore, darling," Peter used to say when he spotted a sexy underwear feature in a magazine or adverts. But then again, he'd never gone into a lingerie shop to buy me a present himself in our entire marriage.

"How am I supposed to know you want sexy underwear if you don't tell me?" Peter demanded one Christmas Day when I laughed out loud as I ripped the wrapping paper off another cookbook. "For heaven's sake, it takes you two hours to buy one bloody shirt! How am I supposed to pick out something you'd like? And underwear at that!"

Instead of turning up with the wrong size or the wrong color, Peter simply thrust money into my hand. "Go on, spoil yourself, Liv; buy some nice clothes, won't you?"

Fourteen years ago, on a glorious, sunny October morning, I had carefully dressed in a white lace gown and placed a coronet of white roses on my hair for my marriage to Peter, the ambitious young man I'd adored since the first time I set eyes on his handsome face.

It had been a wonderful wedding: Mum had held me tight, tears in her eyes, as she whispered, "I hope you'll be happy, darling." Peter and I had run out of the hotel to find Peter's rusty old Renault carefully decorated.

That had been the best day of my life—that is, until the crisp August morning my first baby had been born. Exhausted and drained, I lay back in the hospital bed with my baby in my arms, Peter smiling down at me, an expression of amazement on his face.

When Mark's tiny hand curled around his father's little finger, Peter had actually cried before sitting down on the bed and wrapping his strong arms around his family, his wet cheek against mine. Babies grasp fingers instinctively—I knew that: I had read reams of mother-and-child literature. But I didn't say a word and let Peter believe that Mark was holding his hand.

Just a few days before, I had dusted the ornate silver frame holding a group picture of the wedding. My parents stared stonily at the camera in stark contrast to Peter's father and mother, who had both fallen into developed a fits of giggles whilst the photo was being taken. Who would have guessed that the Nelsons would only stick it out for only fourteen years, instead of "'til death us do part"?

"I know you will make a mess of your marriage," I can still hear my father saying coldly, his gaze contemptuous as he surveyed the daughter who never quite managed to please her father. "You could never do anything right."

Tears welled up in my eyes and spill down my cheeks onto my faded blue sweatshirt. It had belonged to Peter, and I can remember him wearing it.

Maybe this was all a mistake, I thought helplessly. I got up to clear the breakfast table as I did every morning, my mind slipping into housekeeping mode: once, I'd known more about office management than breakfast cereals, more about client servicing than the dietary requirements of thirteen-year-old children. Fourteen years ago, in a trading company, I practically ran one department for months: when the department supervisor had left abruptly for a better job, I was asked to take over, and I didn't hesitate in rising to the occasion.

I sometimes wondered how I had done it all—how I had run my division calmly and capably, responsible for three people and thousands of accounts. I had actually enjoyed it: it had been a challenge for me, the career girl, but would now be a terrifying prospect for Olivia, the housewife. I had always planned to go back to work when the children were old enough, but somehow, the longer I stayed at home, the harder it was to think about entering the job market again.

Delighted with his well-run home, beautifully cooked meals, and happy, well-turned-out children clamoring for fatherly attention when he got home from work, Peter never gave me the push I required to get me back at work—and, as the years flew by and our money problems shrank, we found we had enough money to pay for everything we'd ever want. So, why bother going back to work? I was living comfortably and spending incautiously!

"The children need you, darling," Peter had said every time I mentioned going back to work. "Just because they're at school doesn't mean they don't need their mother when they get home, does it? Anyway, my secretary never stops moaning about leaving her three to her mother, and she's always late every other Monday—one of them has a temperature, or a cold, or some other issue. Be grateful you don't have to work!" Clearly, he did not count running a house as work.

He was probably right: I was familiar with the problems of working mothers—courtesy of the magazines I loved to read. Every second page would have a different story about some woman stuck in an endless cycle of work, kids, and housework, with Saturdays spent cooking giant lasagnas to jam into the freezer for the week. Peter was right: I was lucky he earned enough so I didn't need to work.

Nevertheless, we argued about it several times—and these arguments only worsened when Peter's sister, unbearably smug thanks to a recent promotion in the Bank of New York in which she worked, asked why I was letting my brain rot by sitting at home every day.

"I can't believe she said that to me," I said angrily in the car on the way home. "She treats me like a second-class citizen because I'm not managing a bank, or something. How dare she say that! I'd like to see her running a home and looking after the children! I was working when that little bitch was still in primary school!"

"Don't mind her," Peter had said evenly. "She's just jealous because you've got a husband, two lovely children, and a nice villa. She'd kill to be married—not that any man would be stupid enough to take her." He paused for a moment. "Besides, you'd hate to go out to work. Everything's changed since you last had a job; I mean, where would you even start? You couldn't expect to just walk into a good job after twelve years of housekeeping; you haven't any office skills anymore, have you? Being able to make a perfect quiche isn't much good when you need a degree to get any job these days."

"I want to start my own business," I answered swiftly and somewhat coldly, stung by his words. "I'd always planned for this step, especially for when the children don't need my full attention anymore."

I didn't speak all the way home, silently fuming.

Despite my defense, I resigned myself to being a full-time housewife—and here I was, still stuck in the kitchen with a mountain of ironing, the breakfast dishes to do and the knowledge that my husband was cheating imprinted on my brain.

Please let it be a mistake, God. Of course, it would just be some silly misunderstanding; I mean, I'd know if he was seeing someone else, wouldn't I? He could have bought the underwear for me as a late anniversary present; he could be planning a surprise, and maybe he meant me to find the receipt as a teaser.

Then I remembered the flowers and the large box of chocolates he'd given me, the former from a garage shop. He'd thrust them into my hands with a quick kiss on the cheek. Those multicolored bouquets with not enough chrysanthemums or carnations to make a decent arrangement were always stacked outside garages for last-minute gifts—and that's just what my anniversary present had been: a last-minute gift; an afterthought.

It was unbelievable. I shook my head as I thought of Peter with another woman, his naked body in someone else's arms, his mouth hoovering another woman's body, his tongue tasting another woman's vagina, his eyes dark with desire. Did he murmur her name in the same husky voice he used when it was me in his arms?

Who was this other woman? What did she look like? Questions bubbled in my mind as I tried to picture my rival: she was probably slim, beautiful and clever, with a high-profile job and conversational abilities.

How did this happen to us? Never in a million years would I have dreamed that Peter could sleep with another woman, could betray our marriage.

Passionate affairs happened to people in high-end society where getting divorced and finding another partner was as easy as ordering a bottle of champagne at the most expensive restaurant in town.

Not at any point during our marriage thus far had I felt the desire to look for another man—a younger version of Peter; I had fallen in love with him sixteen years before, and didn't want to replace him. So what if he wanted to replace me?

Every part of my life—every mundane task in the family home—, was suddenly threatened by the existence of some other woman—someone Peter had gone to bed with.

No, this could not be happening. He loved me; we were married. He couldn't go off with someone else— wouldn't go off with someone else. I would take revenge and go off with some other man. Shouldn't I?

Then again, maybe I was jumping to conclusions. That was it: there was probably some perfectly reasonable explanation. Suddenly hopeful again, I realized that there was one way to find out what was going on: whenever Peter bought anything with his credit card, he filed away the statement; he kept several accordion folders in his closet, where he kept bills, bank statements, birth certificates, and, of course, credit card statements.

I untied the ribbons at the top of the first folder with trembling hands and rifled through the alphabetical sections, looking for credit card receipts. I found nothing but bank statements and paid gas and electricity bills, neatly filed with a red pen marking "Paid" on every one.

I tackled the last file, searching quickly through the Cs for credit cards, and then onto V for Visa—and there they were: wedged in-between a sheaf of medical insurance forms.

I carefully removed the familiar credit card statements and spread them onto the soft beige bedroom carpet. It didn't take long to find the debit for Lingerie de Paris; unfortunately, it was nestled in between-other, equally damning expenses that immediately brought a lump to my throat.

Silk knickers followed by numerous debits for costly meals in New York's trendiest restaurants—places I'd only ever dreamed of going to. I then found a debit transaction to a ream of luxurious hotels in Manhattan—one of the dates being two days before our anniversary.

The effortless way he had lied hit me now like a punch in the stomach: with no stuttering or stumbling, he'd lied with the calm of an accomplished liar. He hadn't even told me what hotel he was staying in, and I'd never even thought to ask. Of course, if I had asked, he would, no doubt, have pointed out that I shouldn't bother trying to ring him, since he was out at business dinner.

I dropped the last of Peter's statements onto the floor and rose to my feet slowly. I picked up the telephone by the side of my bed, not registering the empty orange juice glass he'd brought upstairs that morning and left for me to clear away. Under normal circumstances, I would have made the bed by this time, and would probably be busy vacuuming the children's rooms.

Right now, I didn't care if the whole house fell apart: I simply had to know what was happening—who Peter was seeing, and ultimately figure out if our whole relationship was a horrible mistake.

The Labelling Concept: When we want something to be true, we gather information that supports our desire. It does not just affect what information people go looking for, but also what they notice in the first place. Olivia and Peter are in a troubled marriage, each of them having labeled the other's shortcomings (e.g., Peter is labeled as "selfish" and Olivia is labeled as "needy"). These labels become self-fulfilling: the selfish acts become easier to spot, whilst the generous acts go largely unnoticed.

Couples should consciously fight the tendency to only notice what's wrong.

PETER

SIMILAR TO MANY MARRIED females, Olivia seemed to think I was her hostage—a lifetime prisoner that couldn't escape. She took me for granted; I represented no more than a cash cow, a provider for her and the children. She considered me as if I were her property, a form of investment she made so she could always yield some form of profit to keep her secure. It was always my responsibility to make her feel safe, secure, and happy, and to be sympathetic to her mood-swings and female hormones. She could have married an alarm system if she needed safety and security; she could have married a clown if she wanted to feel happy. It was as if I were an emotionless animal, sex being all it took to keep him alive. Until today, I know she would have bet on her life that I would have never dreamt of doing anything more than simply speak with another woman; she felt safe as long as I met her financial demands. If I was meeting her and the children's endless demands, how dare I look after my own self-actualization. Being captured by her endless shopping lists and the children's demands, yet being constantly pushed to feel ashamed because I wasn't meeting her emotional needs, made me feel sick to the teeth. Enough was enough.

"We have to talk." Olivia surprised me with the calmness of her voice as she reached out and tapped me on the shoulder. She was staring into the crowd of coworkers across the room; her eyes seemed to go in and out of focus.

"Are you alright?" I asked.

She turned away, picked up a large tumbler full of gin and tonic—strong and cool, with plenty of ice clinking around the glass—, and took a deep, reviving swig. The gin seemed to hit her system like an injection of adrenaline.

Olivia raised her cool blue eyes to meet mine. From the look in her eyes, I knew something serious had happened.

"What is it?" I asked her impatiently. "Tell me, what's the big fuss?"

"The big fuss is about Jennifer Richard. Does that name sound a bit familiar to you?" She gazed at me expectantly. "I know you're having an affair, Peter; so I think we need a private talk. Don't you? Or do you want everyone on the premises to hear about your sordid secret—if they don't already know, that is." Her eyes glimmered with anger.

My eyes darkening. I stared at her with the same blank look she'd seen when I'd been stuck talking to someone I didn't like: cold and indifferent, my face impassive and my eyes offering nothing.

"How did you find out?" I asked her as casually, as though she'd mentioned that the car was out of petrol.

"You should be more careful with your credit card receipts." She gritted her teeth. "Didn't you know I'd find out if you left a receipt for Lingerie de bloody Paris in your navy suit pocket? Or did you want me to find out?"

"No." I stared down at some spot on the grey speckled office carpet, seemingly miles away, as though contemplating whether 80% wool was more serviceable than pure wool carpet. "I didn't want you to find out, because it would hurt you, and I never meant to do that."

"Yeah, right; you just wanted everyone else to find out you were cheating on your stupid wife. Let her find out by mere coincidence! Is that the way you wanted it? Is there anything else I should know, or are you taking out an advert in next week's paper?"

I stopped looking at the carpet and lifted my gaze to hers sadly— almost pityingly. She was looking at me in a way I couldn't deal with. I averted my gaze to out the window, staring at nothing.

"Maybe I should have asked your secretary if you had a few other women stashed away somewhere. Or was one enough? Did you have a bet with that bloody bitch to see how long you could keep me fooled?"

Olivia paused for breath, taking a huge drink from her glass. Her hands were shaking so much that the ice rattled against the glass noisily. She hung her head and her hair cascaded over her face; I couldn't see if she was crying or not.

"It isn't like that, Olivia," I chided. "I didn't tell anyone; I thought we were discreet—although obviously I was wrong. I never wanted to hurt you, and—"

"Don't tell me," Olivia intercepted. "It didn't mean a thing and you can't even remember her name. Is that your next line? Because I know her name, even if you pretend you've forgotten it. Jennifer Richard, isn't it?"

She looked at me triumphantly, as though we were playing hide-and-seek and she'd just won.

"Just tell me one thing, Peter," she pressed on, her voice wobbling slightly. "Why? Why did you do it? Don't you love me anymore? Don't you care about our marriage and the children?"

We looked at each other silently. I could feel my eyes were still steel-cold. The words had trembled on my tongue dozens of times. "I've loved you for more than fourteen years, Olivia; but I'm not in love with you anymore."

These words seemed to hit her like a bullet. There was a new fire in her eyes, and unusual expression hardened the features of her face. I shrugged and splayed my hands out in a gesture of apology. "I'm sorry," I said unconvincingly, "but it's not as if you wanted to make our marriage work, is it? You just wanted to crawl into your shell and hide from the world." She stared at me disbelievingly. "You, the children, and your damned endless shopping lists—that's all that mattered to you. Not me. You never wanted to be a part of my life; it's always the children. It's like you've forgotten that we got married—that it was us. Not you, me, and two kids, but us." I paused. "No, you don't remember, do you? You cut me out of your cozy little life, and I couldn't deal with that."

I stopped. My words hung in the air like icicles, cold and deadly. I could have stabbed her with them and it wouldn't have hurt as much as the cold look I couldn't wipe from my face.

"You've made it pretty clear you don't want to be part of my life," I continued, "so I wanted someone who did want to be with me."

My voice was calm—maddeningly clam. She'd just confronted me with the biggest crisis a marriage could face, and here I was, looking at her with calm indifference. I spoke about our marriage as if it was already dead as a dodo.

"Don't give me that rubbish, Peter," Olivia breathed. "Lingerie de Paris and nights in hotels is not about our marriage not working; it's about sex—you and some other woman having sex. You just couldn't stop yourself, could you? Everything we had just wasn't enough for you. So don't try and blame me. Don't tell me it's my fault! How dare you—"

"I'm not trying to blame you, Olivia!" I interrupted. "It is just that..." I sighed heavily. "Look, we can't talk about this here with everyone watching and listening. Let's wait 'til we get home, okay?"

"Home! Let's wait 'til we get home!" Olivia repeated shrilly. "You conveniently forgot about home when you were shacked up with that bitch in hotels, lying that you were somewhere else!" Tears sprung to her eyes. "You can forget about coming home with me now; your home is with your bloody bitch, and I don't want to look at you until you've ended things with her!"

"Olivia." I tried to grab her, but she managed to shrug my arm off. "Stop," I commanded. And she did. Spinning her round to face me, I looked her in the eyes, my pupils boring into hers intently. "I never wanted to hurt you, Olivia; you have to believe that." My tone was earnest. "But you've changed. I don't know what's happened to you, but you've become... different. It's as if you shut yourself off from me, and I can't live like that. I'm sorry. You're right about me not coming home; it wouldn't work. It's better if I don't tonight." I exhaled. "I wanted to tell you everything a long time ago, but I could never find the right time... I didn't want to hurt the kids, but there's no time that's right for kids in the middle of a failed marriage." She lifted her gaze to mine. All her anger was gone: instead, her eyes were filled with complete heartbreak. "I'll stay at Tom's tonight; I'll come pick up some stuff in the morning." I looked at her coolly, my eyes taking in the new dress she bought with my credit card and her flushed face, red from the gin.

Her face still left me weak at the knees.

"I better go back in," I said quietly. "The Managing Director is waiting for me to launch the company's new product line in a few minutes."

Olivia slowly drained her glass and turned towards the stairs.

OLIVIA

I FELT THE BLOOD pumping through my body, keeping me alive when all I wanted to do was die. I had given him the chance—the chance to say he still loved me and that it had all been an awful mistake—, but he hadn't used it; he had turned my own words against me.

God, if only I hadn't said he shouldn't come home... If only I'd kept my mouth shut and let him explain, let him beg forgiveness. Surely, then, everything would have been alright. I'd given him a cast-iron excuse to leave.

I'd never quite understood the expression "time stood still", until it did in that moment.

He was standing just a few feet away from me, wearing a pale blue shirt with the top buttons open to reveal a few inches of tanned neck—a neck I had snuggled into countless times, including last night, when we'd sat on the couch watching TV. His aftershave permeated the air and, if I reached out, I could touch him, hold him in my arms and be safe for ever.

Perhaps if I wished hard enough, I could turn back the clock and keep my mouth shut. Then, he would have stayed with me; then, he wouldn't need anyone else.

But it was too late: he didn't want me; instead, he craved another woman in his arms and his life. If someone had told me my feelings for Peter could be reversed in a matter of moments, I would have laughed at the idea: nothing could erase the love I felt for Peter, the bond which tied us to each other.

It was then I started to cry properly: great, heaving sobs that shook my whole body, as if I was coughing my last breath. A perfect house, two lovely children, a wife delighted to play housekeeper-come-nanny, and a successful handsome husband... These pieces hadn't even made an ideal marriage. Reality hadn't conformed to my expectations; my dreams looked as shattered as a broken cup.

On the day I found out Peter was cheating on me with this tall, thin, flame-haired bitch, Jennifer, I went on a major spending spree—and, by the time Peter and the bitch would have been making love, or eating out, or having a romantic conversation, or whatever else they were doing,

I'd have amassed a bright orange jacket, three silk tops, a denim skirt, two pairs of shoes, and an outrageously expensive leather handbag.

It was at the cosmetics counter—where I hadn't originally intended to buy anything at all—that everything went horribly wrong.

The shop assistant smiled brightly at me. It had been a quiet day so far—the weather had kept people out of the shops and on the beaches—, so I knew this sale would help her commission figures considerably.

"I'm sorry, Ms. Nelson," she said as she looked at the machine, "but authorization has been refused. Maybe if you put back one item…?"

I looked at the Christian Dior cleanser, toner, and moisturizer package in front of me, as well as the foundation, lipstick, blusher, and bottle of Dolce Vita. I attempted to calculate how much might be left on the card after all my previous purchases were taken into account.

"Oh." I tried to look nonchalant. "I must have got a bit carried away."

"Carried away" was, of course, an understatement. Before that disastrous day, it had been absolutely wonderful to walk into shops and simply buy things for the sake of it; I'd gotten a buzz every single time a purchase was wrapped in tissue paper and slid into a bag. The sales assistants had been smiling and cheerful, as if I should be smiling and cheerful, too. Every time I signed my card, I felt a little better. My subconscious had been on autopilot—a place where Peter financed my shopping obsession; I'd forgotten there was no Peter anymore.

Now, mortification flooded me.

"I think I'd better forget it," I added, superfluously.

"I'm sure some of it would fit on the card," said the sales assistant. "There's no need to leave everything. Or you could use your store card, if you have one? Or cash, of course."

Cash! I grimaced. "Not right now," I told the sales assistant. "I think that I've done enough spending for the day. I'm sorry."

"Okay." The sales assistant tried to look friendly, the dollar signs clearly fading from her eyes. "See you again, perhaps."

I'd tried to ignore the curious glances of other customers as the sales assistant had taken back the cosmetics. It had been humiliating; I should have known how close I was to my card limit. I usually tried hard to keep track of any purchases I put on it, but I hadn't kept track today; my mind hadn't wanted to.

I gritted my teeth and pushed my way through the crowded street, towards the park in my neighborhood: I needed to sit down and take the weight off my feet. The park was thronged with people—shirtless men and women with skimpy tops—or, in some cases, nothing but lacy Wonderbras. I wished I had the nerve to take off my plain white Calvin Klein T-shirt and sit in the park in nothing more than my bra and skirt—but then again, it was one thing for a girl of eighteen to sit practically topless in the center of New York, and quite another for a woman of forty to flaunt her sagging boobs in public.

There were no pack benches available, so I walked across the grass—past a group of laughing students—and sat down in the shade of a chestnut tree. I arranged my packages around me and closed my eyes.

Forty. I wondered when, exactly, forty had started to feel old; maybe it was when I realized that no exercise in the world was ever going to give me back the body I'd had when I was younger—the slim, taut body of someone who could eat as much as she liked and not gain any weight. It wasn't as though I was fat, exactly—but fourteen years and two children had changed my shape more than I would have liked. Sometimes, when I looked in the mirror, I felt as though I'd turned into someone I didn't even know.

I was quite sure there were hordes of forty-year-old women walking around the city who looked as good as they had when they were twenty-five, and who felt as young as ever. Even worse, I'd opened a magazine the other day and seen a dewy-skinned fashion model smiling out at me—a woman in her fifties. A wrinkle or two would have been nice. I dreaded to think of how I'd look at fifty, given how much my body had let me down already—especially when I compared it to that of the eleven-years-younger, flame-haired bitch, Jennifer.

I'd always thought of her as "The Bitch"—which was stupid, really, since I didn't even know her. It wasn't even as though I cared anymore; I'd been told she was young, red-haired, and absolutely gorgeous. I already knew this.

And then there was when I finally met her, and I almost choked: I'd seen Jennifer's smooth, clear complexion, her riot of tumbling red-gold curls, and her long, long legs shown off to such advantage by her short, short cotton skirt—and I'd wanted to scream with rage. He'd found someone truly lovely, and I couldn't help but feel consumed with envy: the young, beautiful Jennifer was in his life whilst I trundled towards middle age on my own—except for the children, of course. Peter's children. As much as I loved them, they didn't make it easy to start all over again.

I told myself that it wouldn't last; that Peter would get tired of Jennifer's wide, beaming smile and irritating manner of clearing her throat before she spoke. However, even these small reassurances sounded weak in my mind: I'd seen the looks they'd exchanged—the same intimate glances I had once shared with him, ones that voiced the unspoken belief that we were the only people in the world who mattered.

It was funny how clear in my memory the day I'd met Peter Nelson was: It didn't seem like almost sixteen years ago. I smiled faintly. A true sign of age, I thought, that sixteen years seems like a short time. I hadn't for one second ever believed anyone would force him up the altar. I hated to think it had all worked out so neatly for him, whilst I couldn't help feeling a failure.

When I got home, I carefully unwrapped all my purchases and hung the new clothes in the wardrobe. It wouldn't do for Glenda to see them yet; my daughter would be furious if she knew I had blown our monthly budget on feel-good clothes. I wished I felt good about them now. I ran my hand along the back of the orange jacket; it was lovely, though—a classic piece. I'd be able to wear it over and over again, even if orange was only this season's color. And I'd needed the shoes—especially the low-heeled comfortable pair. All the same, I sighed; I really should have paid some of the accumulated bills instead of adding to them.

The Lovers' Reciprocal Altruism Concept: A process of long-term cooperation by which the couples make real sacrifices (emotionally and/or physically) as proof of love and care, based on the expectation that the other party will return the favor at a later time.

COUPLES DON'T END UP in the divorce court because they have arguments; it's the way they argue that massively increases the chance of them splitting up. The high, passionate attachment can't last forever: the body builds up a tolerance to the natural chemicals in the brain associated with being in attachment, to the point where more and more are needed in order to feel the same levels of euphoria. Some people interpret the corresponding decrease in sexual energy to mean they are no longer attached to one another—and, indeed, for some, it does mark the end of a relationship. However, rather than an end to attachment, it may be a transition into the longer-lasting companionate attachment. It appears that the brain cannot tolerate the continually revved-up state of passionate attachment, and so, as the newness of passion fades, new chemicals kick in—endorphins. These are natural, morphine-like substances that clam the mind. Here, whilst the excitement may diminish, the security of a companionate attachment can provide a different—although not necessarily lesser—pleasure.

Olivia—like many women—assumed that all Peter needed to be happy was sex and a home-cooked meal—, and, as long as he got these on occasion, Olivia could treat him however she wanted. However, she failed to realize that Peter had deep-seated emotional needs too—needs he was unwilling (and often unable) to communicate. Hence, when these needs were neglected by Olivia, devastation took over, causing him to take steps back to protect himself—a fight-or-flight response. Men may fight for their rights in the relationship by demanding that their wives submit to meeting certain expectations—or, like Peter, they may prefer the flight response, withdrawing emotionally from the relationship and even looking for a more satisfying attraction outside the home.

The reality is that men aren't all that different from women when it comes to their basic needs: men have emotional needs, too, and they can feel a sense of desperation when those needs aren't being met. As much as a woman longs to have her husband understand and meets her innermost needs, she has to learn to give that which she desires to receive.

A successful marriage is only the product of two people being successfully single.

Marriage is a subtle form of recruitment: when asked, "What can marriage offer you?", most men say something around having a warm safe refuge, having their food cooked for them, and having their clothes ironed; rarely do they mention their emotional needs, and this is because men are generally bad at articulating their emotional needs—not because they didn't have them at all. At base level, they want a cross between their mother and a personal servant—and, unsurprisingly, only few men refer to their female partner as their best friend. The role of the best friend is, for most men, usually taken by another man, who is deemed to understand his thought processes. Similarly, a woman's best friend is usually another woman—someone with similar brain wiring.

If marriage fails as often as it does, why do so many of us keep committing the same crime? If marriage is an outdated institution, why not live on our own, or with our families or friends, and have lovers when the mood takes us? There are several possible answers to this question: firstly, the human being never learns from mistakes; they want to acquire the experience themselves. Secondly, for many, marriage— theoretically— continues to be thought of as a reliable way to raise mentally healthy children. Thirdly, marriage can supposedly have a soothing effect: in a mad world where life is lived at breakneck speed, marriage, at its best, can function, theoretically, like a port in a storm: a place to rest and recuperate from the stresses that face us at every moment. However, these assumptions only apply in theory, and rarely apply to day-to-day life. This is why many still commit the same mistakes within marriage.

Marriage was more important to Olivia than Peter—and this is because, for a woman, marriage is a way of declaration to the world that a man considers her to be special, and intends to have a monogamous relationship with her. This feeling of being special has a dramatic effect on the chemical action in a woman's brain; research on the brains of married women, versus those of non-married women, shows that a woman's orgasm rate is four to five times higher in a marital bed, and two to three times higher in a monogamous relationship.

It is thus no surprise to find in Western society that even non-married partners who live together end up marrying.

Anthropologists have conducted brain scans in order to locate the position of love in the brain, and have as a result located three types of emotion in the brain: lust, infatuation, and attachment. Each one of these emotions has its own specific brain chemistry that lights up the brain when its owner is attracted to someone.

The first stage of Olivia and Peter's story was the lust stage—the physical and non-verbal attraction. Infatuation was the second stage—where Peter kept popping into Olivia's brain and she couldn't get him out—, and it was during this time that her brain focused on the positive qualities of Peter and ignored his bad traits and flaws. Therefore, infatuation is the brain's attempt to form a bond with a potential partner, and it is an emotion so powerful that it can cause incredible euphoria. Similarly, if someone is rejected during this stage, it can also cause extraordinary despair, and can oftentimes lead to obsession. At the infatuation stage, several powerful brain chemicals are released, causing feelings of elation.

Infatuation is a temporary feeling that lasts, on average, from three to twelve months; however, Peter and Olivia mistakenly defined this stage as "love"—when it was, in fact, a biological trick. The danger of this stage is that lovers believe their sex drives are perfectly matched, but this is only because they're still in the infatuation stage; their real sex drive differences reveal themselves only after the infatuation stage ends—or when the attachment stage starts.

When reality finally takes over from infatuation, either one or both of the partners will reject the other, or, the third stage—attachment—will come into play with its focus on building a cooperative bond that will last long enough to raise children.

Understanding these three stages can make it easier to deal with the infatuation stage, as well as to be prepared for its possible downfall.

The Spiderweb Concept: Love is like a spider: the spider finds an innocuous corner in which to spin its web. The longer the web takes, the more eye-catching its eventual construction is; however, few people really notice it, since its threads are nearly invisible. The spider has no need to chase or even to move: it quietly sits in the corner, waiting for its victims to come to it on their own and ensnare themselves in its web.

FOR MEN, LOVE IS CONFUSING: Olivia, who was so exciting before marriage, seemed not-so-attractive after marriage—and not at all intelligent, either. Men are easily led to the lust stage; they are fueled with testosterone, and, during the infatuation stage, Peter was so fired up on testosterone that he got lost and confused. Conversely, because the centers for emotion and reason are better connected in a woman's brain—as well as the fact that she is not plagued with testosterone—, Olivia found it easier at the time to evaluate whether Peter was the right partner for her. This is why most relationships are ended by women, and why so many men are confused about what has happened.

Saying "I love you" was never a problem for Olivia: a woman's brain-wiring makes her world full of feelings, emotions, communication, and words. Olivia knew when she felt warm, wanted, and adored, and was in the attachment stage—and she knew when she was in love. However, Peter was not exactly sure what love was, and had likely confused lust and infatuation with love. All he knew was that he couldn't keep his hands off of Olivia, so maybe that was love? His brain was blinded by testosterone: he had a constant erection, and couldn't think straight. It's often not until a long period after a relationship begins that a man recognizes he was in love, but even then, he does this in retrospect. Meanwhile, women tend to recognize quickly when love does not exist, and that is why most relationships are ended by women.

Similarly to Peter, many men are commitment-phobes: Peter was scared that saying "I love you" would commit him for the rest of his life, and found he would prefer a naked supermodel on the beach than a long-term wife. Most men also tend remain oblivious to the increase in a woman's orgasm rate after he has said he loves her.

The rate of happily married women who have affairs is lower than happily married males who have affairs: more than 90% of affairs are initiated by men, although more than 80% are ended by women. When a woman begins to realize an affair has no lasting emotional promise and will only be physical, she ends it. A man's brain—with its ability to separate love from sex and deal with each item separately because of its compartmentalization—allows him to see just one thing at a time. Therefore, Peter was often happy with just a good physical relationship.

A woman's brain has a network of connections between her love center and her sex center (the hypothalamus), and the former requires activation before her sex center can be switched on. Men, on the other hand, do not appear to have these connections, and so they can often deal with sex and love separately. For a man, sex is sex and love is love—and sometimes it just so happens that they occur together.

A man who has an affair and is asked "Do you love her?" and responds, "No, it was only physical; it didn't mean anything", is likely to be telling the truth: men can separate sex from love. A woman's brain, on the other hand, is not wired to understand or accept this answer, and this is why many women find it difficult to accept/believe this answer: for her, sex equals love. In a woman's mind, it is not the physical act of sex with the other woman that affects her as much as the violation of the emotional contract and trust she had in him. If a woman has an affair and says it didn't mean anything, she is probably lying: for a woman to cross the line to having sex with another person, she would have already had to have established an emotional bond with the new man.

Peter called sex "just sex", but Olivia reacted negatively to this: it was not, by her definition, the way it was. A woman "makes love", meaning she needs to feel loved and have received loving feelings before she wants to have sex; to most women the act of "sex" is generally seen as a loveless, gratuitous act, the wiring of a female brain not identifying with this definition.

Therefore, when Peter said "sex", he wasn't saying didn't love Olivia; when a man wants to "make love", he is still likely to call it "sex". This can have negative effects on a woman—but to use the expression "make love" can make many men feel that they are conning her, since he sometimes feels he just wants sex.

If Peter and Olivia had understood one another's perspective and agreed not to judge the other's definition, this obstacle could have ceased in their relationship.

During their dating, Peter's perception of Olivia related to the depth of his intimate feelings for her: he rated Olivia higher on the physical attractiveness scale, simply because he was madly in love with her. A man rates his partner lower in attractiveness if he doesn't particularly care for her, even though she may be physically stunning. When Peter was turned on by Olivia, her usual physical became irrelevant; in fact, they seemed to be perfect. This demonstrates that whilst a woman's physical attractiveness rates highly in initial meetings for men, a warm, nurturing partnership accounts for a significant part of her attractiveness in the long-term. However, this was not the sole factor of Olivia's attraction to Peter: she also (albeit subconsciously) evaluated Peter's viability as a partner by his personal characteristics above his physical appearance.

Normally, we are drawn to people with similar values, interests, attitudes, and perceptions; they are the people with whom we instantly "click". The same applies to long-term relationships: the chance is higher for a long-term successful relationship if it falls under this "similarity" condition. However, sometimes too many similarities can become boring; thus, partners may require just enough differences to make it interesting and to complement the other's personality, yet not so much that it will interfere with their lifestyles and moral standings. A quiet man may be attracted to an outgoing woman, and a quiet woman may be attracted to an outgoing man—but in general, they will possess many other similarities in values and attitudes.

The books we buy and the type of media we consume are a clear indicator of the things that interest us in romance: women spend millions every year on romance novels, and women's magazines largely focus on love, romance, other people's affairs, or how to exercise, eat, and dress better—with the aim of attracting even more romance. Studies show that women who read romance novels have sex twice as often as those who don't, whilst men will tend to spend millions on books and magazines teaching technical know-how on a range of practical subjects—from computers to fishing, football to mechanical devices.

When Olivia asked Peter to show her more affection, he helped in the household chores and washed and polished her car—which demonstrates how men see "doing things" and "actions" as a way of showing they care. Men's brains are wired for the technical, and not the aesthetic; it's not that a man will not try, but rather the fact that some of them just don't understand the significance of opening a car door, sending flowers, dancing, or cooking for a woman.

Women enter a new relationship looking for romance and love; sex comes as a consequence. However, men frequently enter a relationship with sex as their primary motivator, and then look to see if there could be the possibility of a relationship.

Before getting married, Peter held Olivia's hand in public, rubbed her back, and talked to her endlessly; and after marriage, he occasionally held her hand, didn't want to talk, and only touched her when he wanted sex. During the courtship stage, Peter touched Olivia more than at any other time in their relationship, and this is because he wanted to "get his hands on her", but hadn't yet received the green light for any sexual touching—so, instead, he touched her everywhere else he could. Hence, when he eventually got the go-ahead for sexual touching, his brain saw no point in going back to "the old days"; instead, he just concentrated on the "good bits". He talked a lot during the courtship stage in order to collect information about Olivia, as well as to give her information about himself. Thus, by the time they were married, he knew all he needed to know about her, and saw little point in excessive talk.

However, if Peter had learnt that Olivia's brain was programmed to communicate with talk, and that her sensitivity to touch was ten times greater than his, he would have taught himself to become skillful in such areas, and you can bet that the overall quality of his love life would have dramatically improved.

Oxytocin is known as the "cuddle hormone", and is released when someone's skin is gently stroked or they are cuddled. It increases sensitivity to touch and feelings of bonding, and is a major factor in a woman's behavior towards babies and men. When a woman begins breast-feeding, it triggers the "let down" reflex that releases milk from the breasts.

If a woman wants to pleasure a man by touching him, she normally does it in the way she would like to receive it; hence, Olivia would scratch Peter's head, caress his face, rub his back, and tenderly brush his hair. This childish type of touching had little impact on Peter, and he even found it annoying: men's skin is significantly less sensitive to touch than a woman's so he won't feel excessive pain/injury during hunting. Men prefer to be touched predominantly in one area, and as often as possible, creating major relationship problems as a result of this conflict of interests.

When a man decides to sensually touch a woman, he gives her the things he likes—and so Peter groped Olivia's breasts and crotch. This is at the top of a woman's hate list, and causes resentment on both sides.

Conversely, when a man and woman learn to give each other sensual touches based on their individual needs and skin sensitivity, their relationship is even more enriched.

Love starts with lust—which can last a few hours, a few days, or a few weeks. Next comes infatuation, which lasts on average about 3-12 months before the third stage takes place: attachment.

When the blinding cocktail of hormones had subsided after some years, Peter saw Olivia in a cold light: those little habits he'd found so endearing at first had begun to become irritating. Whilst he once thought it cute that he could never find things in the fridge, it now made him want to scream—and, whilst he used to love hearing her talk about every little thing, he would now be plagued with irritation. Chances are, they didn't have much in common or much to talk about anymore. Men and women fall under the influence of a powerful combination of hormones, there simply for the purpose of urging them to procreate and not think. Finding the right partner means deciding what things you have in common with someone in the long-term—and, more importantly, doing this in advance of nature's blinding hormonal highs. When infatuation has passed, can you maintain a lasting relationship based on friendship and common interest?

Write a list of the traits and interests you want in a long-term partner, and then you will know exactly who you're looking for. A man will have a list of qualities for his ideal mate, but when he goes to a party filled with females, his brain is fired up by testosterone. It then searches for the ideal woman based on hormonal motivation—nice legs, a flat stomach, a round bum, full breasts—, all connected with short-term procreation.

Women typically want a man who is sensitive and caring, has a V-shaped torso, and has a great personality—all things connected with child-rearing and their own protection. These are also short-term biological needs, and have little to do with success in a modern relationship.

When you write a list of the desirable long-term characteristics in your perfect partner and keep it handy, it helps you to remain objective about a new person the next time nature tries to control your thoughts and urges.

Your biological needs want you to procreate as often as possible, and they use powerful chemical brain drugs to push you into it. However, when you understand the game and are armed with a job description of your ideal long-term mate, you are less likely to be tricked, and more likely to be successful in your hunt.

Many modern women have chosen professional careers because they want some of the things men have: money, prestige, and power. However, studies show that career women are now also getting many of the side-effects   usually experienced by working men, such   as heart problems, ulcers, stress, and premature death. Almost half of working women state that their work is now their greatest source of stress, most confessing that if money weren't a factor, they would prefer to be a homemaker or a mother. Still, motherhood is ranked as the number one choice across the board for all women, as compared with 2% for careers, most women still placing raising a child in a traditional family at the top of their list of priorities. These priorities show that the hype produced by the media—as well as feminist waves—have not had as big an impact on women's genuine attitudes and priorities. As is clear from a wealth of surveys, the values and priorities of modern women are basically the same as they have been for centuries—the difference being that most modern women state financial independence as being vital to them. In other words, females don't want to be dependent on men, and this is the only consistent difference between traditional and modern women. Many working women say they work for the money, and most of them live in cities where two incomes are critical for survival. The bottom line is that motherhood still rates top of most women's list of things that give them the greatest satisfaction.

However, some still believe that earning enough money to feed, clothe, and educate the next generation is a more noble cause than rearing it—whilst in reality, all the facts indicate that women enjoy parenting the most.

However, the side-effect of work on women is clear. In a traditional male hierarchy, a woman has two choices: either quit, or adopt the male stereotype. In the majority of political systems, less than 5% of politicians are female—and those within that bracket behave more like men than women.

Male characteristics and value are largely responsible for driving people to the top of the tree, but feminine values are becoming the only way to remain there. Masculine priorities need to be understood by any person aiming for the top of the heap—although now, feminine value systems are much better suited to making the whole show work more efficiently, harmoniously, and, therefore, successfully.

At the top levels, emphasis on masculine values leads to internal power struggles: individuals want to 'go it alone' when unanimous agreements cannot be reached. Intuitive hunches have no place in the fight to look, and be, the best—regardless of whether new strategies or lateral approaches may succeed in encouraging new growth and development. Feminine values, on the other hand, encourage teamwork, collaboration, and interdependence—qualities far better suited to an organization's strategic capabilities and human resources. This does not mean that a man needs to be effeminate, or a woman needs to be masculine; rather, it means that men and women need to understand that each gender system is vital at different times in the rise to the top.

HOW OFTEN HAS OLIVIA or Peter paused before the mirror with sad eyes and asked themselves, "Could it have been different? If I had lived otherwise, could I have saved our home? Was there something I should have known that I don't even know yet?"

Ironically, Olivia also recalled that she was miserable as a single woman, and thought that getting married would solve all her problems; however, as her marriage illustrates, getting rid of her single status only exchanged one set of problems for another—and a more complex set, at that.

There had been several signs indicating they were probably on the road to imminent divorce:

- Harsh startups: Discussions that begin based on criticism, sarcasm, or contempt; what begins badly, ends badly.
- Criticism: There is a difference between complaints—which refer to a particular action by your spouse—and personal criticism.
- Contempt: This includes any form of sneering, eye-rolling, mockery, or name-calling that aims to make the other person feel bad. A worse version of contempt is belligerence, often expressed in the phrase, "What are you going to do about it?"
- Defensiveness: Trying to make the other person seem like they are the problem, as if you have not made any contribution to the problem.
- Stonewalling: When one partner "tunes out", unable to take regular criticism, contempt, and defensiveness. By disengaging, they are less exposed to being hurt. In 85% of marriages, it is the man who is the "stonewaller"; a man's response to conflict is likely to be more indignant, with thoughts of "getting even" or "I do not have to take this"; women, on the other hand, are better able to soothe themselves following a stressful situation—which also explains why women nearly always have to raise the issues of conflict in the relationship, whilst men try to avoid them.
- Flooding: Regular emotional "flooding" is when a partner is overwhelmed by verbal attacks from the other. When we are attacked, heart rate and blood pressure increase and hormones are released, including adrenaline. On a physiological level, we experience verbal attacks as a threat to our survival, and the response is the same—regardless of whether it is a saber-toothed tiger you are facing, or a contemptuous spouse demanding to know

why you can never remember to put the toilet seat back down. When frequent flooding occurs, each partner's wish to avoid the experience results in them emotionally disengaging from the other.

Unhappy Peter and Olivia failed to halt their heated arguments in their tracks by saying, for instance, "Wait, I need to calm down"—or simply employing an amusing expression to prevent the conflict escalating. Happy couples all have this vital ability.

On their own, these signs don't necessarily predict divorce—but because they occurred one top of the other over a sustained period, in combination, they were very likely to end the relationship. Defensiveness, stonewalling, criticism, and contempt were the four horsemen of the apocalypse. The level of negative sentiment slowly started to overtake the positive, hence setting the "set point" of happiness in their relationship, during which time it declined to such a degree that it became too painful. They emotionally disengaged, stopped bothering to try to sort things out, and began leading parallel lives within the same house. This is the time at which affairs are most likely to occur, as now, the partners become lonely and seek attention, support, or care elsewhere. Therefore, an affair is usually a symptom of a dying marriage, rather than the cause.

The mistakes Olivia made in her rows included: raising her voice and using strong emotional tones (i.e., accusing; whining; mockery; sarcasm), when she should have stayed unemotional; using rhetorical questions like, "How could you say that...", rather than directly expressing what she liked or accepted (e.g., "I understand and agree with that, but..."); disregarding Peter by changing the subject back to her feelings (e.g., "I feel angry that you..."), rather than clarifying his own feelings (e.g., "Do you mean that..."); making generalized complaints, rather than being specific (e.g., "You are always watching TV.", when she could have said, "I would love to do something special together" or "Let's take a walk to town"); focusing on complaints, rather than asking for what she wanted—and thus making Peter find the solution (e.g., "I would really like..." or "Would you please...", rather than "I don't like it when..."); expecting Peter to respond like a woman instead of a man, this ignoring the basic male/female differences, rather than acknowledging their differences (e.g., "I understand it is difficult for you to talk about this...", or "I know you want to solve the problem..."); comparing Peter to another, or how he was in the past (e.g., "You used to be much more affectionate" or "Nobody else I dated did that"), rather than appreciating what he had done (e.g., "I love it when..."); starting a fight to express feelings that had been building up (e.g., "You never help" or "You always leave your dishes in the sink"); ranting without giving Peter a chance to express his point of view; expecting Peter to make her feel good, instead of taking responsibility for feeling good on her own (e.g., "Well, that does not make me feel any better" instead of, "I think I'll go run on the treadmill to relax"); expressing resistance with her feelings (e.g., "I feel like you..." or "You make me feel..."), rather than responding by reflecting on what he said (e.g., "So you are saying that..."); bringing up old issues to make a point (e.g., "This is just how I felt when you..."), hence muddying the disagreement by using her emotional memory as a bludgeon; being unwilling to forgive until he would change, apologize, or suffer long enough, rather than being understanding of Peter's needs and being generous with her love; waiting for Peter to make a change before opening her heart, hence making it more difficult for him to make a positive change, rather than opening her heart and then asking for what she wanted; and making demands, rather than expressing preferences (e.g., "You have to do it this way" or "You shouldn't do it like that", instead of, "I would like you to do it this way" or "This way works best for me; would you please do it like this?").

Meanwhile, the mistakes Peter made in his rows included: raising his voice and becoming cold, sharp, or distant in tone—when, since men's voices are deeper than women's, Peter's voice could have seemed threatening and overwhelming when he was angry—something Peter likely didn't realize; making condescending comments (e.g., "Don't worry about it" or "You're making a big deal out of nothing"), rather than acknowledging Olivia's feelings ("I see that you are anxious"); interrupting Olivia with arguments to invalidate her feelings or correct her observations (e.g., "You shouldn't feel that way" or "But that is not what happened"), rather than reflecting on what has been said (e.g., "I understand you think that..."); justifying his actions by perceiving her interpretations as wrong (e.g., "But that is not what I meant" or 'You have the wrong idea"), rather than rephrasing his point (e.g., "Let me put it another way"); criticizing her and putting her down by clarifying what he was saying (e.g., "That is not the point" or "Can't you see...?" or "Isn't it obvious that...?"), rather than restating the point (e.g., "What I mean is..."); expressing frustration with the pace of the argument (e.g., "Why do we have to go over this again and again?" or "I have already said that...", rather than, "I understand you need to absorb what I am saying" and suggesting time out); offering solutions instead of asking more questions (e.g., "You should do this..." or "All you have to do is...", rather than, "What do you think we should do next?"); correcting her priorities instead of supporting her values (e.g., "You don't need to..." or "It is not important to...", rather than, "I see why this matters to you"); minimizing her feelings instead of saying nothing and simply listening (e.g., "You shouldn't get so upset" or "This doesn't have to be such a big deal", rather than, "I see how upset you are"); dismissing her feelings while trying to end the conversation (e.g., "I got it, you want..." or, "I got it; can we now just forget it?" or "Can we now put it to rest?", rather than, "I think I understand; what you are saying is... Is that correct?"); "tit for tat"—when she complained, his coming back with even more complaints about her, with an attitude that she was the one with all the complaints (e.g., "That's true, but...", or, "That's nothing, remember when you..."), rather than validating what she had to say (e.g., "In this case, I understand why you are upset"); and giving in to what she wanted with no logical reasoning, when a reasonable and logical solution should be sought after (e.g., "Then we agree that we should... because...").

You don't have to wait until you have a fight to reflect on this list; instead, one way to avoid fights is to find a time when you are feeling good about yourself, and then read over the list and rate yourself. Find out which common mistakes you make, and imagine having a fight without them. Musicians and athletes use mental role-playing to train their subconscious minds so that they spontaneously act and react in a particular manner, and you can do the same within your relationship.

Women always escalate a fight by asking too many questions, or by talking too much about how they feel; they rarely stay on-topic. They don't realize that mixing feelings and problem solving simply doesn't work.

ABOUT THE MYTH OF "MARRIAGE BRINGS HAPPINESS"

From Olivia's Diary:

IT SEEMS THAT EVERY season of our marriage brings a new hope that things will surely get better soon: we will be happier when we can afford a better car; when we have children of our own; when our children are out of diapers; when Peter finally gets that promotion that will allow us to go to Europe for a long summer vacation; when our children leave for college; when we don't have to pay for college anymore; when Peter and I retire. I have been waiting for a brighter tomorrow almost every day, and frankly, I wonder if we will ever have the marriage I have always longed for.

SOME SPOUSES HOLD ONTO the hope that their unhappiness will eventually disappear and that life will somehow "get better". As Olivia recorded, such hopes for a more fulfilling relationship down the road, are usually dashed.

I have to wonder what part Olivia and Peter have played in undermining their own happiness during the years they have been married; if she/he finds yet another "available man or woman to love", both will more than likely discover that there is one common denominator in all their relationships: him and her. As long as that common denominator is unhappy with herself/himself, she/he will be unhappy with any relational equation.

Let us face the mistake Olivia and Peter made: nothing magical happens once they put those rings on their fingers. If they were unhappy before marriage, chances are they will go back to being unhappy shortly after the honeymoon. Marriage will never make them feel better about themselves or solve their problems in the long run.

Olivia wanted to have children as soon as possible, but Peter did not want them for another two years at least; he always wanted more sex than her; he flirted at parties, which she hated; he wanted to bring the children up as Catholics, and she wanted to raise them as atheists; he hated shopping, but it was a therapy session to her; he hated spending the weekend with her parents talking about disinteresting topics, but she couldn't miss a weekend without seeing them; she hated the arrogance of her mother-in-law, but he was grateful to his mother and didn't consider her behavior as such; she always pushed him to gain more cash to meet her uncontrollable shopping hunger, but he resented feeling like his wife's cash-cow.

Peter and Olivia spent years—as well as huge amount of energy—trying to change one another—but significant disagreements were about values and different perceptions of considering the world—things that are oftentimes difficult to change. Only successful couples know this fact, and, therefore, they decide to accept each other, "warts and all".

Olivia convinced herself that Peter could be the "Mission Impossible" man who would rescue her from all her flaws, personal struggles, and insecurities. However, at some point, you have to learn to take up the work of resolving your own issues, remedying your own insecurities, and becoming happy with yourself, by yourself, before you can truly be happy in marriage.

However, if you fail to acknowledge the need to work on your own issues, it is common that you will end up believing that your relational problems must be your husband's fault; perhaps you mistakenly assume that your life would be so much better if you just had a different man to love, rather than considering the possibility that you may play a part in your own dance of discontent.

The truth is, no marriage is exempt from disillusionment; even the brightest relationship has dark days clouding a couple's history together, raining on their "we have the perfect marriage" parade. On the exterior, a spouse may appear to have the ideal marriage, but the interior landscape of their heart often reveals deep disappointment, anger, bitterness, and regret.

Peter and Olivia struggled in their marriage because, like most spouses, they failed to understand the difference between intensity and intimacy: intensity is a feeling of extreme excitement or euphoria, and is a natural by-product of a spanking-new relationship. Intensity often masquerades as intimacy, and, when you are getting to know new things about a person, you often think you are experiencing intimacy— but such discovering is not intimate, but simply new. It may be exciting, and it may feel intense—but it's often superficial and temporary. At best, it's incomplete. For the most part, you only got to know the sides of these strangers that they wanted you to see. Such relationships often feel intimate, but the intimacy they were feeling was a false intimacy.

Genuine intimacy can only be found at home, where Olivia and Peter both saw not just the good, but also the bad and the ugly in one another. Intimacy can be understood by breaking the word down into syllables: in-to-me-see. It is the ability to see into the heart, mind, and spirit of another person—which is impossible until after you have gotten to know an individual over a long period of time. It comes only after the intensity has worn off and you get to know things that most people cannot possibly know unless they live with that person. Most partners know exactly what it would take to make their significant other happy—they are just too stubborn, egotistical, or lazy to do it.

Most partners who have been together for any reasonable amount of time want their significant other to know exactly what it would take to keep them happy, and so they either drop subtle hints or they outright say it—and when they do not, these things still come across through their actions and reactions. Hence, for the most part, they should know very well what keeps their partner fulfilled. If, however, after all this time they still do not know, they simply have not been paying any attention to each other at all.

The only thing more fragile than a human's heart is a human's ego, and some men and women have convinced themselves so well that a good partner does not exist that they will subconsciously sabotage a relationship with a genuinely good partner, just to prove themselves right. Indeed, if such negative expectations about the partner are strong enough, these feelings will begin to manifest themselves in their actions—and, eventually, this will cause the partner to act in a manner that will ultimately increase the chances of those negative expectations being fulfilled.

In a relationship, the partners should be on the same page; if one or both of them cannot see what the other sees, chances are they are not on the same page—or even in the same book.

What most couples fail to understand is that marriage is a science that should be learned; a marriage based on a young man's experience without knowledge, or a woman's ignorance without experience, is foredoomed to inevitable failure. If love survives despite such an initial handicap, it proves its greatness—although few marriages do. Divorces, separations, ruined lives, cynical husbands, hysterical wives, infidelities, and all manners of family tragedies attest to the failure of the traditional approach to marriage.

If they were to dare to give a frank answer, men and women would tell you that love after marriage disappears, and that happiness in marriage is a gamble, boredom being certain. Marriages built upon the shifting sands of fear, shame, and ignorance can never lead to happiness— yet is undergone with a frank recognition of the central importance of sex in life, alike in its physiological, psychological, and spiritual aspects.

It is possible to increase our number of happy marriages by leaps and bounds through a well-organized system of "marriage education", which would compare favorably with engineering, medical, legal, etc. forms of education. Imagine letting a surgeon open your abdomen whose only qualification for the job was casual conversation with a few other equally unfit surgeons, combined with having read some best-seller novels on the subject of abdominal operations. You would never knowingly let this happen—and yet a young woman or man will risk their lives, and that of their unborn children, on such mountainous ignorance.

The modern medical man is exquisitely trained for his task: he has learned anatomy, psychology, therapeutics, the pathology of all known diseases, diagnoses, and a dozen of other auxiliary branches of medical education. Unless the case is unreasonably obscure, he makes his diagnosis and writes a prescription; every act, every word, every bit of reasoning and psychology that went into his decision, has occurred as a result of careful education.

To a large extent, young couples who marry are the prototype of the medical man: as a wife or husband, they are going to be called upon daily—sometimes hourly—with a "case" that is, in many aspects, as clinical as that of a doctor's patient. The running of the house, with its manifold duties and fairly fixed routine, is comparable to the doctor's running of his office: they have their economics, and he has his. They have their problem of dietetics, as he does; his/her patient—the husband or wife—presents a continuing psychological problem, as do the doctor's patients; and emotional crises will confront them when his/her patient is tired, ill, worried, or discouraged—almost exactly like the crises that confront the doctor when his patients have their similar ups and downs.

To focus this analogy even more, the wife is back from her honeymoon. The little cottage is running well, and the husband's job is paying him well; friends come and go with pleasing regularity, and all is serene. The "patient", so to speak, is well, and there is no professional situation for the couple to face.

Three months later, the wife wakes up to the following profound change in her little world: she is pregnant. She is suffering from the acute nausea of pregnancy, and is irritable and finds it difficult to think as clearly and dispassionately about life as she did three months before. The husband's job requires him to make an unexpected business trip now and then, and he finds his salary is not enough to cover hospital and doctor bills unless he saves carefully, or searches for another job. He becomes anxious, nervous, and worried the majority of the time; he is not as amiable as he used to be, and yet is more affectionate than ever at others.

What the couple does about this depends on two things: first, the kind of female/male she/he is; and second, how logically she/he is able to analyze the whole situation. The former largely depends on the personality of each spouse, and it goes without saying that the strong-minded, sensible, normal spouse will go through this kind of trouble better than the weak-willed gimlet-headed flapper. Between the two types, there is an infinite number of variations and degrees.

What is our interest here is how the two variations of the same spouse will behave—the first type being totally uneducated in marriage, and the second being as well-grounded in being a wife/husband as a trained doctor is in practicing medicine.

Ladies: if you are not happy in your marriage, do not make the mistake of placing all the responsibility on men; instead, turn your marriage relationship around also—it is not completely up to him. Problems are usually the result of both spouses' actions and attitudes. Remember, it takes two to tango!

Of course, when there does seem to be a problem, the wife is usually the first to suggest divorce or marriage counseling—but what are her expectations when she drags her husband through the door of the therapist's office? Her goal is usually for him to change so she can be happy.

An unhappy husband and wife receive from society, their parents, and their friends the traditional agenda: that men are the bad guys, and that women are oppressed. Hence, their cure is either to feminize the husband, or to suggest divorce. Today's modern society insists that it is completely the male's responsibility to change, and that positive improvements to a relationship can only occur if the husband is willing to alter his very nature—in other words, to tune in to his "feminine" side and learn how to think, respond, and "emotionally perceive" the same way as his wife does.

It is true that many women are unhappy—but this is the case for many men, too. These are desperate times, and perhaps this desperation is an indication that it is time for women to take desperate measures and ask themselves, Am I contributing to the demise of the masculine image by how I treat my husband? As much as you may want to throw stones at your partner, you need to stop and ask yourself, What part do I play in my marriage's dance of discontentment?

Ladies: even if you firmly believe that 95% of the issues in your marriage are your husband's fault, are you willing to focus on the 5% that you do have control over?

I know that no man can ever know all about women; however, from the story of Olivia and other wives, it is pretty clear that women don't know very much about themselves. Women are queer characters: they will love you to death one minute, and want to scratch your eyes out the next.

ABOUT THE MYTH OF "SEX IS A MALE CRAVING"

From Olivia's Diary:

MY FANTASIES ARE PRETTY much always better than the actual event.

Getting older, I've had to learn this lesson the hard way: sometimes, fantasies are better off staying fantasies. As soon as I try to play something out in real life, my expectations of them are so high due to my counting on the end result to match the fantasy exactly.

Sexual fantasies are usually the biggest disappointments to play out. Why is that? I think it's because they are so incredibly erotic in my imagination: there are no consequences, no guilt, no insecurities. I have fantasized about having sex with several other men than Peter.

But why the need for fantasies? Isn't Peter enough? Can't I look at him and picture having sex with only him for the rest of my life? Being honest, I don't think so; I cannot imagine spending years and years having sex routinely every time. By now, I know by heart how Peter will initiate the whole thing, what moves he will make, what position we will be in, how he will kiss me, and where, when, and how he will finish this routine.

I like to imagine having more pleasurably, intensive, affectionate, frequent sex than what I currently get from Peter. Something odd; new; different. Sexual boredom is a slow killer; it kills all potential sex-related pleasures—even the whole marriage.

In my opinion, fantasies help increase arousal and desire for more sex; my favorite foreplay isn't having my boobs squeezed, or even oral sex, but dirty talk. That's how I can get in the mood; then, he is welcome to squeeze my breast or go down on me. I think a lot of that has to do with women today being so stressed, at home, at work, in marriage, in family relations... We need mental stimulation to divert us before we are able to fully engage in sex.

What I'm sure of is that one of the fascinating aspects of fantasies is that they are so secretive; not many women dare uncover their fantasies.

Ask someone what he or she fantasizes about, and the look on their face will go from embarrassment, to simply wanting to change the subject. We don't even feel comfortable talking about our fantasies with our best friends. Why is that?

I think I am fearful that my friends—or even Peter—will think I am too perverse; I mean, I know I come up with some pretty crazy and twisted scenarios, so how do I tell my friend that I dream about my boss molesting me in the meeting room at work? I don't: I keep that in my secret dirty world. It's even hard for me to tell Peter about some of the twisted scenarios that I conjure up in my head.

Sleeping with strangers isn't really one of my favorite fantasies because, let's face it, it's more exciting to imagine somebody I know; it's naughtier. Even in romance novels, they don't say, "A stranger walked in and made mad passionate love to me"; it's usually something much more perverse, like the woman's cousin she had been longing for her entire childhood.

It's in rape fantasies that a stranger could actually be useful. This is one fantasy, of course, I never want to have played out—but for some reason, being forced to have sex is at the top of my list.

In terms of being an exhibitionist... Well, who hasn't fantasized about being a model or a stripper at some point during adolescence—or even adulthood? It's funny how incredibly judgmental we are of these professions, yet in my fantasies, I am the star stripper and the naughtiest model.

What I find fascinating is the fact that some women have fantasies while having intercourse, whereas whilst men are in the act, they are simply concentrating on what's in front of them. When it comes to sex, I was shocked to read how many men said, "I'm mainly just focusing on my wife the majority of the time." I think that has to do with men having to do most of the work during intercourse; they have to concentrate, while us women get to close our eyes and imagine having sex with their best friends—not because we want them necessarily, but because we need that trust; that intimacy.

Something Peter and I used to have, before we were man and wife.

Is fantasizing actually a betrayal to Peter? Does it hurt our relationship? Is it a sin? I'm not sure of these answers; unfortunately, my soul is constantly at war with my mind: my soul wants to live in spirituality, but my mind refuses, instead responding with the cruelty of life.

The Adverse Selection Concept: Some women discard the charming, romance-driven prince; the whole thing turns into something deathly boring very quickly. Instead, they go for the wolf. A wolf never misses his target, has an infinite persistence to catch his prey, and can see her better, hear her better, chase her better, kill prospect competitors to win her, and, finally, devour her inside out, like no one could ever do better.

THE SEXES ARE DIFFERENT because their brains are different: the brain—the chief administrative and emotional organ of life—is constructed very differently in men and in women. Their brains process information in a different way, which results in different perceptions, priorities, and behavior.

By the time we emerge from the womb, the majority of the differences between males and females are already formed.

Indeed, just one thing stands in the way of this brave new world of gender equality: science. Whilst we were being taught to believe that there were no differences between men and women that mattered, advances in neuroscience and empirical behavior studies tell us the opposite. The sexes are not just different in a physical way, but worlds apart in terms of priorities, ways of communication, and sexual needs. The idea of gender equality is, at the end of the day, a biological and scientific lie.

Both biology and socialization are at the root of gender clashes in sexual expectations and desires. It is believed that men, generally speaking, seem to want sex more often than women. They are also more likely to use erotica to become aroused, whilst women are more concerned about the emotional relationship they have with their partners: they want verbal communication, gentle touching, and cuddling.

Peter and Olivia came to the bedroom with widely divergent needs and desires—and, because they didn't understand and respect these differences, they faced difficulty in finding common ground between them, on which they could have built a sexually satisfying relationship.

Their problem was compounded by the media's bombardment of false ideas about human sexuality, which reflect and influence cultural values. The majority of the media represent the male role in the sex act as one of technical expertise, wholly neglecting the emotional aspects so vitally important to many women.

Men and women who buy into the movie star mythology of ever-ready sex are burdened with beliefs that are counterproductive to a satisfying sexual relationship: they may believe that the size of a penis is extremely important, that all touching should lead to sex, that the verbal expression of emotions is unmanly, that the goal of sex is orgasm, that the only real intercourse is penetrative sex, that he should take the lead in asking for sex, that women are not interested in sex, that the sex appeal of a woman revolves round her body and curves only, that women should attract the attention of men by revealing clothes, and that the G-spot is the only crucial place for a satisfying sex relation for the woman.

Of course, these aspects would be included in a list of requirements for a satisfying sexual relationship—but the weight of each element on this list may differ between women and men. For both, however, the elements are still important.

Most notably amongst these elements—being one that should be given equal weight for each partner—is the sense of emotional intimacy between partners that comes from the verbal communication of feelings, sharing joys and fears, and the trust that comes from being safely vulnerable with one another. Secondarily, the female (more so than the male) looks for an appreciation of her as the focus of her partner's life, this being the most important ingredient around which his plans revolve. Unfortunately, for the majority of men, this element is not at the forefront of their priorities; for men, there may be different things that occupy him (e.g., his career path; securing his financial future; how to increase bank savings for his retirement; how to secure the next installment for his son's coming academic year). These numerous thoughts not only disturb the man's emotional stability with his partner, but also drain his emotional-giving ability due to the constant pressure he remains under.

Women desire to be touched and caressed in a way that communicates her partner's love to her, but does not necessarily always lead to sexual intercourse; clearly, women are more focused on the emotional relationship, whilst the man is on the physical. Given the fact that men are taught that the expression of emotions is "sissy" and women may crave that very thing for arousal, it is clear that expectations can clash in the bedroom.

Thus, women and men may come to the bedroom with unrealistically high hopes, a host of destructive myths about sexuality, and a great deal of anxiety concerning their ability to please their partner.

In many societies throughout history, women were not expected to enjoy sex; instead, they are expected to participate in it only for reproductive reasons—or simply because it was their marital duty. Men, thus, believed they were entitled to sexual relations with a marital partner upon demand, without consideration of her wishes. This, of course, changed dramatically with the sexual revolution of the 60s and 70s, during which time these basic assumptions were challenged by the publicizing of the capacity for sexual pleasure in women, thus freeing them to explore their sexuality—either within or outside of a committed relationship. The sexual revolution was an attempt to alter these stereotypes by removing the moral judgment placed on sex, as well as by abolishing the double standards in sexual relations. It was, however, only partially and momentarily successful in reaching such a goal; as most movements go, it probably went too far, and society realized free sex was not the answer, either. One result of this revolution was the greater demand placed on men to perform sexually, as well as to be concerned with his partner reaching an orgasm as a matter of mutual pleasure, rather than a power play between the sexually aggressive male and the gatekeeper female.

Women have since been taught that their physical attractiveness is their most important commodity—and, thus, they have been using this as their first-choice ultimate power to facilitate social interactions and obtain what they want in indirect ways. Hence, a woman can often be seen sending out subtle messages that a man could interpret as a sexual invitation—even when the woman has no intention of pursuing a sexual encounter. To complicate matters further, even when a woman is interested in sexual relations, she has been taught that the direct sexual approach is not suitable for a female to undertake—and so instead, women are likely to make use of the same subtle tactics they use in everyday social interactions. Thus, men are oftentimes left confused over such indirect messages, in the worst-case scenario feeling "set up" by a "tease". On the other hand, men are taught to be the initiators of sex in a direct manner—and so they take the risk of being rejected by females.

When these male and female beliefs are compounded by the media-fed belief that women say "no" when they really mean "yes", many men find themselves being accused of rape or sexual harassment—something that can, indeed, be present even in a marital relationship. Today, the accusation of rape in a marital relationship stands up in court as a result of men and women's different views concerning their roles in the sexual relationship.

The sex center is located in the hypothalamus—the part of the brain that also controls emotions, heart rate, and blood pressure. It is the size of a cherry, weighs around 4.5 grams, and is larger in men than in women. This is the area in which hormones—particularly testosterone—stimulate the desire for sex. Men have up to twenty times as much testosterone as women—so combine this with their larger hypothalamus, and we can see why their desire for sex is so powerful.

A woman's hypothalamus is much smaller than a man's, and she only has small amounts of testosterone to activate it; therefore, generally speaking, women have relatively lower sex drives than men, and also tend to be less aggressive.

The male sex drive is like a microwave: it ignites instantly, operates at full capacity within seconds, and can be turned off just as quickly when the meal is cooked. Women's sex drive, on the other hand, is more reminiscent of an electric oven: it heats slowly to a very high temperature, and takes a lot longer to cool down.

The man's testosterone level decreases slowly as he gets older, and his sex drive decreases accordingly; meanwhile, the average woman's sex drive gradually increases so her sexual peak occurs between the age of 36-38—which explains the "toy boy" syndrome of the older woman/younger man: younger men have the physical performance level an older woman craves, and so they are often more sexually compatible with a woman in her late thirties to early forties while they are nineteen, more than any other age. Meanwhile, the sex drive of a man in his forties is compatible with that of a woman's in her early twenties, partially explaining the older man/younger woman phenomenon.

When we say a man's sex drive peaks at the age of nineteen and decreases as he gets older, we are referring to his physical performance level; his interest in sex usually remains high for the majority of his life, meaning that he can be just as interested at seventy as he was at thirty—although his performance level won't match this interest.

A woman can be very interested in sex during her late teens, since it will most probably be related to love at this point; however, she feels less desire for sex than love; this desire tends to heighten during her thirties instead.

We should bear in mind that here, we are talking about the overall sex drive of all men as one group, as well as that of all women as another. Individual sex drives will vary from one person to another, and so here we are discussing a majority. You may indeed find an individual woman that has a high sex drive and a man with a low sex drive, but these are minority cases; they do not reflect the majority. Therefore, the continual high dose of testosterone keeps a man's sex drive high and always ready.

Until her late thirties, a woman will typically complain that a man constantly places pressure on her for sex, leading to resentment on both sides; she would accuse him of using and abusing her, and it is not until her late thirties that a woman's sex drive will begin to match that of the man—and, often, surpass it. Therefore, a man in his early forties will often be caught by surprise by this role reversal, his sex drive now perhaps being lower than a woman's of the same age, her level of assertion also having grown. Therefore, a man at this age may complain about having to "perform on-demand".

The majority of couples do not address these differences, instead expecting the other to just automatically understand their needs. However, this is not how nature intended this exchange to go.

Therefore, testosterone is the main hormone that creates the feeling we call "sex drive". For women, psychological factors (e.g., trust; commitment; closeness; overall wellbeing) all combine to create a list of conditions, under which a stream of hormones are to be released. Men can release this stream at any time, in any place. Hence, you may now be able to understand why when an attractive woman approaches a man and asks him to go to bed with her, most would say yes—whereas more women would say no when approached by an attractive man.

This can be explained as follows: men are stimulated through their eyes; women through their ears. Men's brains are wired to look at female shapes, and this is why erotic images have such a strong impact on them; meanwhile, women have a greater range of sensory information receptors, and so they prefer hearing sweet words and compliments that touch their feelings—"sweet nothings".

When a woman with a nice body walks by, a man—lacking, as he does, good peripheral vision—turns his head to look and goes into a trance-like state: His blinking ceases—a reaction described by women as "drooling". If a couple are walking down the street and an attractive woman comes swaying towards them on the other side of the street, the woman's short-range peripheral vision allows her to spot the woman before the man does. From here, she will make quick comparisons between herself and the potential competitor—usually leaning towards more negative ones when it comes to herself. When the man eventually spots her, he receives a negative reaction from his woman for "ogling".

A woman will usually have two negative thoughts in this situation: she mistakenly thinks the man may prefer to be with a woman like the one he just saw; and, secondly, that she is not as physically attractive as the other woman is. Men are attracted visually to curves, lengths, and shapes. Any woman with the right shape and proportions will catch his attention—but this does not mean that the man immediately wants to be with her. After all, he does not even know the other woman, and could not realistically be thinking about a long-term relationship with her. We are not making excuses for the rude, blatant ogling that some men do; we are simply explaining that ogling does not mean that the man does not love his partner—it is just his biology at work. Indeed, research has shown that in public places, women tend to ogle more than men do—although, being equipped with better peripheral vision, women rarely get caught.

On a similar note, some women think that not experiencing an orgasm during sex means that the sex was bad—either from her side, or from her partner's side. However, this is fiction; rather, it all depends on you. Some women expect to experience an orgasm every time they have sex, whilst others are content with the intimacy and pleasure of the overall experience. It is healthier to consider an orgasm as the icing on the cake. Research shows that 25% of women have never had an orgasm. Indeed, whilst some women have higher sex drives and levels of desire than their male partners, the pressure to emulate stereotypes (men as easily aroused sex fanatics and women are the demure damsel) forces women to suppress their desires.

Hence, a man needs to understand that showing his feelings and emotions before having sex is what turns women on, and is what they primarily find to be seductive.

So, why do things so quickly come to a halt?

At the beginning of a new relationship, sex is always great, and there is an abundance of love being expressed: she gives him plenty of sex, and he gives her plenty of love; one thing feeds the other. After a certain period of time, however, the man becomes preoccupied with chasing for a bigger family and more mouths to feed and take care of. Meanwhile, the woman becomes preoccupied with her nest-caring and defending responsibilities—which is why sex and love seem to fade away simultaneously and gradually from the scene.

Men and women are equally responsible for whether they have a good or bad sex life, but each often blames the other when things do not go well. Indeed, whilst men need to understand that a woman requires attention, praise, pampering, and lots of time before she heats her electric oven, women also have to remember that these are the feelings that men are more likely to express after a session of great sex. Further, a man should remember how he felt after sex and relive such feelings with a woman when he wants sex next time—and a woman should be prepared to help him in this. The key here is always sex, for when sex is great, the whole relationship dramatically improves.

So, how do you satisfy a woman every time? Simply: caress; hug; pamper; compliment; phone; protect; acknowledge; indulge; accessorize; entertain; embrace; excite; stimulate; support; tease; idolize; forgive mistakes; forget rudeness; use humor; soothe; ignore faults; defend; trust; and worship.

And what about satisfying a man every time? Simply: arrive naked to bed!

For a man, sex represents a means to empty; for women, sex represents a means to fill.

For a man to feel fulfilled during sex, he needs to feel he can release his tension; whilst for a woman, she needs to feel the build-up of tension over a longer period, including lots of attention and talk.

The release of this built-up tension is the orgasm: after sex, a man weighs less, since he has lost a part of his body and needs to rest to recover. This is why men often fall asleep after sex—something women become angry about, feeling he is selfish or does not care about her needs. Here, women often form the assumption that what he aimed for was just sex, and that he does not care for her feelings.

Men use sex to express physically what they cannot express emotionally; thus, if a man has a problem to resolve, he is likely to use sex to relieve the intensity of his emotions. However, women do not understand this need, and become resentful at being "used" for sex only. However, this misses the point: that the man had a problem that he could not deal with.

After sex, a woman is high on hormones and is ready to take on the world: she wants to touch, cuddle, and talk more. However, a man—if he has not already fallen asleep-sometimes withdraws, getting up and "doing something" (e.g., making coffee; smoking). After sex, each gender goes back to their regular state of behavior: a woman goes back to bonding, talking, and loving, whilst a man goes back to the need to feel in control of himself.

Understanding these subtle differences can ensure men are more caring lovers, and women more considerate.

For a man to talk during sex, he needs to switch to his left-brain—and this is why a man tends not to. A woman, however, can multitask, and therefore can comfortably speak and engage in sex.

As mentioned above, men can only do one thing at a time—and so when a man has an erection, he finds it difficult to speak or hear. This is why men rarely talk much during sex, meaning a woman will often need to listen to his breathing to gain an idea of his feelings, rather than his romantic words or compliments about the beauty of her body or breasts. A man may experience a loss of direction—and sometimes even his erection—when a woman talks to him during sex.

During sex, a man uses his right brain, brain scans showing that he is so intent on what he is doing that he becomes virtually deaf. For a woman, however, talk is a crucial part of foreplay; words are all-important to her. Hence, when a man stops talking during sex, a woman may think he is not interested in her, that her body is no more attractive to him, and/or sex with her is no more pleasurable to him.

When a woman talks during sex, a man feels obliged to respond, and the moment can be lost; therefore, a woman needs to stop talking during sex and instead use vocal sounds to keep a man interested; these would be enough to give a man the positive feedback he needs in order to achieve his fulfilment. On the other hand, a man needs to practice lots of love-talk during foreplay in order to similarly fulfil the woman's needs.

A woman's brain is not pre-wired to respond to the chemicals of sex drive as dramatically as a man's brain is. During sex, a woman is acutely aware of outside sounds and environmental changes, but a man will be totally focused and undistracted. Further, with a woman (generally speaking), attempting to entice her to make love in an open area, in an unlocked room's door, or in a room with an open window, could be a challenge—and sometimes will be faced with total refusal.

Does she need an orgasm in order to feel fulfilled? Indeed, a man's criterion for fulfilment is orgasm—and yet when it comes to the woman in the sexual relationship, she is typically more focused on the emotions, feelings of closeness and warmth, and build-up of tension for great sex, rather than just the orgasm. She usually considers the orgasm as something extra—not the objective, but a nice thing to have, nonetheless.

Women can fake orgasms, whilst men do not: no man wants to pull a face like that on purpose! A man's measurement of his prowess as a lover is directly related to the woman's level of satisfaction, and so he constantly monitors her reactions to see how well she is doing. Most men do not have the ability to sense a woman's intimate feelings and emotions during sex—another reason why her orgasm is so important to him. It proves to him that he must have done a good job and achieved the required result.

The majority of men never understand that the compulsory orgasm is a man's criterion for success—not necessarily a woman's. However, when a man and woman understand the history and evolution of their desires from a biological standpoint, it is much easier for them to understand and accept one another's needs without anger, resentment, or guilt; having an open discussion about these needs can, instead, help to enhance a more loving relationship.

If aliens arrived to Earth and surveyed our selection of media channels—either online or offline—, they would quickly conclude that human females are a highly sexual group, all of which experiencing multiple orgasms every time they engage in sexual intercourse. Further, if they read female-targeted articles and watched the kind of pornography we produce, they would be convinced that women have an insatiable sexual appetite, and will sleep with almost any man under nearly any circumstances. Unfortunately, the feminist movement has freed modern women's attitudes to their sexuality, leading to many falling into the trap of using such media channels to express their sexuality—explicitly and implicitly—, either through sexual photos, postures, sexual selfies, or body gestures. Because of what women have been exposing about themselves with the help of media, men have been coaxed into believing that women now have high sex drives—and this ultimately makes men feel angry or frustrated when women don't respond positively to his sexual pursuits often.

The sex drive of women has probably remained the same for thousands of years; all that has changed is that women and the media now openly discuss sexuality. This does not mean, however, that women do not have sexual desires and sex drives; it just means that these desires and drives are the same as they have always been. The difference is that in the old days, female sexuality was not so openly exposed to all media channels and was not so explicitly discussed.

PART IV: SIN HAPPENS TO OTHERS

Our desires are fruitful sources of every kind of error and misjudgment.

OLIVIA

GLENDA LOOKED AT ME with disgust when I told her that Mia and her daughter, Suzy, were coming over, and that I wanted her to look after her niece.

Mia arrived right on time, carrying a bottle of wine and a box of chocolates. I looked at her in amazement. "I'm trying to lose weight; I'll never manage to do that on Faustino and Ferrero Rocher."

"You look fine," Mia said impatiently.

"Not as fine as you, Mia."

Mia had always been the pettier one, with her smooth skin, high cheekbones, and sparkling blue eyes. Her auburn hair gleamed with health and vitality. She was wearing a white cotton shirt and stonewashed jeans pulled tight at the waist—a waist that looked a lot slimmer than the last time I'd seen her.

Mia poured her wine into her glass and took a swig. "Mum used to ask me if I'd been drinking. She sniffed my breath every evening when I went out."

My mouth tilted in a half-smile. "I remember."

"You only had to put up with it when you were in your teens; I'm a grown woman—not, I'll admit, always the world's most sensible woman, but I'm still old enough not to have my mother sniffing my breath!"

"She'll never change." I took a sip of my own wine.

"I know. Controlling old bitch!"

"Mia!" I look at her in horror. "You can't say that about Mum."

"Why?" She tucked a stray hair behind her ears. "Why can't I call her controlling? Or manipulative? Or patronizing? Take your pick."

I bit my lip. I agreed that Mum had all those qualities—but she was also our mother, and it seemed disloyal to say those words out loud. One could just think about them, but never to reveal them. "It's just the way she is."

"She should never have had kids," Mia pressed on, popping a cereal snacks into her mouth. "At least, not daughters. Daughters that might have become nuns, maybe. But not normal daughters."

I giggled. "Maybe if we'd spent more time reading housekeeping magazines and less time on romance novels, it might have been different."

"She's just so old-fashioned." Mia sighed. "She couldn't cope with us being out late and having multiple boyfriends."

"Repressed," I said in a tone that left much doubt as to whether I actually meant it.

"Do you think so?"

"Could be." I shrugged. "I don't know; she wants perfection all the time. She likes things that I hate."

Mia nodded. "I know; it must have been her upbringing. She'd have done better with sons. It's us that have been the problem."

"But maybe not always," I pointed out. "You know, she was so proud of you when you got married; I was quite jealous."

"Really?" Mia drained her glass.

I nodded. "Absolutely. And even though my divorce is somewhat traumatic for her, she goes on and on at me about how at least you had a decent marriage."

For a moment, I wondered whether or not Glenda had these types of conversation with her friend, Shauna—complaining that I didn't love her enough, that I was always out at work, that I didn't spend enough money on her, that I was always nagging at her to tidy her room and hang up her clothes, that I was a boring mum—as my mother was. Maybe I'm looking at Mum the wrong way, I thought. Maybe I'm exactly like her.

I hoped not: I wanted to believe my children loved me and didn't see me as simply a figure of authority. But then again, I had no authority over my kids.

"Anyway, I didn't come here to talk about Mum," Mia said, breaking into my thoughts. "I wanted to ask you about something."

"Fire ahead. Although I've never been good for giving you advice, Mia."

Mia sat back in her chair. "I've met someone."

"A man?"

"Well, of course a man," Mia grinned.

"You're joking!"

"Why should I be joking?" Mia looked offended.

"I didn't mean it like that. It's just that I didn't realize you were looking to meet someone."

"I'm not. It's one of those really stupid things; I'd taken Suzy to the local park, we were running around having fun, I tripped—and this bloke helped me up."

"Mia!"

She grinned. "He's a nice guy, Liv; he really is. He works in a bank—always good news!—and he's forty-six."

With these words, I was invaded by a sudden spurt of jealousy toward Mia; she was already married and her husband adored her—and she'd found another nice man, while I was still struggling alone like an old cow.

"We clicked straightway," Mia was saying. "He asked if he could give me a hand, and I said another ankle would be better. He then helped me to one of the benches."

"I won't believe that. You're definitely not making this up?"

I wanted to remind Mia she was already married, and that Paul loved her madly. Why should she be dragged to this, anyway? I refrained, however, and held my tongue, curious to know the full story.

"He's not bad at all: dark hair, a little bit of grey—not much. He's tall; a tiny bit overweight, but just enough that I feel okay with having an extra pound or two myself."

"Mia, you can't weigh more than seven stone."

Mia smiled. "I've lost a few pounds, to tell you the truth."

"Bitch. That's the bloody best thing about falling for someone." I sighed. "Weight just slides off."

"I didn't say I'd fallen for him."

I eyed her thoughtfully. "It sounds like it. Does he have kids?"

"He has two: a boy and a girl."

"And the mother of his children?"

"They're in the process of a divorce."

I couldn't swallow my words no longer. "What if they decide they want to get back together?"

"And what if they don't?" Mia challenged, deadpan.

"Why are they getting a divorce?"

"That's what I want to know, Olivia; why does a woman decide to walk out on her husband? I mean, why did you decide to divorce Peter? What was the trigger?"

I sat back in my seat and stared into space.

"Well?" pressed Mia after a minute's silence. "What is it, Olivia? I've never asked you before... I didn't want to influence you or get involved. Maybe that was wrong, but—"

"I didn't want anyone to be involved," I interjected. "You know, I'd thought about it for ages and ages before I realized the way it would end up."

"And why?"

"Because we lost our feelings towards each other," I answered truthfully. "He doesn't love me anymore. Everything died with time—not like when we met the first time: in the beginning, I showed my best and he showed his best—and as time went by, all our flaws rose to the surface."

"But you were married to him for a long time."

"It didn't take long to realize everything was dying; it took a lot longer to realize it wasn't one I could live with."

"Okay." Mia lit a cigarette. I made a face at her. "I only smoke when I'm under pressure," she huffed, "and I feel a bit pressurized right now. So, Liv, you decided you didn't love Peter anymore and you wanted a divorce. Do you ever feel you shouldn't have gone through with it? Do you ever regret divorcing him?"

I wriggled uncomfortably on my seat. These were questions I didn't really want to answer—mainly because I sometimes wasn't sure of the answers myself.

"There were times I thought I should say to him that I'd changed my mind; that I didn't want the divorce," I admit. "But that was copping out, Mia; it wouldn't have changed anything, and I would have ended up being even more miserable. This thing is, Peter and I changed—and we didn't love each other enough to accommodate such changes. I still care about him, but I don't love him. It's funny, but love can disappear in a split second: one minute it's there, and then suddenly it's gone."

Mia exhaled slowly. "Do you think it's a good idea? Me and Ross?"

"How the hell would I know? I'm the first wife, Mia—not the new and improved model!"

"Neither am I," Mia shrugged. "I'm the same age as his ex-wife. It's not quite the same as Peter and Jennifer—presuming you're assigning the role of the new and improved model to her?"

I smiled ruefully. "Of course she's new and improved. That's why he married her."

"I thought you were dealing with it okay."

"What, the divorce? Or his re-marriage?"

"Both."

I paused. "Getting a divorce isn't even the worst part; you think it will be, but it isn't, and there is a great sense of freedom afterwards: I don't have to plan my life around someone who isn't at all dependable anymore. But seeing him married again—that's more difficult. I can't conceal my envy of him—especially to someone with legs like Jennifer."

"I don't know why Ross's wife left him," Mia mused. "I haven't asked him yet, and I have a horrible feeling he'll say something like, 'Because she didn't understand me.'"

"Aren't you jumping the gun a bit?" I pointed out. "After all, you've only just met the guy."

"I know, but I have a feeling that he's the one, Liv. I can't stop thinking about him. I want to be with him all the time. Every moment I'm not with him and I'm with Paul seems such a waste."

"Wow," I murmured. "You've completely fallen for him, haven't you?"

Mia nodded. "But you're right; maybe I should wait and discover what his fatal flaw is before getting in too deep."

"The problem is that most of us don't find the fatal flaw until it's far too late."

Mia stared blankly into the distance for a moment before bringing her gaze back to mine. "I know you're right, but I never thought I'd feel like this about anyone, Liv. It's wonderful and scary, all at the same time."

I nodded; I remembered what it was like, too. I just wondered if I would ever feel that way again. "But what about Paul? I thought you loved him as much as he loves you! And what about Suzy?"

"It's a long story, Liv," Mia sighed. "A miserable long story if you get to know it." She bit her lip. "I really need to leave now; I have a doctor appointment. We'll catch up later, dear. See you soon."

I remained in my seat, motionless. I was bewildered: what had looked so perfect from the outside could not have been more chaotic from the inside. The person that appeared to be of virtue had turned out to be evil!

But why was she going to the doctor? My shock had taken such hold of my thinking that I had forgotten to ask what was wrong with her.

MIA

I AM THREE YEARS older than Olivia, boasting an almost overdeveloped figure and the fresh color of perfect health glimmering through the creamy texture of my skin. I have always been the vivacious type—the one that must always be at the center of a group of men at a social gathering. I have personal charm, full red lips, white regular teeth, luxurious and naturally golden hair, slender, eager fingers, and trim ankles. To set forth the delights of my femininity, I always dress in clinging outfits—ones that leave little to a man's imagination.

Throughout my childhood, I always heard—as everyone does—the question of what you would change about your life if you knew you only had a couple of years left to live being flung around. It sounded to me like a question we hear in a sermon at church, or were asked to contemplate in a personal growth seminar during a self-discovery exercise—until one day, this question became a reality to me.

I used to joke that my life was uneventful. That was until the day I was diagnosed with liver cancer. I went to the doctor for a checkup—I'd been feeling tired—, and had never imagined I would hear him announce the words that confirmed I had cancer, and that I probably only had two more years—at the most—to live. Sat there in his office, all I could think was, But I'm only forty-five years old; I'm supposed to live until I'm at least seventy. I'm too young to die.

The doctor told me I would be able to remain active for some time before my liver began to fail, and then I would deteriorate pretty fast. Listening to all this, I felt like I was having a horrible dream, except that I wasn't: it was very real.

As Paul and I got up to leave, my doctor came over to give me a hug and tell me how sorry he was. He had tears in his eyes.

"Is there anything at all I can do?" I asked him, tears filling my own eyes.

"Just make sure you live every moment the way you want to. Don't lose a moment in sadness," had been his answer.

Sleepless nights became my new companion, and, as I lay in the dark, I began thinking about my life—or what I had left of it. The doctor's words echoed in my head, and I began to ask myself, How am I supposed to live happily every moment when the remaining moments of my life will be loaded with sadness and regret? I began to lose count of how many days I awoke—broken, furious, and aching that I could barely breathe as a result of my all-consuming fear of death—as if someone was throttling me.

Following one of my routine rows with Paul, the answer to my question arose from deep down in my soul— one that I didn't expect, but knew was as honest an answer as I'd ever given to anything: I wanted to leave my husband and try to find true love; I had no more time to waste.

The idea wasn't new; in fact, I'd been thinking about divorce for years. I'd been with Paul since we were kids in high school, and, for the past decade, we'd been more like friends than lovers. Paul and I were very different people, and, in order to keep the peace between us, I'd given up a lot of my own interests. I had always loved Paul, but I'd never really been in love with him. You could say I'd been living part of a life, but not a whole one.

I'd never been the kind of person who did anything I knew would hurt anyone—I'd always worried about what people thought of me—, and yet suddenly, none of this mattered anymore: I didn't want to die without tasting true love, if I could find it. I didn't want to die without doing all the things I'd been putting off doing. Tears ran down my cheeks as I realized how much time I had wasted already, and how little time I had left.

One month later, I rented a little studio apartment near the beach—something I'd always wanted to do. My parents were horrified. I don't know what shocked Olivia and my parents more: finding out I wasn't happy, or finding out I'd left Paul. They warned me that to turn my back on Paul was foolish and selfish—but then again, nobody knew what I was going through; nobody yet knew about my cancer.

I started doing all I'd missed doing before—and, for the first time, I felt like the "real Mia" had come back to life. Pretty sad, I know, considering I was dying, but in many ways, I felt more alive than I'd ever been. It was then something amazing happened, faster than I could ever have imagined—as if life was responding to my before-death-wish: I met the man. I met Ross. And fell madly in love.

Ross was everything I'd always wanted in a partner: he was warm and adventurous, and lived fully in the moment. I refused to believe that he'd want to be with me—a dying woman—, but whenever I brought it up, he replied, "Hey, I could die before you, you know!" I'd always been such a cautious person, but now, I felt free to indulge in my every whim. Thus, when Ross suggested we take a trip around the world, I thought, What the hell. Let's do it.

At the time, almost no one from my former life was speaking to me—with the exception of Olivia and a few good friends and my parents, that is, who were all still hoping my decisions had just been made irrationally, and that I'd quickly realize my mistakes and reclaim my old life. What other explanation was there for my foolish behavior? I was the main subject of all the hot gossip at my old job, and even at church, according to my girlfriends. I was behaving shamelessly and senselessly, people said. How could I do this to my husband and my family?

Whenever my doctor heard these things, I would laugh and ask him, "So, what is a respectable way for a forty-five-year-old woman to die?"

He'd answer, "With a smile on her face!" This became our little joke every visit to his office.

The biggest lesson I learned from all this was, "There are more ways than one to die."

I would look back on my years before cancer and honestly be able to say the half-life I'd been living at the time was when I had really been dying. It was when I was diagnosed and began dying that I started living. Little by little, you leave the voices behind; little by little, you are left with just your one true voice—and as soon as you hear it, you know what you have to do.

And then one day, finally, you do it. You leap. Your new wings unfurl. And you fly.

The fact of the matter is that Paul and I were two entirely different sorts of people; we were unhappy since his work kept him in a small college town, from which he could get away only four weeks a year. This didn't feel worth it considering even if his salary hadn't been entirely sufficient, I had some money of my own that could have contributed to our living.

The trouble lay in the lives we individually wished to live—entirely different to the other's ideal vision. Whilst he was quite content with the few friends amongst the faculty and small college gatherings we occasionally attended, I was not. With my income—which was substantial, though not large—, I felt we should have had a home in high-end neighborhoods, our circle of acquaintances being several times what it was at the time. Then, I could have kept up with the shopping malls, theatres, concerts, and other events of the day. Suzy could have grown up in an atmosphere of culture that would make her woman of the new world.

Many years ago, I married Paul because he had one of the most brilliant minds I had ever known, and I understood he was going to be a technical adviser for a big corporation. However, when he proved to be unmanageable, the president of the corporation declared his brains were insufficient, and so he went back to the college town—and has been there ever since.

I was discontented, and Paul was irritated by the annoyances of our incompatibility.

One might naturally suspect that Paul and I were breaking up because we were obviously mismatched in a sexual way. Paul was a small, dry, nervous, bespectacled gentleman who looked closer to sixty than to forties. He was ill at ease, though very discerning and apt in his behavior with others. The difference between the physical natures of both of us was too striking for anybody to ignore. My Mum's feeling, though, was telling her that our sexual relationship was part of our problem; at least not to be ignored. But we were not.

This was something I right before I married Paul, during which time we talked it over superficially. It was then that he admitted he was not a passionate man, and would prefer to work than spend a passionate evening with me. Despite this being a major hang-up for me, he then somewhat proudly showed me his credentials from his past regular medical check-ups, proving there to be no reason for why he should not become the father of my child—and he lived up to his claim.

However, as I had anticipated, his idea of living up to life was far from mine. He had never had much virility—and the amount he did have was largely sublimated by the strain of his highly scientific research. I found myself almost disgusted by his fatuous inefficiency as a lover, but then again, my honest affection for him—combined with my determination to make our marriage a success, if I could—sustained me at such moments.

What saved me was the fact that I'd had the good fortune to have experienced a skillful lover before I'd was married—a real gentleman of decency, imagination, and experience with women. We enjoyed one another with studied thoroughness. He was the complete opposite of Paul—and now Ross, my new man, was identical to my old lover. Both, however, are admittedly no comparison to him.

It was when I realized this about Paul that I realized I couldn't stand continuing with him anymore.

The Veracity Concept: Even when we have reason to be suspicious, we generally act as if we expect honest dealings from other people. Most of us carry a foundational assumption that people will communicate honestly to the best of their conscious knowledge. Social life, as we know it nowadays, would be impossible without this assumption—yet such a trust-based system is easily exploited by cheaters.

OLIVIA

WE ARE DISHONEST, AND yet we expect others to be honest to us. All this time I had become somewhat of an actress, fabricating my dissatisfaction with false happiness—and it was a matter of time before my dark side got uncovered after being hidden for so long.

Things with Peter had frequently become up and down, and we were constantly breaking up and getting back together. I fought with him countless times, and always warned him that there was no coming back from the one currently being dealt with. In one such moment of despair, I decided to hang out in distinctly not-me places with distinctly not-me, bizarre people. The thought of taking revenge controlled my mind: I wanted to find my lost self elsewhere, outside home, since I couldn't find it inside home. I felt a disaster coming my way, and yet I blindfolded myself.

One night, I was at the casino. Peter didn't know I frequented casinos when he wasn't around. It was when I glanced out into the crowd that I saw Nick, sitting there in the corner with people I didn't know. We made eye contact and he walked through his entourage to greet me. Nick was one of mine and Peter's old schoolmates. I hadn't seen him in years.

"Liv, what are you doing here?" he laughed. "You're the last person I thought I'd see in a casino. Do you want to join me for a drink?"

"Can we go outside instead?" I asked. There was no harm in getting one little drink, but I was worried word would get back to Peter and that he would come and find me, dragging me from the casino—from my fun. Even though it was close to over with Peter—at least from my side—,saying hello to Nick still felt like a betrayal.

"Of course," he said. "Let's go to my car."

We sat in his car and talked for three or four hours—until dawn crept over the horizon. Not once was there an awkward break in conversation; rather, his words were cajoling. He told me he was working as a scuba-diving instructor—something I'd dreamt of doing one day. Few things had ever seemed so natural, so right—but it was on the drive home that I started thinking, What am I doing? I felt an attraction to Nick, and it was certainly something deeper to I had with Peter. Mind you, I hadn't done anything—and besides, Peter and I weren't even on good terms that night, nor were we the many nights before. Even still, my stomach was in knots, like I had just cheated. I knew I was making a mistake, but I just couldn't help it; I was so attracted to Nick. We caught up, and it felt organic. I began to miss his friendship and the old days, and the connection we'd had always harbored—way before I knew Peter. I had lost that connection with Peter, though. Deep down, I knew it had become a toxic relationship.

One night, Nick came by our house: Peter had invited him for dinner and forgotten to tell me about it. The possibility of such a situation happening had never even crossed my mind, until I was in the kitchen, making dinner, and Peter called Nick inside.

"Hey, bro!" Peter welcomed Nick. "My wife, Olivia," he introduced me. "My schoolmate and friend, Nick."

In that moment, I fully wanted to force the knife in my hand through my chest; that would have been better than facing the shame I was about to endure. Not once while we'd talked had I thought of telling Nick that I was married to Peter—someone who had also gone to our school. I hadn't known we'd all meet one another, by coincidence, the night before; Peter hadn't mentioned it.

As I stood there with Nick and Peter before me, I began to reason with myself: why should I tell Peter when there was nothing serious between me and Nick? It was just an attraction—at least from my side. And why should I tell Nick that I was married to Peter? These thoughts screamed in my head like a bomb ready to explode at any moment.

"Oh, bro, you're married to Olivia!" Nick exclaimed with an odd, twisted smile. "I didn't know." He didn't sound upset; just shocked.

I was beyond embarrassed. It wasn't that I wanted to be with Nick; I was still faithful to Peter. I hadn't fallen in love with him; I was just a little attracted to him. He was a gentleman, after all—and he was nice to me. I knew my feelings had been confused at the time, but I still felt that Nick suspected what I felt deep down: I wasn't happy in my marriage, and I was struggling to make it work with Peter. He knew I was searching for a new love—a new adventure. I could see right through him. His glazed eyes said everything.

After that night, Nick had disappeared, and I found a new level of respect for him: he was a real gentleman to withdraw when he knew I was married to Peter, his old friend. But then again, deep in my heart, I felt Nick backed off because he knew the me he'd come to know wasn't real: I'd been in an unbalanced mood when I'd first met him at the casino, and I was in turmoil now.

On one hand, I was happy and felt lucky that my story with Nick had been cut so short—or hadn't even had the chance to start. But then again, on the other hand, I was ashamed: I'd lied to Peter and to Nick. I hadn't been authentic in my feelings or my words. I felt so humiliated, and began to hate myself for my actions—although then again, it wasn't just my fault, but Peter's, too: he was the cause of my desperate life; he had pushed me to my limit. I'd had enough of him; I wanted my dignity, happiness, and life back. It was unfair for me to take all the blame.

I had always believed Peter would change; I always loved him— even when he betrayed me with his little cow, Jennifer. He was frustrated; I was frustrated. He betrayed me, and to take revenge, I wanted to betray him.

Where were we in all of that? Nowhere. We'd killed our souls so our bodies could live together. We became passive and more distant than ever before. I refused to do anything that would drive me crazy—like arguing with him about important topics—, and he became more silent at home, never willing to discuss anything or to open up. Any topic he had felt I would argue with him about, he preferred to ignore simply and never talk about again.

Little by little, the drama disappeared—and so did we.

I leaned my head back, closed my eyes, and allowed a breath to shudder from me as I pushed past the initial agony. What is a sin, Olivia? I thought to myself.

It is the act that contradicts our personal conscience. It is something relative. A specific act could be considered a sin in a particular situation, but not be in another. I was trying to convince my conscience that what I'd done was not a sin—Peter had pushed me to do it; I'd responded equally to his acts. This had been a fair, normal reaction—so why should I blame myself for it?

The "Evil Design" Concept: People act knowingly with evil design. Most often, an erroneous perception of what will result in maximum pleasure provides the motivation behind the error that leads to the evil, as well as the tragedy that so frequently accompanies it.

MIA

I DIDN'T SET OUT to date a married man like Ross—and I never in a million years thought I'd be in this position. The relationship I had with Ross was very different from a lot of "Other Woman/Married Man" relationships: first of all, we didn't hide; we went out all the time, we had our favorite restaurants, we went shopping, and we went to concerts.

Apparently, his wife had never gotten along with anyone in his family and had refused to see any of them since well before I came along, and the more I got to know him, the more I began to understand the type of man he really was: he was fun, loving, and willing to do anything he could to help those he loved. Quickly, I also came to know his family more, and it was from them that I heard the things his wife had done to make them dislike her. I hadn't asked; they'd simply volunteered the information, and, as much as I felt a little uncomfortable at what they told me, I was still glad to have a better understanding of the situation.

There are a lot of people out there who think in black and white when it comes to the "other woman" and her still-married lover. It is not, however, black and white: there are shades of grey—many shades of grey.

I learned a lot during those first few days of being with Ross: I knew when he was being honest and when he was lying—usually a lie of omission—, and what I also knew for a fact was that his wife just didn't care. She'd called a few times while he'd been with me, but this was usually to complain about something, or to inform him of an emergency concerning their kids. Other than that, there had been no contact.

At the time, I still knew I could be history at any time: I was under no illusions about him divorcing his wife and moving in with me. His wife had made it clear that if he left her, she would make his life miserable, and he would never see his kids.

Even with the knowledge that his wife didn't care about what he had been doing, did I wanted her to "catch" him with me? Absolutely not. Why? Because, as women, we all know the drill: even if you don't want a man you've been with, you also don't want to see him happy with another woman; no woman wants that rubbed in her face. It's the "I don't want him but you, bitch, can't have him, either" syndrome.

Ross and I didn't take many precautions when we were together; again, nobody he knew thought he should be with his wife. They really disliked her because of her ugly personality, and his family and friends—even his mother—had stopped going to his house because of his wife.

In her heart, his wife must have known he was seeing someone—even just because of the sheer amount of time he spent with me. Saying that, this didn't mean she wanted the affair "confirmed": she had her house, car, and someone to pay her bills and do the yard work. She'd go out with friends almost every Friday night while Ross was home babysitting his kids. She also got an all-expenses-paid vacation every year—courtesy of him.

At the time, I knew Ross wouldn't leave his wife right there and then: his kids depended on him a lot, and his wife had several health issues—both mental and physical—that meant she needed his health insurance coverage.

Regardless, I spent plenty of time with Ross, and, after some time, I realized I didn't need him to live with me: whenever he left my house, we'd talk on the phone until he got home—and after he hung up, I'd be free to do whatever I wanted. I realized that I, finally, got what I'd been unconsciously needing: a semi-committed and semi-free lifestyle—especially when considering the fact that I didn't have much left to live in this life. Thus, I would never sit by the phone waiting for Ross to call; instead, I'd make plans and let Ross know when I wouldn't be around. On those nights, he'd stop by my house for a quick kiss and to hang out with me until I left to go out. The point was, I knew that I could be dumped at any time—and Ross knew he wasn't safe from being dumped, either.

I know being with a married man isn't the optimal choice, but sometimes, things just happen.

Despite their broken marriage, Ross never talked negatively about his wife; instead, he'd say, "She gave birth to my children, and this entitles her to some respect. Even if our marriage isn't working for whatever reason—whether cause is her or me—, I won't talk negatively about Carol. She deserves to have some dignity."

I was sure his wife knew, in her heart, that he was seeing another woman, but she didn't need to hear it from me; anyway, she didn't care about him anymore as long as her lifestyle was safe—so really, it was a win-win situation.

The "Becoming" Concept: What you think you lack determines what you will become in the future. It is the feeling of inferiority, inadequacy, and insecurity that determines the goals of an individual. A thousand talents, capabilities, and even devilish actions will arise from such feelings of inadequacy.

SIN, TO THE AVERAGE person, means an offense against the command and will of God—and, because Olivia and Mia are non-believers, God took the microcosmic form of "Personal Conscience". Sin is, therefore, not necessarily an offense against the civil law—though it may so happen coincide with such an offense.

If I were to ask every person around me (e.g., my spouse/coworkers/family/neighbors) to keep a diary for one week and to record every single social interaction they had and every time they lied, I would doubtless be amazed at the results—assuming they'd be honest in such recordings! The conclusion cited in thousands of academic papers suggest that people tell an average of one to two lies per day, and are lying in 20% to 30% of all their social interactions.

Olivia, Peter, and Mia lied about their feelings for their spouses mostly, but also their actions; meanwhile, other people lie about their future plans, whereabouts, and as well as facts about themselves, their achievements, and their possessions. Most lies tend to be self-serving, told with the aim of protecting the self from embarrassment or from missing opportunities to look good. Some lies, however, are chiefly altruistic—told to help or protect others from distress.

Everyone has an instinctive sense of what it meant to lie, but sometimes, it's as though they've been tricked; they struggle to distinguish between lying and other types of human communication. They may have thought a lie as simply being the opposite of the truth, yet the objective truth is hard to know and is always up for debate: everyone has their own version and perspective about what truth is—especially in a postmodern society shaped to seek out divergent perspectives on reality. Mankind is "condemned to tell lies," as written by the philosopher Maria Golaszewska, "because he never knows what the truth is." The same set of events can reveal different aspects of a person, depending on the nature and mood of the witness. Dishonesty, then, cannot be defined in opposition to absolute truth, but rather as a misrepresentation of what the liar believes to be true. Such a standard is central in law and everyday social life.

Philosophers determine four criteria to define a lie: they are communications that the speaker knows to be false; they are intended to mislead others; they are used for some identifiable purpose; and they occur without notification or warning.

A lie occurs any time you intentionally try to mislead someone—like when a woman gets breast implants with the objective of luring her prospect prey. The intention to mislead serves to distinguish lying from situations in which the speaker is simply wrong. Kids will often categorize any counterfactual statement as a lie because they have not yet developed the cognitive capacity to fully imagine the mental experience of others— but in deception, it is not enough to merely speak inaccurately. As much as the moral question of whether you are lying or not is not settled by establishing the truth or falsity of what you say, you first must know whether you intend for your statement or action to mislead.

Intentionality also helps to distinguish lies from more bizarre behaviors (e.g., the delusional claims of those who believe they are God or the devil while experiencing psychosis). Although untrue, the emphatic claims of a delusional person are not intended to mislead the listener; quite the contrary, such patients are often quite driven to reveal their version of the truth.

Purpose is another aspect of deception, and this requirement behind a lie serves to distinguish deliberate lying from pathological lying—the latter being defined by its lack of any discernable goal or practical reasoning. In 2001, there was a case of disgraced California judge who could not stop making false claims about his education and military service, even with his job and reputation at stake. Indeed, pathological liars may be highly functional people who face great costs for their compulsive deceptions.

Another element of lying that is often overlooked is a lack of notification, which we could think of as the failure to be honest about the fact that one is lying. It is a deliberate choice to mislead a target without giving any notification of the intent to do so. Therefore, lying is making a false claim in situations when the truth is expected, this element of "notification" helping us separate lying from a diverse set of communications on which listeners are alerted that the speaker is not being truthful. These include sarcastic remarks that are meant to convey the opposite of their literal content (e.g., "I am just loving this painful skin rash; it's a real treat"). This also includes theatrical performances, when everyone who enters the theater knows the actors onstage are likely to be saying things which are, strictly speaking, not true.

Perhaps the best example of the notification issue is offered by President Donald J. Trump. In a quoted passage from his 1987 book The

Art of the Deal, Trump wrote, "The final key to the way I promote is bravado. I play to people's fantasies. People may not always think big [of] themselves, but they can still get very excited by those who do. That is why a little hyperbole never hurts. People want to believe that something is the biggest and the greatest and the most spectacular. I call it truthful hyperbole."

Trump's essential point is that because showmanship is a recognized element of sales, his exaggerations are merely giving the audience what they want and expect—making him innocent in terms of lying. Trump believes his audience has been notified by the context of real-estate sales, just as theatergoers are warned when they take their seats in a playhouse.

What we call lying, then, is not a unitary phenomenon, but rather comprises a host of behaviors in which some advantages can be gained, or loss prevented—materially, socially, or psychologically—by failing to tell the truth. Lies can benefit the liar in a self-serving fashion, or they can serve to help someone about whom the liar cares. The liar has access to a variety of tools and techniques, each useful for a range of tasks. For example, exaggeration was handy for securing Olivia's plan to attract Peter, and is generally useful when it comes to jobs and self-esteem. Omission and secret-keeping are useful for escaping criminal prosecution, mollifying Mia's worried mother, or saving Olivia's marriage. If you have an aggressive goal (e.g., ruining the reputation of an enemy), your weapon of choice may be fabrication—the invention of a false version of events.

Lying does not require speech; ne does not have to actually tell a lie to be lying. Indeed, the most common form of deceptive communication involve the omission of relevant information, rather than the utterance of untrue statements. Olivia and Nick hid from Peter their previous meeting in the casino—and, worse, they hid their long conversation in Nick's car. Olivia also didn't tell Nick she was married to Peter, their common schoolmate. Omission is the most common form of dishonesty reported by therapy clients, politicians, actors, singers, and media figures in general, these professions being heavily weighted toward passive dishonesty (e.g., omission) more than active dishonesty (e.g., fabrication, also known as commission); they omit important information whilst peaking to their therapists, audience, citizens, and media.

Nonverbal communication is another ballgame altogether when it comes to deception: the many muscles in the face allow people to simulate emotions they are not really feeling. We fake smiles so often it probably escapes our awareness until our faces start hurt from the effort; we pretend to nod in agreement with our managers, wives, fathers, mothers, or even leaders with whom we disagree or disrespect; and we raise our eyebrows in artificial delight when tasting a mother's-in-law or wife's inedible baked cakes.

Humans have four common strategies of nonverbal deceit: we use minimization—where we dampen the expression of strong emotions (as when Mia's doctor, whose patient's health had been deteriorating, simulated a calm demeanor to conceal Mia's panic); exaggeration—the false heightening of one's emotional expression (as when Olivia simulated sorrowful anger to pressure Peter to marry her); neutralization—the adoption of a poker face (an especially important skill for Peter as he listened to Olivia's continuous complaints and accusations without conveying even the slightest hint of judgment); and substitution—the replacement of one emotional expression (e.g., indifference; disgust) with a more acceptable one (affection; delight). The latter is handy when friends invite you to adore their badly behaved children or pets.

The majority of us tacitly endorse other forms of deception (e.g., white lies, which serve as a social lubricant and thus support the social order); we teach our children to conceal their opinions when they may be true but offensive (e.g., "If you can't say anything nice, do not say anything at all"), and we all know adults are routinely expected to tell outright lies in the name of politeness. The degree of compassion we feel toward others increases the intensity of prosocial lying: we eschew white lies in favor of dishing out the unvarnished truth, which would inevitably provoke the shocked outrage of coworkers, family, and friends.

Try for a month to speak only the truth to everyone in your life, and you will find it to be the worst month of your life. Continuously being absolutely honest puts you at clear risk of being (to put it frankly) beat up, fired, and divorced. Behavior at the extremes of honesty and dishonesty can, thus, leave one at risk of adverse consequences, and it is perhaps for this reason that the flow of natural discourse features little total honesty or total dishonesty, containing few of what is called bold-faced lies or bold-faced truths. The most deceptive messages are mixtures of true and false information that must be judiciously blended to meet the goals of the communicator.

The Social Desirability Concept: People claim something that is not real in order to project a particular image of themselves.

People do not present anything near what we could call their real selves in society; instead, they attempt to enact social roles appropriate to the occasion, engaging in constant modulations of their appearance and behavior intended to manage the impressions they are making on their audience. The presentation of the self in everyday life is one that is edited to appear coherent, believable, and worthy of respect. As with actors in the theater, these performances change strikingly, depending on whether they happen in front-stage public spaces (e.g., office; street; party) or backstage private spaces (bedroom; kitchen; bathroom), where the social actor can be more genuine—though almost never entirely genuine. Blunders in self-presentation result in a painful loss of persona; indeed, even when alone, we may experience social judgments of our performance.

Therefore, the nature and significance of any given lie can be understood by examining four features: the technique/means of deception used by the liar; the moral status or harm potential of the lie—for the self and others involved; the external goal that the lie is designed to achieve; and the internal function the lie may serve for the liar's psyche.

How do people judge the moral status of their lies now? Lies that benefit others are seen to be most acceptable, whilst lies that benefit both the liar and the target are deemed slightly less acceptable. Lies that harm others, meanwhile, are seen to be least acceptable. Lies with severe consequences are not okay, whereas low stake lies are often fine. Further, in most cases, lying to strangers is seen to be far more acceptable than lying to a spouse, or someone in another close relationship. The moral logic that unifies these findings appears consistent with evolutionary logic—specifically in terms of humankind's evolutionary reliance on reciprocal altruism for survival. The basic rule seems to be lie to strangers and about trivial matters if you must, but never lie to people you are close to about important things.

OLIVIA

I FELT BAD ABOUT myself and my life.
For about four years, I had always preferred silence. I spent my time lonely: no more arguing with Peter and the kids; no appetite for hanging out with friends, or even Peter. Life was unfair; I hated it. Very quickly, suicidal thoughts began to infiltrate my mind and cloud my reason. I felt like my life was crumbling and that there was no way out. I also didn't want to direct any extra effort to making my marriage work again, and so I just gave up trying; I just let things go. It was always any excuse to get out of it—reading, gardening, talking to Mia—, but once I was done, the same feelings controlled me again. I didn't know what was actually happening to me; it was hard to explain in any depth to anyone. I knew I was going through something abnormal, but was not aware of what it was exactly.

The morning the trouble began—years before I realized there was even trouble in the first place—, I was sitting at home, lonely and staring at the walls—so bored that I was giving serious thought to reorganizing the living room. It was one of many times that feelings of desperation had crept up on me, and my mind reverted to the turmoil I had been going through. It was eleven-thirty in the morning, and I had resorted—again— to taping a kitchen towel over the clock on the wall to stop myself from looking at it every two minutes.

I had no idea what to do next.

That day, I made a deal with myself: if I could make it to noon without going crazy or devouring whatever was in the fridge, I would leave the house and do something fun, instead of resting at house like a pregnant cow all day long.

I spent the next ninety minutes trying to figure out what exactly that would be, and, when the clock ticked to one o'clock, I forced myself to put on some makeup and a revealing dress, and drove to a nearby casino about twenty minutes away from home. Even on a Thursday, the casino was filled with people. There was a band playing near the entrance, and a woman was circling the venue, handing out free cocktails. I ate shrimp from a buffet and allowed my head to tilt back in my seat and my eyes to flutter closed: the whole experience felt luxurious. I made my way to a blackjack table, where a dealer was patiently explaining the rules. When my fifty dollars of chips were gone, I glanced at my watch and saw two hours had flown by; I needed to hurry home to pick the children up from school.

That night at dinner, for the first time in years, I had something to think about besides what the children would like to eat for lunch the next day.

After that first trip, I started going to the casino once a week, on Friday afternoons. I considered it a reward for making it through empty days: keeping the house clean, staying sane, and laying on the bed, open-legged, preparing to fulfil my role as Peter's sex toy. I knew gambling could lead to trouble, so I set strict rules for myself: no more than one hour at the blackjack table per trip, and no gambling for any more than fifty bucks. I was deceived myself into thinking it was kind of like a job; I never left the house before noon, and I was always home in time to pick my kids. I was very disciplined.

I got good at this—quick. At first, I could hardly make my money last an hour, but six months down the road, I had picked up enough tricks that I adjusted my rules to allow for two-hour shifts, cash still sitting in my pocket when I walked away. There was one afternoon that I sat at the blackjack table with $200 in my purse, and left with $760. What a hell of an amount—and in just a few hours! I was astonished. By then, the casino was sending me coupons for free meals, which I would treat the children to on Saturday nights.

Long before then, my marriage with Peter had started to show signs of hopelessness: he was only growing more interested in his work than my anxieties, and I couldn't help but feel resentful of my children, who of course didn't realize I needed them then more than ever before. To tell you the truth, whenever I hit the casino, those tensions floated away; it was a truly amazing feeling. It started out with me going a couple of times a week—and then every Monday, Wednesday, and Friday. With every win, my rules started to loosen. I had been gambling for almost two years at this point, and began to experience the axioms serious players lived by. I never put down less than $200 a hand, and always played two hands at once; I learnt that one has better odds at a higher limit table than at a lower limit table. One has to be able to play through the rough patches until their luck turns. I began to see people walking in with $500 out with $10,000, and was admittedly decoyed: what if I were to gain such a fortune in just a few hours? I wouldn't need Peter's money anymore. I imagined myself setting up my own business; I could even buy a house by the sea! Slowly but surely, I began to convince myself that all of this could be possible—if I followed my rules.

By then, I didn't have to think about whether to take another card, or whether I should double my bet; I was acting automatically. One day, I went home from the casino with $6,000 in my pocket. I felt completely numb with shock; I simply couldn't believe what had just happened. It was like a dream come true. Then, there was another time that I walked away with $3,000. Sometimes I lost—of course I did—, but that was part of the game: smart gamblers knew one had to go down to go up. Eventually, the casino gave me a line of credit so I wouldn't have to carry so much cash. Other players sought me out and sat at my table because they knew I knew what I was doing. At the buffet, the hosts would let me go to the front of the queue—all because I knew how to play.

I know this sounds like I was somebody who had a problem without recognizing it, and this is true—and the biggest mistake I made was not quitting.

Gradually, my rules became more flexible as the size of my winnings and losses expanded: one day, I lost $2,000 in an hour—and then earned $3,200 in forty minutes. My luck then turned again, and I walked away down $7,000. The casino began to keep records of how much I owed and what I'd earned; frankly, I'd stopped keeping track myself long ago.

Then, the month came where I didn't have enough for the electricity bill; I'd lost the money for the house's monthly bills, as well as everything in my bank account. I started to ask my father for small loans every now and then, and what started as $2,000 a month climbed to $4,000. It wasn't a big deal; my mother didn't know anything, and my father had the money.

At the time, I frequented the casino almost every day. I went whenever I fought with Peter, or felt even slightly unappreciated by him or the kids. At the tables, I was both exhilarated and numb all at once, and my anxiety would grow so rapidly that my mind would simply block everything out besides what was right in front of me. The high of winning was so immediate, and the pain of losing passed so fast.

"You want to be a big shot," my friend Nicole told me when I called to borrow some money. "You keep gambling because you want the attention, don't you?"

That wasn't it, though. "I just want to feel good at something, Nicole," I'd admitted. "This is the only thing I've ever done where it feels like I have a skill."

The desperation started once I realized how much I'd lost—and at that point, I felt like I couldn't stop: I then had to win it back. Sometimes I'd started feeling jumpy, like I couldn't think straight, and I'd know that if I pretended to take another trip soon, it would calm me down. The casino would call, and I'd say yes, simply because it was so easy to give in. I really believed I might win it back: I'd won before. Besides, if you couldn't win, then gambling wouldn't be legal, right? Soon, though, the losses were too big to ignore, and some nights, after Peter was asleep, I would crawl out of bed, sit at the kitchen table, and scribble out figures, trying to make sense of how much was gone. The depression seemed to only be growing larger. I felt so tired all the time—and the casino just kept calling.

By the end of my third year of gambling, my debts to the casino hit $80,000. I had, of course, been keeping the losses a secret from Peter. It was, however, when my father finally cut off the stipends that I broke down and confessed everything to Peter.

It was a disastrous day to Peter; he had discovered a completely different Olivia to the one he had known for all those years.

At the time, it was almost as if the scale of loss hadn't registered; when I thought about it afterwards, it just didn't seem real. I had lied to myself about so much already, to the point where only two choices remained: to continue lying to myself, or to admit I had dishonored everything Peter, my mother, my father, had worked so hard to earn.

Peter hired a bankruptcy attorney, cut up my credit cards, and sat in the living room writing out a plan for a more austere, responsible life. Eventually, it started to feel like the worst was over; finally, I thought, the compulsion has gone. But, of course, it wasn't even close to the end; I simply couldn't withstand the humiliation. The disgust I constantly saw in Peter's eyes was too devastating to ignore. The depression that had become a huge, gaping hole in my life after my confession seemed only to be growing larger and larger.

After I had lost everything and ruined my life—no, all our lives—; after I had thrown away thousands of dollars and my lawyer had argued before the state's highest court that I had gambled not by choice, but out of habit, and thus shouldn't bear culpability for my losses; after I had become an object of scorn in the family; I wondered, How much responsibility actually rests on my shoulders?

"I honestly believe anyone in my shoes would have done the same things," I told Nicole at the time.

Three months after I was declared bankrupt, my father passed away. His death was a blow; he had always been my hero. Then, eight months later, my mother died. I was broken; my entire world disintegrated, more than I ever knew it could. I woke up every morning and, for a blissful second, I would forget they had passed—and then it would always come crashing back down on me that they were gone, and from then, I wouldn't be able to think about anything else. I'd had enough; my life was falling apart all around me, and I quickly found myself unable to find the energy too even get out of bed.

Ten months after, the casino tried to collect the money I owed, only for the promissory notes I signed to bounce. Thus, the casino sued me, demanding I paid my debts, as well as an additional $275,000 penalty—a civil punishment, in effect, for committing a crime.

My lawyer argued I shouldn't have been held accountable; the casino, after all, had lured me in all the ways possible, and it has largely been this that had changed my previous straight behavior. Indeed, my attorney managed to prove that the casino in question was known within the industry for the sophistication of its customer-tracking systems: at the core of that system were computer programs, comprised of predictive algorithms that studied their gamblers' habits and, in line with these, tried to figure out how to persuade them to spend more. The casino's software would also build calendars anticipating how often I would visit and how much I would spend, tracking me through loyalty cards and mailed-out coupons for free meals and cash vouchers. Telemarketers would call me at home to ask where I had been; the employees were trained to encourage visitors to discuss their lives in the hopes they may reveal information that could be used to predict how much they had at their disposal to gamble with; the casino offered free limos to take players to any of the casino's branches across the US, to fly me and my family to Lake Tahoe, to put us in a suite, to give me tickets to a Pink Floyd concert. I had, of course, accepted all of these offers at the time—and, at the concert, I had sat in the front row. The casino once gave me $10,000 to play with—compliments of the house—, and the offers still kept coming. Every week the casino called, asking if I wanted a free limo, free entry to shows, and free plane tickets. Suddenly, everything I had ever dreamed of was free. I said yes each time an invitation arrived.

Peter countersued, claiming that by extending my credit, free suites, and booze, the casino had preyed on someone they knew had no control over their habits. My case went all the way to the state Supreme Court. My lawyer consistently stated that I shouldn't be held accountable, since I had been reacting automatically to temptations that the casino placed in front of me; once the offers from them had started rolling in, he maintained, my habits took over and it became impossible for me to control my behavior.

The jury, however, would state that these were wrong. "There is no common law duty obligating a casino operator to refrain from attempting to entice or contact gamblers that it knows, or should know, are compulsive gamblers," the court wrote. Hence, I was held responsible for all my acts, and it lay on Peter's shoulders to pay the full amount; otherwise, I would be thrown into prison.

He paid.

At the time, I couldn't bear to think that Peter's disgust and agony were understandable reasons for his ultimate cheating on me; I saw no relation between the two events. Sure, I had lost some money; but cheating was a different game altogether... Wasn't it?

The Self-Deception Concept: We manage to think of ourselves as great thinkers, rational humans, talented lovers, and brilliant leaders—and so when the facts of our lives reveal a pathetic parade of broken families, crumbled social relations, disappointed partners, and deflated souffles, we simply fabricate the facts and ignore the alarm bells that ring.

B ASIC MILITARY TRAINING TEACHES soldiers carefully designed habits for how to shoot, think, and communicate under fire; hence, on the battlefield, every command that's issued draws on behaviors practiced to the point of automation. From this, we can see that the entire military organization relies on endlessly rehearsed routines for building bases, setting strategic priorities, and deciding how to respond to attacks. Understanding human habits is the most important lesson you would get to learn from military reads.

Olivia never had problems with alcohol or drugs: she was a normal mother, with the same highs and lows in her marriage life as everyone else. The compulsion she felt to gamble—the insistent pull that led to her feelings of distraction or irritableness on the days when she didn't visit the casino; the way she found herself thinking about it all the time; the rush she felt on a good run—caught her completely off guard. During her marriage's downfall, winning and losing had been a new sensation—a sensation so unexpected that she hardly knew it was a problem until it had taken hold of her life. In retrospect, it seemed like there had been no dividing line: one day it was fun; the next it was uncontrollable.

Science tells us that, neurologically speaking, pathological gamblers get more excited about winning than the average player; even when such gamblers don't actually win any money, the areas in their brains related to emotions and rewards are much more active than in nonpathological gamblers. What is more interesting are the near-misses experienced by such players: to Olivia, near-misses appeared to be wins; her brain reacted in almost exactly the same way. To a nonpathological gambler, however, a near-miss is like a loss. Hence, people without a gambling problem are better at recognizing that a near-miss means they still lost. Indeed, although these two groups ultimately undergo the exact same event, from a neurological perspective, they view it completely differently: Olivia, who had gambling problems, got a mental high from near-misses—probably being the main reason behind why she gambled for so much longer than nonpathological gamblers—, and it was these near misses that triggered her ultimately destructive habits, prompting her to place yet another bet. The nonproblematic gamblers, however, receive a dose of apprehension with a near miss that triggers a different habit—one that says, "I should quit before this gets worse."

The depression Olivia was feeling as a result of her failing marriage heightened her sense of reward with slot machines, online poker, and casinos—all combining to develop new behaviors in Olivia. These drastically altered how her brain functioned—namely, how it processed information—, which helps to explain why she lost control every time she walked into a casino.

Because of her marriage's slow failure, Olivia was so disoriented that she failed to realize her own intellect until she stepped into the casino; before then, she had spent days crying, binge-eating, lying awake at night, and feeling ashamed, helpless, depressed, and angry—all at once. She felt like everything she had ever wanted had crumbled. Thus, she made the decision to prove her own self-worth—in an albeit unusual way. It was this one small shift in Olivia's perception—the conviction that she had to prove her self-worth—that triggered a series of behavioral changes that ultimately began to take a toll on every aspect of her life.

As written by William James in 1892, "All our life, so far as it has definite form, is but a mass of habits." The majority of the choices we make each day may feel like the products of well-considered decision-making, but they are not: they're mere habits, and though each habit means relatively little on its own, over time, the food we eat, what we say to our children, whether we save or overspend, how often we exercise, and the way we organize our thoughts and work routines, have enormous impacts on our health, productivity, financial security, and happiness.

The process in which the brain converts a sequence of actions into an automatic routine is known as "chunking", and it is this that is at the root of how habits form. There are dozens—if not hundreds—of behavioral chunks that we rely on every day: some are simple (like when you automatically put toothpaste on your toothbrush before sticking it in your mouth), whilst others (such as making lunch) are a little more complex. Others are very complicated, but, nonetheless, the repetition of such actions rapidly turns them into habits (e.g., driving). To use driving as our example, how we do so when we first learn to drive is drastically different to now, which we do with apparently hardly any thought: as soon as we pull out our car keys and our basal ganglia kicks in, identifying the habit we've stored in our brains related to driving a car into the streets, our gray matter is free to either quiet itself or to chase other thoughts—which is why we have enough mental capacity left to remember that we forgot to drop of our son's lunchbox. The routine occurs through habit.

The habit of gambling was formed in Olivia's brain in a three-step loop: first, there was a cue—a trigger that told her brain to go into autopilot. By going to the casino a couple of times, she understood that time began to fly by when she was truly enjoying herself, making three or four hours barely noticeable. She quickly realized that passing the time in this way was far more enjoyable than staying home, lonely and bored. Several times after—when she started to properly gamble—, she felt as though she was doing something new and interesting for the first time in a while—something different to the household chores and empty, boring days. Thus, when she started to win—even when they were just small amounts—, she felt smart and skillful, proving to herself that not only could she do something skillful, but also that she was smart enough to excel at it.

Then there was the routine, which can be physical, mental, or emotional: Olivia's brain had developed the routine of going to the casino, as well as the routine of gambling. Both were done automatically.

Finally, there was a reward; this helped her brain to figure out if this particular loop was worth remembering for the future. Going to the casino helped her to not feel lonely; gambling helped her to feel worth something, skillful, and smart.

Over time, this loop—cue, routine, reward; cue, routine, reward— became more and more automatic; the cue and reward aspects became intertwined, until a powerful sense of anticipation and craving emerged. Eventually, a habit was formed in Olivia's mind.

Gaming companies are well aware of this tendency, of course; this is why slot machines have been reprogrammed to deliver a more constant supply of near-misses. Gamblers' (like Olivia) consistent betting after every near-miss is what make casinos, racetracks, and state lotteries so profitable: adding a near-miss to a lottery is like pouring jet fuel on a fire. Sales explode because every other scratch-off ticket is designed to make the gambler feel like he almost won. To pathological gamblers, near-misses look like wins; but to a nonpathological gambler, a near-miss is like a loss.

However, habits are not destiny: habits can be ignored, changed, or replaced. It is important to study the self-habit loop; it reveals to us a basic truth: when a habit emerges, our brains stop fully participating in decision-making. It stops working so hard and instead diverts focus to other tasks. So, unless we deliberately fight a habit and find new routines, the pattern will unfold automatically. Thus, simply understanding how our habits work—learning the structure of the habit loop—makes them easier to control—, and, once you break a habit into its components (cue, routine, reward), you are in a position where you can fiddle with the gears.

Olivia's habits occurred for so long that she stopped paying attention to what caused them; however, once one becomes aware of how their habit works—once one recognizes the cues and rewards—, they will be halfway to changing it. The truth is, our brain can be reprogrammed; we just have to be deliberate about it. If we identify the cues and rewards, we can change the routine—at least, most of the time. For some habits, however, there's one other ingredient that's necessary: belief. Belief is the ingredient that makes a reworked habit loop into a permanent behavior; it is about the capacity to believe that things will get better when you implement the efforts required to change the routine.

The will to believe is the most important ingredient in creating belief in change: habits are what allow us to do something initially with difficulty, soon with more and more ease—before finally, with sufficient practice, it is done semi-mechanically—or with hardly any consciousness at all. If you believe you can change—that is, if you make it a habit—, the change becomes real. This is the real power of habit: the insight that your habits are what you want them to be. Once that choice occurs and becomes automatic, this not only seems to be real, but also inevitable— the thing that bears us irresistibly toward our destiny, whatever that may be.

The golden rule of habit-change is to keep the same cue and the same reward, and to only change the routine; this way, if you want to change a habit, you must find an alternative routine. This leads to the odds of your success increasing dramatically when you commit to changing as part of a group. Belief is essential, and it grows out of a communal experience—even if that community is only as large as two people.

If you want to lose weight, study your habits to determine why you really leave your desk for a snack each day, and then find someone else to take a walk with you, or to gossip with you at their desk, rather than in the cafeteria. Form a group that tracks weight-loss goals together.

Once you diagnose the cue, routine, and reward, you gain power over your habit.

Changing a habit may not be fast, and it isn't always as easy as it seems to be—but with time and effort, almost any habit can be reshaped.

This part isn't meant to be comprehensive; rather a practical guide, or a place to start.

The framework of changing a habit is as follows:
- Identify the routine;
- Experiment with rewards;
- Isolate the cue;
- Have a plan.

Olivia formed a bad habit—one that caused her to lose a significant amount of money. She knew this, and Nicole had even made a few pointed comments to her. She tried to force herself to stop in what she felt was every possible way, but failed every time: every day she got up, wandered around, found herself alone, and, whilst feeling bored, she put on her makeup and ran to the casino. It felt good—and then it felt impossibly bad. Tomorrow, she would promise herself, I'll muster the willpower to resist. Tomorrow will be different.

But tomorrow never came, and the habit took hold again.

Unfortunately, Olivia didn't know how to change her bad habits. Thus, our first step is to learn how to go about diagnosing—and then changing—our unwanted behavior.

First, identify the routine—the routine in this case being the behavior Olivia wanted to change (i.e., getting up from her bed, feeling lonely at home, and thus going to the casino).

Next, some less obvious questions: what was the cue for this routine? Was it boredom? Her failed marriage? Proving herself? A lack of self-esteem? There could be multiple reasons triggering the same routine. And what was the perceived reward? The money she gained? The change of scenery? The temporary distraction from her daily problems with Peter? Socializing with strangers? Or the burst of self-confidence that came from proving herself as smart and worthy?

In order to figure this out, one needs to consider carrying out a little experimentation.

PETER

IT WAS BEYOND MY own imagination to ever imagine Olivia as a professional gambler—for three whole years! How on earth hadn't I noticed any symptoms of the depression Olivia was apparently suffering from? Admittedly, with hindsight, I could see she occasionally acted a little strangely—her behavior had definitely altered—, but depression and gambling? They hadn't crossed my mind for one second.

I'd messed up at the time: I decided to distant myself as much as possible from Olivia, and was too arrogant to realize Olivia was suffering and anxious, and as distant as I. And yet I didn't even bother to ask. Then again, that was because Olivia was acting as if we were enemies—as if our relationship and life together was a battle for which she must be the winner, and must appear the strongest and capable of standing strong.

That dark day—when I so happened to discover Olivia's gambling addiction and the fortune she had lost to the casino—was also the day when I had discovered her medical records, where it was clearly stated she had been suffering from depression.

Depression? Gambling? Debts? Medical records? Lawsuit by the casino? And that was without our shattered marriage! It was like the skies had crumbled into dust over my head over the course of one night.

When Olivia's medical records were examined during her trial before the State Court, they revealed she harbored four of the six common symptoms of depression. High-risk depression is typically diagnosed when someone experiences either the first two symptoms in the list, and at least four or more of the other symptoms, continuously, over at least a two-week period and in a way that departs from natural functioning. Olivia had symptoms 1, 2, 3, and 7 from the following specification:

1- Feeling depressed or sad most of the day;

2- Loss of interest or ability to derive pleasure from all or nearly all activities that were previously enjoyed;

3- Significant weight loss when not dieting, or weight gain, or a significant decrease or increase in appetite;

4- Difficulty sleeping through the night, or a need for more sleep during the day;

5- Noticeably slower or more agitated throughout the day;

6- Feeling fatigued or low in energy nearly every day;

7- Feelings of worthlessness or extreme/inappropriate guilt;

8- Difficulties with concentration or the ability to think, which can also be seen by others as indecisiveness;

9- Recurrent thoughts of death, or ideas about suicide (with or without a specific plan for committing suicide), or a suicide attempt.

I—intentionally, as well as ignorantly—hadn't paid any attention to any of these symptoms.

When asked to think back to the last time she began to feel unhappy and to describe her feelings during such a time, Olivia used a range of similar words: sad; blue; downhearted; miserable; despondent; low; feeling sorry for myself. The strength, however, of such feelings varied; she felt anywhere from slightly sad to extremely sad. Olivia frequently felt irritated, and when down, she felt particularly impatient, frequently feeling "at the end of her tether" with me. She was also more prone than usual to angry outbursts over little to nothing.

Olivia described herself as dumb; why could she not just get over this and move on? Of course, such thoughts were rather counterproductive; they just dragged her down further, serving to be extremely powerful and potentially toxic. Her feelings were both an end point and a starting point of her depression.

Despite her medical records—as well as the fact that her depressive state played a huge role in altering her behavior—, the judicial system declared her responsible and, thus, guilty for her acts. Depression was not seen as a reason to not pay her debts.

Feelings are not facts; one can change their feelings by changing their thinking.

THE FEELINGS BY WHICH Olivia had defined her depression are usually thought of as an end point: she was depressed and felt sad, low, blue, miserable, despondent, and desperate. However, these feelings were also a starting point; research suggests that the more one has been depressed in the past, the more corresponding feelings of low self-esteem and self-blame will be experienced. Not only did Olivia feel sad, but she also felt like failure and like she was useless, unlovable, and a loser. These feelings triggered powerful self-critical thoughts, and, thus, she turned on herself, berating herself for the emotion she was experiencing.

Olivia and Peter were deeply in love at the early beginning of their marriage, but over time, their deceptive behaviors to one another began to unfold, to the point where they seriously began to hate each other. Every time they humiliated one another yet again, this hatred grew more and more, their emotional reactions depending wholly on the story they had been telling themselves—the running commentary in their minds that interpreted the data they had received through their senses: he hates me; she hates me. Even if Peter hadn't been feeling as depressed as Olivia, this sort of self-talk made him feel much worse each time they rowed.

Our world is like a silent film on which we each write our own commentary: our varying interpretations of the events unfolding can wield a massive impact on what happens next. With a benign interpretation, we may quickly forget the incident—and with a negative one, we may be turn to self-chiding.

As we can see here, your handling of the situation depends on the way in which you interpret them. This is the ABC model of emotions: A being the facts of the situation (i.e., what a video camera would see and record); B being your interpretation of such facts (i.e., the "running story" often just below the surface of awareness, running in the subconscious); and C being your reaction (i.e., your emotions/bodily sensations/behavior). You often see the situation A and the reaction C, but remain unaware of the interpretation phase (B); instead, we think it was the situation itself that caused our emotional and physical reactions, when in fact, it's our interpretations of a situation that causes this.

To make things worse, Olivia's reactions then had an impact all on their own: when she felt low, she was likely to pick out and act on the most negative interpretation. Olivia did not only feel that Peter hated her, but also that he was likely making fun of her with his friends. Hence, whenever he laughed while talking on the phone with one of his friends, her low mood would cause such an interpretation to form in her mind, making her feel even lower.

If you are familiar with this kind of stream of thoughts, it may be helpful to know that you are not alone in this pattern of negative thinking. If you are feeling okay at the moment, you may see quite clearly that some thoughts are mere distortions; and, similarly, when you are depressed, you will probably be able to identify that they can seem like the absolute truth. It is as if depression is a war you wage against yourself, and you marshal every bit of negative propaganda you can muster as ammunition.

The fact that Olivia often took these toxic and distorted thoughts about herself as unassailable truths only cemented the connection between her negative feelings and self-critical streams of thought. Knowing this is vitally important when it comes to understanding why depression took a hold of Olivia and not others, or on some occasions but not on others.

There were many specific self-critical (automatic) thoughts that led Olivia to a depressive state that frequent the minds of depressed people:

1- I feel like I am up against the world;
2- I am not good;
3- Why can I never succeed?;
4- No one understands me;
5- I have let people down;
6- I do not think I can go on;
7- I wish I were a better person;
8- I am so weak;
9- My life is not going the way I want it to;
10- I am so disappointed in myself;
11- Nothing feels good anymore;
12- I cannot stand this anymore;
13- I cannot get started;
14- What is wrong with me?;
15- I wish I were somewhere else;
16- I cannot get things together;
17- I hate myself;
18- I am worthless;

19- I wish I could just disappear;

20- I am a loser.

When such thoughts affected Olivia on one occasion, they remained ready to be triggered on other occasions—and when they were triggered, they dragged her mood down even further, draining what little energy she had left at a time when she needed all her resources most. Imagine what effect it would have on you if someone stood behind you all day, telling you how useless you were when you were trying desperately to cope with a difficult experience—and now imagine how much worse it would be if the criticism and harsh judgment came from inside your own mind. No wonder it seems so real; after all, who knows us better than ourselves?

Unhappiness in and of itself is not the problem—sadness is an inherent and unavoidable part of being alive—but, rather, it was the harshly negative views that Olivia had towards herself that were the key issue. It was such views that transformed passing sadness into persistent unhappiness and depression—and, once these harsh, negative views of herself were activated, not only did they affect her mind, but also her body—and so the cycle continues.

Depression affects the body drastically; Olivia had been suffering from insomnia before she decided to go to the casino the first time, and depression also led to the dysregulation of her eating habits, sleep, and energy levels. She gained an appetite, eventually resulting in unhealthy weight gain—although in other cases, some people may lose their appetite and those lose drastic amounts of weight. Her sleep cycle was disrupted in both ways: whilst she was sometimes extremely low in energy and overslept to compensate, she also sometimes found it difficult to get enough sleep, waking in the middle of the night or early in the morning and being unable to get back to sleep.

The bodily changes Olivia had experienced during her depression also had profound effects on how she felt and thought about herself; when these bodily changes activated old feelings of inadequacy and worthlessness she was, even further changes that were minor and temporary made her low mood deepen even more.

Around 80% of those who suffer from depression consult their physician due to aches and pains in the body they cannot explain, and much of this is linked to the tiredness and fatigue that oftentimes accompanies depression. Generally speaking, when you encounter something negative, the body will usually tense up. Our bodies are quite literally built to prepare us for action when it perceives a threat in the environment, and, when such a threat arises, your heart rate speeds up and blood is transferred from the surface of the skin and digestive tract to the large muscles of the body. The brain, however, makes no distinction between the external threat of the tiger, for example, and internal threats (e.g., worries about the future; memories from the past). When a negative thought or image arises in the mind, a sense of contraction, tightening, or bracing occurs somewhere in the body—whether that be in the form of a frown, stomach-churning, a pallor in the skin, or a tension in the lower back—, and they are all part of a preparation to fight, run, or freeze.

Once Olivia's body reacted in this way, the original "threatening" information was reinforced in her mind; indeed, research suggests that the state of your body affects the state of your mind without you having any awareness of it, since our bodies function as highly sensitive emotion detectors. Your body's subconscious mechanisms are giving you constant moment-to-moment readouts of your emotional state without you even realizing. Many of us have been brought up to ignore the body in the interest of achieving whatever goals we are striving to attain, and yet we can see here that this is completely counterproductive: physical issues can be symptoms of perceived hurdles in reaching such achievements.

When Olivia was struggling with depression, she felt a strong aversion to any signals that her body was putting out—including constant inner tension, exhaustion, and chaos. She preferred to ignore such feelings in the hope that this interior turbulence would run its course and subside on its own—and, naturally, this avoidance only led to more unconscious contractions in the body and the mind. Gradually, she slowed down and was less and less able to function, until her depression began to impact a huge aspect of her life: her behavior.

As a child and young adult, Olivia was constantly counseled by her parents to "soldier on", "fight it", and "just get over it" when she was feeling downhearted or miserable—and, somewhere along the way, she picked up the message that it was shameful or a sign of weakness to show her emotions. Consequently, she assumed people would think the worst of her if they knew she was depressed.

The thought processes that accompany depression—usually including themes of inadequacy and unworthiness—are infinitely transportable to any situation. Unconsciously, Olivia became stuck in the belief that any stress or difficulty she was to experience was her fault, and that it was her responsibility to sort it out for herself. Hence, when working harder hadn't solved anything, she felt this was her fault, too. The result of this was, predictably, terminal exhaustion.

Whenever Olivia's mood began to sink and she felt her energy draining out of her, she consciously adopted a strategy of giving up her "unimportant" and "nonessential" leisure activities—ones which actually gave her pleasure—, such as going out with her friends for a coffee and playing guitar with them; to her, such strategies made complete sense, since they meant she was able to focus her dwindling energy (which she viewed as a strictly limited, fixed resource) on her more "important" and "essential" commitments and responsibilities. This was understandable— except that her essential commitments included being the perfect wife (obedient to her husband, father, kids), regardless of whether this was actually a realistic goal or not. In giving up the "nonessential" and "unimportant" leisure activities that may have lifted her mood and extended (rather than depleted) her reserves of energy, Olivia deprived herself of one of the simplest and most effective strategies of reversing a decline into depression, instead plunging herself into gambling.

This phenomenon of "giving up" is described as drifting down a funnel of exhaustion, which is created when the circles of your life becomes smaller and smaller; the narrower the funnel becomes, the more likely a person is to experience burnout or exhaustion.

Olivia had noticed she no longer felt any urge to see her friends in the way she normally did, and that she wasn't getting the same kick out of the things she used to enjoy, like playing the guitar. Each time she considered going out, all she'd think was, What's the point? Nothing is going to make any difference to the way I feel, so I'll save myself the effort and stay in or try to sleep... That will make me feel better. Unfortunately, as Olivia stayed in alone, her mind simply drifted into her well-worn self-critical grooves—, and, of course, these combined to create the perfect setup for the persistence and deepening of her depression. It was ultimately these feelings that led to her going to the casino to gamble, and, thus, Olivia's "giving up" behavior ended up making her a criminal.

Take, as an example, the Exhaustion Funnel:

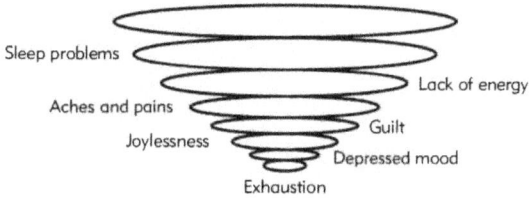

Sleep problems
Lack of energy
Aches and pains
Guilt
Joylessness
Depressed mood
Exhaustion

The narrowing area of the circles above illustrates the narrowing of life as Olivia started to give up the things in life she enjoyed, but perceived as an "option." The result was her stopping doing the activities that would ultimately nourish her, leaving only stressors that often depleted her resources. Therefore, depression caused her to behave differently, and it was these behaviors that fueled her depression. If she was convinced that she was "no good" or "unworthy", how likely was she to pursue the things that she valued in life? Indeed, when she made choices informed solely by a depressive state of mind, they were more than likely to keep her stuck in her unhappiness and to result in more troubles.

Because Olivia had been going through depression for a long time during her marriage, her low moods became easier to be triggered over time—and, with each time it returned, the thoughts, feelings, bodily sensations, and behaviors that accompanied it formed stronger and stronger connections to one another. Eventually, any one element triggered the complete depression all by itself: a fleeting thought of failure triggered a huge sense of fatigue; a small comment by Peter triggered an avalanche of emotions (e.g., humiliation; regret; being invaluable), feeding her sense of inadequacy. Because these downward spirals were so easily triggered by small events or mood shifts, they felt as if they came out of nowhere, and, once the depression took hold, she felt powerless in preventing it from getting worse. All her attempts to control her thoughts or to snap out of her feelings were to no avail.

It wasn't Olivia's fault that she repeatedly felt depressed; she would initially start by just feeling bad, and before she knew it, she would have been pulled down into a spiral, no amount of struggle getting her out. In fact, the more she struggled, the deeper into the abyss she seemed to fall. She blamed herself for feeling bad in the first place—and especially for feeling worse from dwelling on it. However, what was really at work was a mental pattern—or mode of mind—triggered so automatically that she hardly noticed or knew what was actually happening.

Freedom from depression is possible, but such freedom grows from an entirely different perspective and understanding of what the problem actually is. A gaining of the correct perspective will serve as a map to guide you into a new territory within your own being and experience, as well as to tap into and harness the deep interior resources of the mind that you never suspected you had.

Olivia's emotions played an essential role in the depression she repeatedly felt: her emotions had been vital messengers, evolving as signals to help her meet her basic needs for self-preservation and safety. The human emotional repertoire is remarkably sophisticated, its inner and outer expressions and messages often being eloquent and complex. The most prominent families of emotions are happiness, sadness, fear, disgust, and anger, each emotion being a full-body reaction to a characteristic situation—fear's being danger; sadness and grief being when something precious is lost; disgust being when something highly unpleasant is to be dealt with; anger being when a goal is blocked; and happiness being when your needs are met. Naturally, you pay attention to these signals: they tell you what to do to survive and thrive.

Our emotional reactions are designed to be temporary: the messenger needs to be alert to the signal of the next alarm, and our initial emotional reaction lasts only as long as the subject of this alarm continues. Some situations are very short, so our emotional reaction is, by the same token, short—and, indeed, when other situations endure, so do our emotional reactions. The sadness Olivia felt surrounding the loss of her dad continued for a long time; grief tends to come in unexpected waves that well up and overwhelm for lengthy amounts of time. Even in such cases, however, the mind has ways of healing itself. Indeed, even with something as brutal as grief, most people find that, over time, life eventually returns to some sense of normalcy, and they can then begin to discover the possibility of smiling and laughing once again.

Why, then, did Olivia's depression and unhappiness outlast the situations that triggered such feelings? Why had her feelings of malaise and dissatisfaction continued for so long? The answer is simple: these emotions persisted because Olivia had emotional reactions to her own emotions, which kept them going in a vicious cycle.

The problem with persistent and recurrent depression isn't "getting sad" in the first place; sadness is a natural state of mind. Rather, the problem lies in what happened next, immediately after the sadness came. The problem wasn't the sadness itself, but how her mind reacted to the sadness.

The fact is, when her emotions were telling Olivia that something wasn't quite right, she felt distinctly uncomfortable. The signals were inherently designed to push her to act—to do something to rectify the situation—, so, if the signal hadn't felt uncomfortable and created an urge to act, would she have acted in the wrong way and plunged herself into gambling to prove herself as smart and worthy? Probably not. It is only when the mind registers that the situation is resolved that the signal shuts itself off.

When the signaled problem persisted, Olivia reacted in a way that would allow her to avoid it or escape from it, her brain mobilizing a whole pattern of mostly automatic reactions that helped her to deal with whatever was threatening her survival. This is called "initial pattern of reactions", and it was during this time that she felt negatively toward and wanted to avoid or eliminate something—something known as aversion. Aversion forced her to act (through gambling) in some appropriate way (from her point of view) to the situation, and thereby turned off the warning signal. Thus, every time she walked into the casino to gamble, she felt satisfied and calm. In this regard, aversion can, indeed, serve us well, and even save lives—sometimes.

In Olivia's case, it is not hard to see that these reactions were counterproductive and even dangerous to her wellbeing when directed at what was going on "in here"—within her own thoughts, feelings, and sense of self. In fact, none of us can run fast enough to escape our own inner experience, nor can we eliminate unpleasant, oppressive, and threatening thoughts and feelings by fighting with and trying to annihilate them.

When Olivia reacted to her own negative thoughts and feelings with aversion, her brain circuitry involved in physical avoidance, submission, or defensive attacks (the avoidance system of the brain) was activated, from which point her body tensed (as if it were either getting ready to run, or bracing itself for an assault). She also sensed the effects of aversion in her mind: when she was preoccupied, dwelling on how to get rid of her feelings of sadness or disconnection, her whole experience was one of contraction; her mind, driven to focus on the compelling yet futile task of getting rid of these feelings, closed in on itself. With this, her life experience itself narrowed, leaving her feeling cramped and "boxed in". The choices available to her seemed to dwindle, and she came to feel increasingly cut off from the wider space of possibilities that she longed to connect with.

When Olivia reacted with aversion to her own negative emotions, treating them as enemies to be overcome, eradicated, and defeated, she got into trouble. Hence, we can see here that understanding aversion becomes fundamental to understanding what gets us stuck in persistent unhappiness. Olivia ran into problems because the unhappiness she was feeling triggered old, extraordinarily unhelpful patterns of thinking from the past.

Have you ever visited a place you haven't been to for many years? Before the visit, memories of things that happened at that time of your life may be quite sketchy, but once you get there—walking down the streets and taking in the smells and the sounds—, it all comes rushing back—not just the memories, but also any feelings of excitement, of sorrow, of first love. Returning to the place—the old context—does something that our best efforts to remember could not do nearly as well.

Context has incredibly powerful effects on memory; a particular study into memory found that if deep-sea divers tried to commit something to memory whilst on the beach, they tended to forget it when underwater—and were able to recall it fully when they were back on dry land. It worked the other way around, too: if they learned a list of words underwater, their memory of that list when on dry land was not so good, but came back when they returned to the water. The sea and the beach acted as powerful contexts for the memory, just like a visit to a childhood town.

Olivia's emotional state had such pervasive effects on her mind: her mood functioned as an internal context, acting in the same way that the sea did for the divers, bringing back memories and patterns of thinking associated with other times when she was in that mood. Hence, whenever she felt feelings of unhappiness, thoughts and memories relating to whatever was going on in her mind or world to make her unhappy came back quite automatically—whether she wanted it to happen or not.

Because we live different lives, the experiences that may have provoked unhappiness in the past will differ from one person to another. For that reason, we all differ in terms of the kinds of memories and thinking patterns that get reactivated by the moods we are experiencing in this moment. If the main things that made us sad in the past were losses (e.g., death of a beloved grandparent), when we feel passing sadness now, these will be the memories that come to mind. We may feel sad again, but we may have no trouble acknowledging our loss and then shifting the focus of the mind to other things while the echo of the grief fades in its own time.

But what if our previous moods of unhappiness or depression were evoked by situations that somehow led to our thinking and feeling that we were not good enough—that we were worthless, or frauds? What if in childhood or adolescence, at a time when we didn't have the life skills we now have, we experienced overwhelming feelings of being abandoned, abused, lonely, or just plain no good? Sadly, we now know that many people who become depressed as adults have had such experiences—and, if they had also been commonplace experiences for us, the thinking patterns that made us depressed then—as well as the sense that we are not good enough in some way—are highly likely to be reactivated in the present by even a tiny passing feeling of depression.

This is why we can react so negatively to unhappiness: our experience isn't one simply of sadness, but is colored powerfully by reawakened feelings of deficiency or inadequacy. What may make these reactivated thinking patterns most damaging is that we often don't realize they are memories at all; we simply don't feel good enough, and are unaware that it is a thinking pattern from the past that is evoking such a feeling.

When caught up in such absorbing emotions, how can we possibly contemplate switching our attention away from these pressing and understandable concerns to focus on other topics or approaches, even if doing so may contribute to a lightening of our mood? Sorting things out and forcing a solution will always appear to be the most compelling thing to do: figuring out what it is that is not good enough about ourselves and sorting out what we need to in order to minimize the havoc our unhappiness will wreak in our life if it persists. However, perhaps counterintuitively, focusing on these issues in this way leads to us using the opposite tools that we should be; rather, it simply fuels further unhappiness and keeps us fixated on the very thoughts and memories that are making us unhappy, as if a horror story were being enacted in front of us; you hate looking, but, at the same time, you cannot turn away.

It is difficult to change the fact that past memories and self-critical and judgmental ways of thinking are triggered when we feel unhappy, as it all happens quite automatically; however, we may be in a position to change what happens next.

If Olivia had realized how a slight shift in her mood managed to reactivate old thought patterns concerning a time in her life when she felt most alone, misunderstood, and devalued, she would have been able to let it float by and to continue with her day; she may have even been able to treat herself with a little kindness.

We can learn to relate differently to our unhappiness in such ways, the first step of such a process being to clearly see the ways in which we entangle ourselves; specifically, we need to become more aware of the pattern (or mode) of mind that gets switched on and can cause so much suffering.

When the thought processes triggered by Olivia's depressed mood told her that she was the problem, her automatic urge was to get rid of those feelings immediately—but larger issues had also been triggered. This mean that it wasn't just that today wasn't going well, her that her whole life felt as if it wasn't going well. She felt caught in a prison without a way to escape.

The problem was in the fact that she tried to think her way out of her mood by working out what had gone wrong. Questions like, "What is wrong with me?" and "Why do I always feel overwhelmed?" would be her first thoughts, and, from that point, she would compulsively try, over and over, to get to the bottom of what was wrong with her as a person, or with the way she lived her life, so as to fix it. She directed all of her mental power—all of her critical thinking skills—to working on the problem.

Unfortunately, such critical thinking skills, as we have established, had been the exact wrong tools for the job at hand.

Rightly so, the majority of us are proud of what we can do just with critical, analytical thinking; it is one of the highest achievements of our evolutionary history as human beings, and gets us out of a whole slew of fixes in life. Thus, when Olivia saw things weren't going well in her internal, emotional life, it was hardly surprising that her mind quickly reacted by employing a rational perspective that had worked so effectively in solving problems in her external world before. This mode of careful analysis, problem-solving, judgement, and comparison was aimed at closing the gap between the way things were and the way she thought they should have been—or, put simply, at solving the perceived immediate problems. In line with this, scientists call this state of mind the "doing mode of mind"—and this was the mode by which she responded to what she heard as a "call to action".

The "doing mode" is recognized to (usually) work very well in helping to achieve goals in everyday situations, as well as in solving work-related technical problems. Consider the simple everyday action of driving across town: in order to make a journey, the "doing mode of mind" enables you to reach the goal by creating an idea of where you are now (i.e., at home) and an idea of where you want to be (.e., at work); it then automatically focuses on the mismatch between these two ideas, generating actions aimed at narrowing the gap (i.e., get in the car and drive). It continuously monitors whether the gap is getting bigger or smaller to ascertain whether these actions are having the desired effect of reducing the "distance left to travel" between the two ideas. If needed, it will adjust the employed actions so as to ensure the gap is decreasing rather than increasing, then repeating the process over and over again.

Finally, the gap is closed, you have reached your destination, the goal has been achieved, and the doing mode is ready to take on the next task.

This strategy offers us a very general approach for attaining our goals and solving our problems: if there is something you want to happen, you focus on narrowing the gap between your idea of where you are and your idea of where you want to be—and, by the same token, if there is something you don't want to happen, you focus on increasing the gap between your idea of where you are and your idea of what you want to avoid. This doing mode of mind not only enables you to manage the routine details of your daily life, but also underlies some of the most awe-inspiring accomplishments of the human species in transforming the external world—from the construction of the pyramids and skyscrapers, to putting a man on the moon. All these achievements require exquisite and elegant problem-solving. Hence, we can suppose that it would be quite natural that the same mental strategies would be recruited when you want to transform your interior world—in other words, to change yourself so that you can attain happiness, or get rid of unhappiness. Unfortunately, this is where things can start to go horribly wrong.

Imagine yourself walking along a path by a river on a sunny day. You are feeling a little down; a little out-of-sorts. At first, you're not really aware of your mood, but then you realize that you don't feel happy. You are also aware that the sun is shining. You think, It's a lovely day; I should be felling happy.

Let that thought sink in: I should be feeling happy.

How do you feel now? If you feel worse, you are not alone: virtually everyone reports the same response. Why? Because, in the case of Olivia's moods, the very act of focusing on the gap—comparing how she currently felt with how she wanted to feel (or how she thinks she should feel)—made her feel even more unhappy, taking her even further away from how she wanted to be. Focusing on the gap in this way is actually a reflection of the mind's habitual strategy for trying to sort out situations in which things are not as it wants them to be.

Focusing on the mismatch between her idea of the person she wanted to be and her idea of the person she saw herself as made her feel worse than she had been in the first place—and all this is is the doing mode's attempts to help. It uses mental time travel to "help", calling up past times when she may have felt like this in an effort to understand what went wrong, and imagining a future, blighted by unhappiness, to remind her that this was what she desperately needed to avoid. The memories of previous failures, combined with the images of feared future scenarios, add their own twist to spiral of worsening mood: the more she had suffered from low moods in the past, the more negative the images and self-talk unlocked by her present mood were—and the more her mind felt dominated by these old patterns. Hence, this only heightens the familiarity felt surrounding such patterns worthlessness or loneliness—which makes the mind feel it is going down an old mental groove. She took these feelings of familiarity to mean that her low feelings must be a true reflection of her character, and that was why she couldn't snap out of it. However, the truth of the matter is that she couldn't let go simply because the doing mode of her mind insisted that her highest priority was to sort herself out by identifying and solving this "problem". Thus, she hammered herself with more questions: why do I always react this way? Why can't I handle this better? Why do I have problems other people don't have? What am I doing to deserve this?

You may think of this self-focused, self-critical frame of mind as brooding—something psychologists also call rumination. When Olivia ruminated, she became fruitlessly preoccupied with the fact that she was unhappy, as well as with the supposed causes, meanings, and consequences of her unhappiness. Research suggests that if you have tended to react to your sad or depressed moods in these ways in the past, then you are likely to find the same strategy volunteering to "help" again and again when your mood starts to slide—and, of course, every time, it will have the same effect, as demonstrated by Olivia's getting stuck in the very mood from which she was trying to escape. As a consequence, she was at an even higher risk of experiencing repeated bouts of unhappiness.

Why, then, did Olivia keep ruminating? Why did she continue to dwell on thoughts about her unhappiness, when this just seemed to make things worse? When researchers asked people who ruminated a lot why they did it, a simple answer emerged: they do it because they believe it will help them overcome their unhappiness and depression, believing that not doing it will make their condition worse and worse.

Olivia ruminated when she felt low because she believed it would reveal a way to solve her problems—when on the contrary, research shows that rumination does exactly the opposite: Olivia's ability to solve problems actually deteriorated markedly during rumination. Indeed, all the evidence seems to point towards the stark truth that rumination is part of the problem—not part of the solution.

Imagine a car trip, during which every time you check to see how close you are to your destination, you find that the car has moved farther away from it. This is tantamount to what happens in the interior world of emotions and feelings when Olivia employed the doing mode of mind. This is was why she often found herself saying things like, "I do not know why I feel so depressed; I have got nothing to be depressed about," and then discovering that she felt even more unhappy: she had checked her destination of feeling happy, and found herself to be even farther away from it. She couldn't seem to stop reminding herself how bad she felt.

Rumination invariably backfires—as we can see in the fact that it merely compounded Olivia's misery. It was a heroic attempt to solve a problem that it was just not capable of solving. Indeed, it is another mode of mind altogether that is required when it comes to dealing with unhappiness: awareness.

In a sense, we are all somewhat familiar with this alternative capacity of ours—it's just that the doing mode of mind has eclipsed it. This capacity does not work by critical thinking, but through awareness itself. We call it the being mode of mind.

You don't only think about things; you also experience them directly through your senses. You are capable of directly sensing and responding to things like cars and tulips, and you can also be aware of yourself experiencing such experiences. You have intuitions about things and feelings; you can come to know things not only with the head, but also with the heart and with the senses. Furthermore, you can be aware of yourself thinking, and so thinking is not all there is to conscious experience. The being mode is an entirely different way of knowing from the thinking of doing mode—not necessarily a better, just different. This mode of mind, however, gives you a whole other way of living yourself and of relating to your emotions, stress, thoughts, and body—and it is a capacity that you already have, having just been a little neglected and underdeveloped.

The being mode is the antidote to the problems that the doing mode of mind creates.

MINDFULNESS

MINDFULNESS IS THE AWARENESS that emerges through actively paying attention, in the present moment and non-judgmentally, to things as they are—to anything, but especially to those aspects of life that you most take for granted or ignore. For instance, you may start paying attention to the basic components of experience, like how you feel, what is on your mind, and how you perceive or know anything at all. Mindfulness means paying attention to things as they actually are in any given moment, rather than as how you want them to be. It is the exact antithesis to the type of ruminative thinking that causes low moods to persist and return.

Mindfulness is intentional; when you are cultivating mindfulness, you can be more aware of present reality and the choices available to you. You can act with awareness, whilst rumination is an often-automatic reaction to whatever triggers you—tantamount to unawareness (being lost in thought).

Mindfulness is experiential, focusing directly on present-moment experience. By contrast, when you ruminate, your mind is preoccupied with thoughts and abstractions that are far away from direct sensory experience, propelling your thoughts into the past or into an imagined future.

Mindfulness is non-judgmental; its virtue is that it allows you to see things as they actually are in the present moment, and to allow them to be as they already are. By contrast, judging and evaluating are integral to rumination, as well as the entire doing mode of the mind; judgments of any sort (good or bad, right or wrong) imply that you—or the things around you—have to measure up in some way to an internal or external standard. This habit of judging yourself severely disguises itself as an attempt to help you to live better life and to become a better person—when in actuality, the habit of judging leads to irrational tyranny that can never be satisfied.

By cultivating mindfulness, you can become aware of the intricate interconnections between external events, your feelings, your thoughts, and your behavior—which, in turn, can allow you to take more and more notice of the ways in which you can trigger other emotions—and, thus, the entire depressive spiral. You may no longer repeatedly feel quite so stuck in a seemingly never-ending depression, since you now have new and wiser ways to relate to your experience in the present moment; indeed, you may even find a way to be kind to yourself in such times that you feel at your most vulnerable—and this, in turn, may increase your enthusiasm for taking up new interests and making new friends.

Practicing mindfulness is more than just noticing things around you that you had not noticed before; it is learning to become aware of the particular mode of mind that gets you stuck in the first place. You have to acquire the practical skills that will allow you to disengage from such a mode when it is not serving you, and shifting to an alternative mode of mind that will not get you stuck. With an increasing ability to sustain mindfulness, you can explore what happens when your emotions are allowed to come and go in awareness, with a non-judgmental attitude and self-compassion. Such practice of mindfulness teaches you to shift into the being mode of mind, so that you can be more at peace with your emotions; after all, your emotions are not the enemy, but messages that reconnect you, in the most basic and intimate of ways, with the adventure and experience of being alive.

Awareness—also known as mindfulness—is much more than paying attention more thoroughly; it is paying attention differently—changing how we pay attention.

If asked, the majority of us would probably say we already pay attention; we have to, just to get everything done we need to. Similarly, if we have been chronically unhappy, we may also feel that we already far too self-aware—at least in terms of the pain we feel when we are at our lowest. However, the kind of attention the majority of us customarily pay—particularly when depressed—is attention via tunnel vision, only being aimed at a problem to be solved. Everything that the mind tells us that is irrelevant to the problem at hand tends to drop out our field of vision. However, through mindfulness, we can experience a moment of life that will not drag us somewhere we were not going in the first place. Mindfulness can free us from the trap of rumination and endless "doing" that only imprisons us in further unhappiness and depression; it is a way of shifting from doing to being so that we take in all the information that an experience offers us before we act. Being mindful means the complete suspension of judgment and the setting aside of any goals for the immediate future, and instead taking in the present moment—as it is, rather than as you would like it to be. This means that you can approach situations with openness, even if you notice that they bring feelings such as fear. Being mindful means intentionally turning off the autopilot mode in which you spend so much time brooding about the past or worrying about the future, instead tuning into things as they are in the present, with full awareness. It means acknowledging your thoughts as mere passing mental events—not reality itself—, as well as the fact that you are more in touch with life as it is when you allow yourself to experience things through the body and your senses, rather than mostly through your unexamined and habitual thoughts.

If we can be present for experience—with it and during it—, we could bring to that mood a mind that is ready to experience just that moment, with no presuppositions or assumptions about it whatsoever. Eventually, it may be that you reach a point where every moment of sadness is no longer experienced as a supposition that this means your whole life is going badly, but just as a fleeting moment of sadness. This shift in and of itself will not necessarily make you feel better. but it may very well send you down a different path to the one that does not lead so inexorably to depression.

During such a mental state, you can easily forget that you are in the present, since your mind begins travelling down the road of the past, or future situations. This leads to you becoming absorbed within such ideas, as if you were actually there, often reliving remembered emotions or pre-lived, anticipated ones. In this way, not only do you remove yourself from the only reality that you can directly experience—the here and now—, but you also suffer the agonies of events that are either long past or may never actually happen. No wonder you can end up feeling worse than you started out.

In the being mode of mind, you learn you can inhabit the present with a sense of spaciousness; there is no place else you need to be in this very moment, and nothing to do other than what is required in this moment. Your mind can thus be trained to be dedicated exclusively to the awareness of now, allowing you to be fully present in what life offers you in each moment. This does not mean that you are forbidden from thinking about the past or planning for the future; it only means that when you do think about them, you're aware that you are doing so.

The tremendous power of the mind to think about things allows you to solve problems mentally before you actually put the solutions into action, enabling you to plan, imagine, and write novels. The difficulty occurs when you confuse the thoughts about things with the things themselves; thoughts inherently involve interpretations and judgments, which are not in themselves facts, but merely more thoughts.

The fact that you can be thinking about an imaginary chair in your mind and know that it is not the same as the chair in which you are seated in the living room is relatively easy to grasp—but when the mind brings up ideas of things that are not physically tangible to begin with (e.g., your worth as individual), the distinction can be much harder to see. Ideas about your own self-worth are no more real than thoughts about an imaginary chair; however, if you switch to the being mode through mindfulness in this moment, you can see this much more clearly, learning to observe your thoughts—and your feelings, for that matter—as experiences that come and go in the mind. Just as the sound of a car on the street outside passes, and the sight of a bird in the sky is momentary, the thoughts that come to you are mental events that naturally arise, stay for a while, and then fade on their own accord.

This ever-so simple yet challenging shift in the way in which you relate to thoughts releases you from their control; for when you have thoughts such as, This unhappiness will always be with me, or, I am an unlovable person, you don't have to take them as realities. When you do, you succumb to an endless struggle with them. The reality is that these ideas are mental events, akin to weather patterns your mind generates for whatever reason in that particular moment. If you can see and accept them in this way (through mindful awareness), you may eventually gain some insight into when and how they appear; in the meantime, however, you certainly do not have to treat them as tyrants to be toppled.

Unawareness pervades your life, eating being a prime example: despite the fact it engages all your senses, you eat with almost no awareness. It is possible to go for weeks on end, eating several times each day, and never even tasting your food; you may be eating and talking, eating and reading, or simply eating while thinking of other things. You are fully entangled in your stream of thoughts unrelated to eating. Dieticians have suggested that eating in this way is one reason behind why some of us end up overweight: we pay no attention to the body's signals of satiation. In the same way as this, the patterns of the mind that get you stuck in unhappiness and depression are old, overlearned habits that get dredged up from your memory and take control when you are not fully awake and present. You have passed the reins over to the autopilot aspect of your mind, creating the conditions in which these subconscious mechanisms can operate freely.

We have all been on autopilot at some point in our everyday situations, and this often takes us where we had not planned to go. Let's say you have to deviate from your usual route home to deliver a package; what then happens if you drive an autopilot—daydreaming, problem-solving, and ruminating? It is quite likely you will find you still have the package in the car when you get home: whilst your mind was elsewhere, the older habit of following the well-worn route home took control. You have probably laughed in the past when you have discovered your grocery bag is filled with everything but the item you went out to get, or when you have found yourself repeatedly dialing a number that changed some time ago.

Awareness keeps the old habits favored by the automatic pilot from having the final say in determining your behavior, even enabling you to spot them on the horizon and recognize them for what they are. Ultimately, you may even be able to view your ruminative thought patterns with the same detached, self-compassionate amusement with which you view the lapses that make you forget that not to dial a changed phone number, that your best friend has moved, or that you went shopping because you needed something different than what you ended up buying. In doing mode, your mind is so often preoccupied with thoughts about what is going on that you may be only vaguely aware of what is actually happening in the present moment; whilst by contrast, the being mode is characterized by an awareness of the immediate, sensory experience of the present: you are in direct contact with life in each moment. This fresh, direct intimacy with your experience is accompanied by an entirely different way of knowing—an implicit, intuitive, nonconceptual, direct knowing of what is unfolding as it is unfolding; a knowing of what you are doing as you are doing it.

Without this awareness, you are stuck in a groove that grows deeper and deeper the longer you tread that path. Your automatic thought patterns take you down the same road over and over, and you respond with the same actions—which, of course, bring about the same worsening feelings. This leads to every part of the anatomy of depression triggering the others and the whole. A lack of awareness in this regard blinds you to other possibilities—and to change in general.

When you are interrupted and given the task of responding to a question that requires some problem-solving, you instantly lock onto the goal of solving the problem, the mind (in doing mode) selecting only the information that is immediately relevant to attaining that goal. Without being conscious of doing it at all, you screen out much of what is available to your senses—even to the extent of not noticing the person to whom you may have been speaking to. Psychologists call this change blindness.

Further, doing mode narrows your attention to the issues it is preoccupied with, creating a veil of ideas that ordinarily keeps you out of touch with direct experience. When you eat whilst in doing mode, the majority of your attention is absorbed in, or colored by, thinking that is related to achieving the goals set by the unfinished business you seem to carry around with you all the time in the background of the mind: daydreaming; planning; problem-solving; rehashing; rehearsing. From the narrow goal focus of doing mode, the sights, smells, sensations, and tastes of eating are simply irrelevant—and, for that reason, are given only scant attention. Indeed, most of us are unaware of how much of life we miss as a consequence.

You mortgage your present moments for some future promise; for example, when you are completing the household chores whilst in doing mode, you want to get them done as soon as possible so you can get onto the next activity—although chances are that you are also preoccupied with other things, so you don't give the chores at hand your full attention. Perhaps you are hoping to have an hour to yourself with your friends; or perhaps you are thinking about having a cup of coffee, and how relaxing that will be. If you then come across a dirty pot that you somehow missed (or, even, worse, someone else finds a dirty pot that you have missed), you may feel irritated, since the offending pot has temporarily thwarted your desire to get finished as quickly as possible. Finally, even when you do finish and, say, go out with your friends, your mind (when in doing mode) still remains to be preoccupied with its various plans and goals—meaning it is very likely that you are already thinking of the next task you have to do (e.g., business calls; paying the bills; getting back to work).

In this way—little by little, moment by moment—, life can slip by without you being fully aware of it; always preoccupied with getting somewhere else, you are hardly ever where you actually are, and attentive to what is actually unfolding in this moment. You imagine you will be happy only when you get somewhere else—wherever and whenever that may be—, as then, you will have "time to relax and enjoy". Hence, you postpone your happiness, rather than opening to the quality of the experience you are having right now. As a consequence, you may miss the quality of the unfolding moments in your day, just as you missed doing the dirty pots—and, if you are not careful, you may actually miss most of your life in this way.

The doing mode of the mind is all about reaching preset goals by focusing on the gap between your ideas of where you are now and your ideas of where you want to be; by contrast, the being mode is not concerned with the gap between how things are and how you want them to be. In principle, there is no attachment to achieving any goal at all, and this non-striving orientation in itself helps to release you from the narrow-goal focus of the doing mode. It also has two very important further implications.

First, in the being mode, there is no need for constant monitoring and evaluation to see whether the state of the world is approximating to your idea of the goal state you have set—which is reflected in the non-judgmental, accepting quality of the way that you pay attention. In the being mode, however, you find you can stop evaluating your experience in terms of how it "should" or "ought" to be, of whether it is "correct" or "incorrect," of whether it is "good enough" or "not good enough," or of whether you are "succeeding" or "failing"—or even of in terms of whether you are "feeling good" or "feeling bad." Each present moment can be embraced as it is, in its full depth, width, and richness, without a "hidden agenda" constantly judging how far your world falls short of your ideas of how you need it to be. What a relief!

Saying this, it is very important to be clear that when you let go of constantly evaluating your experience in this way, you are not left to float—rudderless, without any purpose or aim to your actions; of course, you can still act with intention and direction. Compulsive, habitual, and unconscious doing is not the only source of motivation available to you, for we can also take action in the being mode—the difference is that we are no longer so narrowly focused on (or attached to) our concepts around our goals. This means that you may not be quite as upset or as paralyzed when reality does not conform to your expectations or to the goals you have conceptualized—whatever they may be. Alternatively, you may in some moments be very upset, and perhaps even paralyzed—yet by allowing your awareness to include even those feelings, that very gesture of awareness brings with it new degrees of freedom that allow you to be with things as they are (including how upset you are feeling), without having to have them be different from how they actually are in this moment.

Secondly, when you shift to the being mode, you may no longer experience the entire range of unpleasant feelings and emotions that are automatically generated whenever you focus on the discrepancy between how you are feeling and how you want to feel in the same way. This is because the shift in your awareness that occurs can, with one stroke, cut through the source of much of the additional unhappiness you experience when you are "making extra" by becoming unhappy about your unhappiness, fearful of your fear, angry with your anger, or frustrated with the failure of your attempts to think your way out of your suffering. In this way, you remove one of the primary sources fueling the escalating cycles of dissatisfaction and depression to which you may be vulnerable: you allow yourself to no longer be so constantly concerned with what is wrong with your experience. Instead, you can open to the possibility of feeling a greater sense of harmony and at-oneness, with yourself and the world.

Peace can only exist in the present moment. It is ridiculous to say, "Wait until I finish this; then I will be free to live in peace." What is "this"? A diploma, a job, a house, the payment of debt? If you think that way, peace will never come; there is always another "this" that will follow the present one. If you are not living in peace at this very moment, you will never be able to. Thus, if you truly want to be at peace, you must be at peace right now; otherwise, there is only the hope of peace "someday".

You have been taught that setting goals and working toward them is the way to get where you want to go: to a place of happiness. Hence, it may be difficult to believe that it is the not clinging to goals—even highly worthy goals—that may be the core way out of unhappiness, since these can easily lead you into a downward spiral of rumination and depression. Perhaps now you can see how the non-striving orientation of mindfulness may help you avoid that trap altogether, allowing you to refrain from judging and condemning your moods and trying to escape from emotions you do not want to be feeling. As a result, you can "pull the plug" on the habit of depressive rumination, giving yourself the chance to free yourself from its relentless pull.

The quality of mindfulness is not a neutral or blank presence; true mindfulness is imbued with warmth, compassion, and interest. In light of this engaged attention, you discover it is impossible to have or fear anything or anyone you truly understand. Indeed, the nature of mindfulness is engagement: where there is interest, a natural, unforced attention follows.

Non-striving does not mean floating around without a rudder; rather, it means broadening your focus beyond what is needed to reach a particular goal. It also means that, instead of triggering fervent efforts to reject the "unacceptable" emotions that pass through you, you meet them with a sense of acceptance. Saying this, mindfulness is hardly a passive resignation; it is a stance by which you intentionally welcome and turn towards whatever arises—including inner experiences that you would have normally fought or tried to escape from.

The openhearted approach to mindfulness provides an antidote to the instinctive avoidance that can fuel rumination; it provides a new way to relate to yourself and the world in the face of external threats and internal stress. By regaining intentional control of your attention, you can rescue yourself from becoming stuck in a cycle of unhappiness and depression.

BRINGING AWARENESS TO ROUTINE ACTIVITIES

ONE WAY TO PRACTICE being more mindful is to choose some routine activity that you do every day, resolving that each time you do it, you will bring a fresh quality of deliberate and gentle moment-to-moment awareness to the task or activity as best you can. Bringing awareness into these activities of daily living can make it much easier for you to recognize when you are operating in doing mode (on autopilot) and providing you with an instant alternative—namely, an opportunity to enter and dwell in the mode of being. In this way, knowing full well what you are doing while you are actually doing it.

When you stop trying to force pleasant feelings, they are freer to emerge on their own. When you stop trying to resist unpleasant feelings, you may find that they can drift away by themselves. When you stop trying to make something happen, a whole world of fresh and unanticipated experiences may become accessible to you.

Gently asking yourself, What is this? and actively living the experience when you encounter something unpleasant keeps the mind from leaping in with, I hate this; get me out of here!

You can cultivate an awareness of your feelings from a range of different angles: either pay attention to the moment and take note of what sensations arise, or take note of a particular pleasant/unpleasant feeling and pay attention to the thoughts, feelings, and sensations that accompany it.

Deliberately attracting attention to the difficulties you are facing with the hope that it will help you to get rid of it is more likely to, on the contrary, get you more stuck. Radical acceptance can keep you from becoming progressively constricted and diminished in the face of painful experiences; it invites you to fully experience the richness of life, even when things seem to be at their worst.

Your thinking will often reflect your mood and your mode of mind, not what is "actually" here or who you actually are. Thoughts are not facts.

Intellectualizing and analyzing does not work when a low mood has been triggered; remembering that thoughts are "just thoughts" is a wiser strategy. Clearly viewing our thoughts as mental events is particularly difficult when they are related to a painful event in the past, or when the brain tells you they are high-priority, unfinished business.

Sometimes, simply acknowledging what is actually going on—instead of dwelling on what "should" be happening—is all that is needed in order to transform your experience.

People often say that what they are all seeking is the "meaning" of life, but I believe they are mistaken; what they are really seeking is an experience that makes them feel they are still alive.

A little kindness and gentleness toward yourself is a wiser and more skillful response to feeling threatened than any amount of analytical problem solving.

Six steps for practicing Mindfulness throughout the day:
1. When possible, do just one thing at a time;
2. Pay full attention to what you are doing;
3. When your mind wanders from what you are doing, consciously bring it back to the task at hand;
4. Repeat the above step several billion times;
5. Investigate your distractions;
6. Aim to let go of happiness as a goal so as to pave the way for happiness to appear on its own.

ABOUT COMMUNICATION AS A REASON FOR MISUNDERSTANDING

From Peter's Diary:

THE WEDDING PARTY WAS already full when Olivia and I arrived. Inside the hall, Olivia looked at me, and, without even appearing to move her head and her lips, she said, "Look at that couple over there! The lady's dress is so inappropriate... She looks like a whore."

The flare of surprise in my eyes told all: she'd shocked the hell out of me. I turned my head to take a look. "Don't look now; she'll notice!" Olivia hissed. "You're so obvious, you piece of shit."

Olivia couldn't understand why I'd turned my head so indiscreetly and let myself look like a fool while staring at the couple. I, for one, couldn't believe that she was able to see the couple in the room—a fully packed room, at that—without even moving her head towards them—and even could speak to me without moving her lips. I was amazed at how quick she was in noticing such details just after five minutes of entering the wedding hall—and to also comment on them in that short a space of time.

I am amazed how after just five minutes, Olivia had given me an almost instantaneous commentary of everything in the hall—from the hall decorations, to the attendees' dresses—, while I had barely noticed the color of the groom's suit. Olivia couldn't believe how unobservant I was; she thought I was joking at first.

She became angry at me when I turned my head to take a look—when she'd asked me to! What had she expected me to do? I don't have eyes in the back of my head; I'm not an Indian Cobra. I didn't understand her logic, and quickly began to feel depressed; it was supposed to be a nice night, and here we were, already in the middle of a row.

Have you ever heard of a man asking his male friend to accompany him to the toilet? Even if you have, I'm sure you can attest that it rarely happens; everyone around them would be instantly suspicious... Correct?

"Hey, Catherine! I'm going to the toilet—come with me," Olivia said.

"Sure," came the addressee's instantaneous response.

"I'm coming with you," added Sue.

"Me, too," came Sandra's voice.

Sound familiar to you? Have you ever felt suspicious upon hearing such an exchange? Never, actually—but then again, you might ask yourself why four women go to the toilet, all together, at the same time; surely they didn't all suddenly decide they needed to piss at the same exact time?

The answer is obvious: when a man goes to the toilet, he usually goes for one single reason; however, women use toilets as social lounges and therapy rooms. Women who go to a toilet as strangers can come out as best friends. A woman in the toilet can talk about her shitty husband; her disastrous marriage life; her kids; her parents; her neighbors; her weight gain. She can even go to the toilet to cry! Countless topics could be discussed in the women's toilets, whereas for a man, a quick selfie is probably the most exotic thing they would do. Hence, it's of no surprise that women can stay in the toilet for half an hour at a time, whilst a man couldn't spend more than five minutes—well, unless they were gay, or doing drugs, but that's not our subject matter here.

I had been amazed at how Olivia hadn't noticed a red flashing oil light on her car dashboard for a full week—for so long that it caused a total motor breakdown. Meanwhile, she found it very easy indeed to detect Jennifer's hair—from one kilometer away—on my coat.

I'd always asked myself why Olivia could always find my missing car keys that were under the couch, hidden under the carpet, in the living room, but could rarely find the most direct route to her destination. I also wondered how Olivia could detect a cat crossing the street—again, from a kilometer away—and respond swiftly by slowing down the car speed, whilst this same woman hit the wall while trying to park her car.

We've had countless conversations taking the following format:

Olivia: Darling, what should I wear with this dress: the gold or blue shoes?

Me: Hmmm... Whichever you like, sweetie.

Olivia: Come on, Peter. Which one looks better? I need your opinion.

Me: The gold ones.

Olivia: What's wrong with the blue? You've never liked them. I paid a fortune for them, and now you tell me that you don't like them!

What the hell did this woman want? If she didn't want my opinion, why the hell did she ask for it?

After many occasions of trial-and-error, I came up with several insights: such a conversation is a typical trait of women, and these kinds of question are traps. Never fall for them. Instead, remember: she has already decided which shoes she was going to wear; consequently, she didn't want another opinion on it, but wanted confirmation that she looks beautiful; thus, her question was, in the main, to give her the kind of answer that she wanted to hear—which doesn't even always have to have anything to do with choosing which shoes to wear.

Yes, my poor friend; that's the truth.

Hence, when faced with such questions, never give an answer; instead, your answer should be in the form of another question, following a format similar to this:

You: Have you chosen a pair? You're the most beautiful woman on the planet; you'll have picked something perfect.

Her: No, not really... I'm lost.

Don't believe her; this is another trap.

You: But I can see that you're swaying more towards the gold ones. Have you chosen them?

Her: Well... I think I could possibly wear the blue shoes.

You: Why the blue?

Her: Because I'm wearing red accessories and a white dress, so the blue goes well with them.

You: Wow, what a hell of a choice. You look fabulous, darling; you'll easily be the most beautiful lady in the party. I love the blue.

And that, my friend, is a job well done.

From Olivia's Diary:

I am bewildered by Peter: he is an expert in parking his car in a tight spot without even using the rear-view mirror, but can never even find my G-spot!

When Peter stops his car to read a street sign, what's the first thing he does with his radio? He turns it down! Why on earth is this the case? I can read while listening and talking; I can drive while my babies are playing in the back of the car; I can text while driving while monitoring my kids, plying and crying in the back of the car.

So, why can't he hear what I just told him? He prefers watching the match over answering my questions. I truly believe that if I could take a brain scan of Peter's head while he's watching TV, or listening to music, or reading the newspaper, I'd find that he's virtually deaf; his concentration is always wholly absorbed in the task he's engaged in—not with what I said. Because of this, he almost never hears what I have to say; he'd hear my voice in general, but wouldn't register my words.

The "Modes of Thinking" Concept: People choose between two ways of coming to conclusions or judgments; by thinking—which uses an impersonal process of logic—and feeling—whereby what something means to them is decided. Trusting their own way, the thinkers consider the feelers to be irrational and subjective, whilst the feelers wonder how the thinkers can possibly be objective about the things that matter to them—so cold and impersonal.

IN A WOMAN'S WORLD of higher perceptiveness, Olivia expected Peter to read her verbal, vocal, and body language signals and, in turn, to anticipate her needs—just as another woman would. However, for evolutionary reasons, this simply wasn't the case: Olivia assumed Peter would know what she wanted or needed, and, when he didn't pick up on her cues, she accused him of being "insensitive". Meanwhile, men everywhere can be heard screaming, "Am I supposed to be a mind reader?"

Peter was a poor mind reader, and Olivia didn't understand that: men need evidence, clear, specific cues, specific words, specific actions, and a very clear-cut communication system—not the kind of read-between-the-lines communication system preferred by most women.

In the past, the concept of communication styles concerned how people communicate; however, with the emergence of the modern societies, complications in marriages, and the rise of divorce rate across almost all societies, this area has become more focused on how men and women communicate, separately. It became crucial not only to study how each gender communicates, but also for each gender to recognize and acknowledge these key differences in communication styles, and to act toward one another with these differences in mind.

Several factors contribute to such differences, including: the natural brain-wiring system; relative power in a relationship; stereotypical value systems; language skills; and the use of communication.

Power differences play out within interpersonal communication on two levels: the type of communication between equals (or symmetrical interactions), and the type of communication between non-equals (or complementary interactions). Healthy relationships are those in which the participants are able to move freely between complementary and symmetrical interactions, depending on the demands of the situation.

Peter and Olivia should have been able to nurture one another during times of adversity; neither should have been frozen into either a protector/savior posture or a protected/saved posture; likewise, when a conflict of interest occurs, each partner should feel comfortable in engaging in negotiations with the other. Thus, unhealthy relationships then are those in which a healthy conflict is not possible.

Traditionally, men have possessed far greater political, socioeconomic, and physical power than women, whilst women usually have more relationship and communication skills due to their position as the dependent and subservient gender. During power imbalances, communication problems occur: a woman that fears physical/financial retaliation will be reluctant to engage in symmetrical interactions, instead being likely to resort to a more indirect communication style. Meanwhile, men—socialized to view dominance and leadership as the main characteristics of their duties—may feel distressed when women interact symmetrically and get too pushy, and may feel the need to "keep her in her place".

A woman's more effective communication skills and "relationship power" also creates communication problems: in situations requiring interpersonal relationship skills (e.g., nurturing children; dealing with extended family), men typically defer to women, putting themselves in a one-down position. However, when it comes to the critical area of the relationship's maintenance, men often feel threatened by the woman's greater verbal skills and ability to identify affective states.

Men are more physiologically reactive to stressful stimuli than women are, and so Peter frequently avoided emotional conflict—or, in many cases, tried to suppress any pressures to communicate by exerting his superior physical and financial power. Peter's avoidance of intimate communication likely came about as a result of his greater arousal and subjective discomfort in the face of interpersonal conflict.

In a similar vein, authenticity and appropriate self-disclosure enhance interpersonal communication—and, thus, it is logical to conclude that the communication that occurs between men and women should be characterized by abundant sharing about differences in backgrounds and experiences, as well as by efforts to describe accurately gender-based reactions to all situations. Unfortunately, this is nearly the opposite of what actually happens most of the time.

Peter was taught that he was not supposed to share with Olivia—or even with other men—his innermost thoughts and feelings, since Olivia then would either see him as weak and reject him, or misunderstand and criticize him. Therefore, men and women often hide their private lives from each other due to these gender role pressures.

Hence, a man facing a devastating personal loss is trained to believe that masculinity requires him to be as strong as possible, eliciting only emotionless reactions. Therefore, Peter neither communicated his pain to

Olivia, nor was he able to explain why he was emotionally constricted. Likewise, a woman who sees nurturing, caretaking, and self-sacrifice as an integral part of her femininity will have great difficulty in acknowledging the part of herself that is enraged by the need to care for a husband with a debilitating illness.

Olivia couldn't understand that Peter's brain differed so much from hers. His brain was configured to concentrate on one specific, dedicated task at any one time due to the fewer connecting fibers between his left and right hemispheres.

It is of no doubt that females are equipped with far more finely tuned sensory skills than men—and, because she is the child-bearer and nest-defender, she also requires the ability to sense subtle changes in mood and attitude in others—colloquially referred to as the "female intuition". Hence, it is no wonder that, for Olivia, it had been obvious when her sister was upset or feeling hurt—whilst for Peter, generally speaking, he had to physically witness tears or an obvious bad temper before he would even have a clue anything was going on with Olivia.

Therefore, in order to safeguard her family's survival, the nest-defender needed to be able to take notice of the small changes in the behavior of Peter and her kids that could signal pain, hunger, sickness, depression, or injury—whilst Peter, on the contrary, was weak in reading non-verbal signals, and was also weaker than Olivia in his interpersonal communication skills.

Research involving fMRI scans suggest that in a man's resting state, around 70% of the brain's electrical activity is shut down; meanwhile, for a woman's brain in a state of rest, 90% of her mind is still active—which confirms that women are constantly receiving and analyzing information from their surroundings.

These are just a few examples of many that you may have experienced and noticed throughout your life with women.

Still, the answer to all these wonders is very simple: men and women are fundamentally different—not for the better or the worst, but just different. They live in different worlds, living by different values and sets of rules. You may need to take into consideration that the word "different" has a meaning that is very distant from the word "equal": men and women are equal, but they are different.

Men and women should be equal regarding their opportunities to exercise their full potential in life, but they are definitely not identical in their innate abilities; therefore, whilst the question of whether men and women are equal is a political and moral one, whether they are identical is a scientific one. Hence, we can say they are different (and thus not identical) by nature. Men and women have evolved differently—because they had to. In order for them to excel in the duties they were created for, God granted them different physical and mental abilities that suit their specific role—which are, again, not better or worse, but different.

Whilst men hunted, women gathered; and whilst men protected, women nurtured. As a result, their bodies and brains are completely different—the former being physically adapted to their specific functions in the same way as their brains. Men tend to be taller and stronger than women, whilst women tend to have brains that are more detail-oriented than those of men in order to fulfil her caring and nurturing role.

It took the world 100 million years to evolve into a society sophisticated enough to put a man on the moon, but he still has to go the toilet—just the same as his primitive ancestors—whilst doing so. Therefore, whilst people may indeed look a little different from one culture to another, underneath, their biological needs and urges are the same: an Australian woman's biological are the same the Egyptian or Malaysian woman—and the same goes for men.

More than 90% of male and female genetic coding is exactly the same; out of the 30,000 genes in the human genome, variations between the sexes are few and far between. However, those few differences influence every single cell in our bodies—from the nerves that register pleasure and pain, to the neurons that transmit perception, thoughts, feelings, and emotions.

Thus, many researchers attribute the differences in personality between males and females to the "social conditioning" factor, rather than the "natural brain-wiring system" factor. Thus, characteristics such as being nurturing, verbally expressive, emotional, and cooperative are attributed to females more than they are to males—whilst characteristics such as competitiveness, aggression, assertiveness, and logic are all attributed to males more than they are to females.

Although we can agree that social conditioning wields a significant impact on gender personality characteristics, this impact is limited to the moderating role of reinforcing and deepening such differences in personality characteristics. This means that the natural brain-wiring system is the primary cause of gender differences, whilst social conditioning helps to reinforce and, sometimes, deepen, these differences.

Unfortunately, gender socialization only encourages personality characteristics that support the masculine principle for men and the feminine principle for women—meaning that men and women who step outside such boundaries are often negatively perceived by society, and end up paying the price. Hence, gender socialization impacts the male/female relationship in general, and particularly in marriage.

Men and women often not only expect, but also demand at least one certain quota of gender-appropriate personality characteristics in their partners, anything otherwise posing the risk of a potential spouse being rejected on the grounds of them being unsuitable. Therefore, with the continuous development of modern society, men and women seem to be intuitively aware that they need to possess the full range of personality variables in order to live a satisfying life in such a society—either that, or that they need the attributes of the other gender in order to complement their own. In fact, men and women who require opposite-sex traits in their mates often become frustrated when the negative side of such attributes interfere with the realization of a satisfying relationship.

Generally speaking, women want men to protect them, as well as to be more emotional and compassionate; however, as is reinforced in military training, a pressuring work life, a depressing social environment, and ever-pressurizing economic situations, a man must completely eliminate his gentleness and soft emotions in order to act as the strong protector and gain his bread. He must not give in to fear, pain, or compassion; instead, he must be aggressive, place a high priority on physical strength or the use of weaponry, be action-oriented and decisive, and be able to exploit the weaknesses of his enemy and attack quickly. Saying this, when a man does not share his anxieties, fears, grief, and depression with his wife, she may feel shut out or distanced from him. This is exacerbated when he prefers to go out, isolate himself, disconnect, or even plunge in some other mental activities, rather than sit and chat with his wife.

Hence, when Peter provided a quick solution to a problem instead of providing Olivia with emotional support, she felt unheard; when he criticized the way she did something in an effort to problem-solve, she felt devalued; and when he got angry in response to what he perceived as an attack from her, she felt hopeless—and yet all of these characteristics are required for the protector role, and are constantly reinforced by social conditioning.

On the other hand, a man expects his wife to be his nurturer and his friend for life, supplying him with the emotional side that is undeveloped within him. In order for Olivia to do so, she should have been in-tune to emotions—both his and her own—, expressive (so that he would have felt appreciated), and accommodating (so he would feel supported). She should have drawn him out so he would have had permission to talk about the things deemed "unmanly", and she should have not criticized him or demanded too much from him, since it would hurt his ego. It often went that when she had wanted to talk about emotions, Peter would feel inadequate and confused; when she cried in the middle of an argument due to an inability to hold back her emotions, Peter felt stymied and manipulated.

When Olivia grew resentful and began to make digs towards Peter, he began to wonder why she did not simply say what she wanted in the first place. Whenever she'd insist on asking him what he was thinking or feeling, he would feel annoyed and want to be left alone; when she spoke to him in indirect ways about changes she'd like to see about him, he did not get the message, and would ultimately feel manipulated. However, once again, her actions were merely a result of her brain's wiring, reinforced by the social conditioning she had been subjected to over time, constantly telling her to be a "good wife".

Of course, not all men and women are programmed to behave in the ways we have described above—but there are enough to render therapy and court institutions fully booked!

THE MOUTH

WOMEN USE THEIR MOUTHS as an integral part of their communication system and processes with anybody—including men, for sure. Talking is the best talent a woman possesses, regardless of whether the content of their chatter has substance or not. For women, talking is a way to fill time, bridging the gap that silence creates between the moments. Women constantly feel the urge to talk; to express what goes on in their minds. It does not have to be a specific feeling that urges the woman to do so, but rather could just be a story/situation she's currently thinking about. She feels the urge to express these ideas, stories, and situations in the form of spoken words.

Since the creation of the universe, nature has constantly signaled to women that men don't listen to them—and yet all attempts always go in vain, simply because staying quiet is inherently against the female's natural building blocks. For females, the most efficient communication medium is the mouth—and yet females rarely realize that, as much as her mouth could indeed prove very efficient with her female counterparts, children, and mother, it never will with a male.

Hence, it's no wonder that Olivia's key complaints about Peter surrounded the fact he didn't talk to her much—particularly after their marriage. Still, females don't realize that, for males, the mouth plays a specific role—a goal the man wants to reach—, and, once this goal is reached and the mission is completed, the mouth is useless for the male. It is no wonder, then, that Peter used his mouth frequently during the dating period, but largely stopped once everything had been settled.

THE EARS

A S IS COMMON KNOWLEDGE, the ears are the other twin-organ to the female mouth in her communication system and processes: a woman can never talk and feel satisfied without getting back a response back, and so listening is clearly another talent women possess. An urge to talk automatically necessitates an urge to listen.

Have you ever noticed that the first attraction point in a male for any female are the words she listens to from him—even if those words are short and in brief? It took Peter just a few words to successfully seduce Olivia. However, females are not attracted to the male who talks too much: women's ears have the ability to sensor the male's false, intentionally manipulative talk from his real, and sincere talk—even if the latter are very short and brief. Females are able to detect when a male is talking too much and is thus being insincere in his words. Hence, the ears are an essential aspect of the communication process for females.

When women listen, the conversation enters from one ear and doesn't go out the other: the conversation remains in the mind, in a state of processing, analyzing, and digesting. Still, females don't realize that when a male listens, the words she speaks enter from one ear and go out instantly the other. It is no wonder, then, that Olivia didn't receive any response from Peter about what she had just talked about so often; she hadn't realized her words had already left Peter's brain, no processing having occurred. In a man's world, the ears are always in a state of filtration, whereby only important words remain in his brain.

Have you noticed how Olivia was able to remember every single detail, word, and facial expression of a conversation that had occurred ages ago? This is simply due to the fact that females are naturally talented in listening carefully—not because females have better memories than males, which is a complete myth. Rather, females are talented in listening, listening carefully and processing it so deeply that everything remains in her memory in a fresh condition, all to be retrieved when needed. Whilst one ear is for listening, the other serves as a concrete wall that does not permit the conversation to fly away.

On the contrary, have you ever noticed the number of males that don't remember the vast majority of the words said by a female? Again, this is not because males have a bad memory compared to that of females, but rather because the majority of female conversations does not remain in his brain, within seconds already flying away through the other ear. Hence, this is not at all about having a bad or a good memory.

Therefore, the female is way better at remembering everything her partner says, generally being better at processing words, analyzing conversations, and remembering details.

THE EYES

ALTHOUGH FEMALES USE THEIR eyes effectively, males are far better than females in this specific talent: sight.

Males don't use their mouths and ears as often as females; and so face minimal distraction from the many things to do and focus on; hence, they are able to focus more with their eyes—and this is putting aside the fact that females themselves already help males to use their eyes more than anything else with their physical looks.

You certainly know now why women tend to give optimal attention to their physical looks, the one who feels she is ugly or not physically fit feeling the urge to have plastic surgery, or always being keen to apply make-up before she goes out. So, does she do so because she wants to feel better about herself? Because she wants to take care of herself for her own self-satisfaction? The simple answer here is no; rather, these are the reasons feminists oftentimes try to convince themselves (and males) of.

Do you remember what had Olivia used to seduce Peter when he didn't give her any attention? Have you ever come across a woman who says, "I will seduce this man with my personality"? Of course personality is still important—but it comes second to her physical looks, simply because she is well-aware of the fact that the male uses his eyes better than anything else, and that this is just his weak point.

Again, personality is important for the male, but physical looks is the first point of contact with any female. Hence, whilst a female may focus on her personality, when it comes to attracting a man, it comes second on her priority list.

Have you ever heard of a male saying he wants to approach a specific female because he finds her to have a good personality—particularly during his first time ever seeing her? The answer is no; he first judges her looks and whether she is worth approaching on this basis, and then personality comes after, when he gets to know her. On the contrary, you may find a female saying she wants to approach a specific male because he seems to be funny, honest, strong, decisive, etc. In other words, she is not initially attracted to a male mainly by his looks. She may view him as smartest male she has ever come across, but she still will not be attracted to him, simply because she still does not know his personality. Hence, for a female, personality comes first, and looks come second. Of course, this does not mean that a male's looks do not count; rather, our point here is that his physical looks are not the first attraction point for a female.

Have you ever asked yourself why the most beautiful women date the most unsavory males—and oftentimes the unattractive ones, too? The reason for this becomes clear above: whilst the male in question may be unlikeable and unattractive, the female can see the parts of his personality she deems to be amazing. She finds in him the personality she needs, to the extent that she oftentimes ignores the most flawed aspects of his personality, only focusing on the characteristics she seeks that he possesses.

And now, is it really a surprise that females are easily deceived by the words of cruel males? Is it a surprise that they are deceived by the fake personality characteristics that some males show to them at first? Is it a surprise to you that the most beautiful women tend to date the most unsavory and unattractive of males?

THE TOUCH

"**D**ON'T TOUCH ME." THIS phrase is reminiscent of the woman that is emotionally cut-off or angry at a man—a phrase that has very little meaning to men, since the majority of the time these words are uttered, the husband hadn't tried to touch the woman at all!

Have you ever noticed that during female conversations, women are more likely to touch one another whilst talking—four to six times more often than a man is likely to touch another man?

Touch can be life-giving, and it is because of this that many "non-touching" cultures love cats and dogs; they allow them to experience touch via stroking and patting their pets.

The skin is the largest organ in the body, measuring at around two square meters. Distributed unevenly across it are 2,800,000 receptors of pain—200,000 for cold, and 500,000 for touch and pressure. From birth, girls are significantly more sensitive to touch than boys, and, as an adult, a woman's skin is at least ten times more sensitive to touch and pressure than a man's. Female skin is also thinner than male skin, and possesses an extra layer of fat below it for more warmth in winter, as well as to provide her with greater endurance.

The skin on a man's back, meanwhile, is four times thicker than his stomach skin—something left behind from his four-legged animal past, which offered him more protection from a rear attack whilst chasing food for his family. This could also explain why women tend to get more wrinkles than men: her skin is much thinner and more receptive than a man's skin.

Males require desensitized skin in order to run through the prickly bushes, wrestle animals, and fight enemies without pain slowing them down.

Have you ever wondered why the majority of the males are unlikely to be aware of an injury when they are focused on a physical task? Our answer to this lies in the hormone oxytocin, which stimulates the urge to be touched and fires up our touch receptors. It is, hence, no wonder that women with receptors that are ten times more sensitive than a man's attach so much importance on cuddling their men, children, and friends.

We have up to 10,000 taste receptors, all for detecting a least four major tastes: sweet and salt on the tip of the tongue; sour on the sides; and bitter at the back. Men score higher on discerning salt and bitter tastes, which is why they tend to favor beer; meanwhile, women are the superior in discerning between sweet and sugary tastes, which is why they tend to prefer chocolate.

Our evolutionary roles have equipped us with the biological skills and senses we require for basic survival—which is why women are simply better at picking up the small nuances in body language, vocal cues, tone of voice, and other sensory stimuli. They can also read attitudes and emotions in animals.

A woman's highly refined senses contribute significantly to the early maturity of adolescent girls; by the age of seventeen, the majority of girls can function as adults—whilst the boys are still lighting their own farts.

To conclude, it is not so much that women have super-senses; it is more that men's senses have been dulled, comparatively speaking.

THE SPEECH

HAVE YOU EVER ASKED yourself why the below examples take place?:

When males get together to watch a football game on TV, the only conversation that occurs tends to be something around, "Pass the chips", "Give me a cigarette", "Do you have a drink here?", and, "Let's order some food till the second half starts". Meanwhile, for a group of women, meeting up to a watch a TV program is usually just viewed as a chance to have a chat with one another. They will discuss everything in life that you could never imagine, and such a conversation could extend for hours after the program's conclusion.

Ask your daughter about the party she attended the week before, and you will be amazed at the articulate recitation of everything that happened there that day she provides—including all the mundane details.

Meanwhile, ask your son the same exact question about an event from this morning, and he will provide very little information besides, "Everything was good; it was a good gathering."

Again, no one is better or worse; males and females are just different.

For males, speech and language are not critical brain skills: they are inherent lunch-chasers—not communicators—, and the hunt was conducted with a series of non-verbal signals, the hunters often sitting for hours, silently watching for their prey, not talking or bonding with one another.

Have you ever noticed that fishing is not an activity typically preferred by women? Rather, it is viewed a male sport: you sit there for hours and say nothing—even if you have a group of friends fishing with you.

Males greatly enjoy one another's company, but they never feel the need to express this in words—yet if women were spending time together and not talking, it would be indicative of a major problem. This is why greeting cards were primarily invented for men, not women—particularly pre-written greeting cards. Men are not usually good with saying things or expressing their feelings in words, and so these cards are very crucial to men, since there is then less space for them to write. Buying a greeting card is never a problem for a man: it is what to write inside the card that embarrasses him.

This is also perhaps why flowers are a good escape for men to express their feelings towards a woman; for him, flowers would say it all.

For men, speech and language are not critical skills of theirs due to the nature of his responsibilities and duties, as explained above. This is why these two skills operate mainly in the left-brain hemisphere, with no specific location for them—and is also why men find it hard to find the words to say.

On the other hand, for women, speech has a specific known area, located primarily in the front-left hemisphere—alongside another location, which is a smaller, specific area in the right hemisphere. Therefore, having a specific location for speech on both sides of the brain makes women good conversationalists, leading to them enjoying it and engaging in lots of it. Further, considering they have their specific areas to control speech, the rest of the woman's brain is free and available for other tasks, enabling her to engage in other activities at once whilst talking. She also finds it very easy to find the right words and to express her emotions, since she has the specific location of speech in her brain—ready to retrieve the words.

Have you ever noticed that newborn babies can recognize their mother's voice, but not their father's? This is because babies were exposed to their mother's voice resonating throughout her body while he/she was still in the womb.

Further, because females possess a specific brain zone/location for speech and language, they are better at learning foreign languages, and are typically better at grammar, punctuation, and spelling.

For women, speech has a clear purpose: to build relationships and make friends. However, for men, to talk means to state the facts and relate them together.

Have you ever wondered how a woman can spend two weeks on vacation with her girlfriend, and yet when she returns, she'll phone the same girlfriend and talk for another two hours? How could that even be?

Men see the phone as a communication tool for relaying facts and information to other people, making sense of things, and exchanging porn clips; meanwhile, for women, this simply means an avenue for bonding. She could talk over the phone for two consecutive hours, talking complete nonsense, and yet that is the whole point: she is bonding with others.

Men cannot concentrate on watching TV and having a serious discussion at the same time; he would have to pick between one or another. This s why when Peter and Olivia were watching a movie together, he usually ended up telling her to be quiet; men can either talk or watch the screen, whilst Olivia felt the point of getting together was to have good time and develop relationships.

Indeed, Olivia couldn't understand why Peter oftentimes kept his thoughts to himself, remaining quiet the majority of the time as all of his thoughts occurred inwardly, in his mind. Because of this, Olivia would feel uninvolved and got embarrassed, since he didn't seem to want to initiate conversation the majority of the time.

When Peter was asked to solve a problem, he often responded by saying, "Leave it with me; I'll think it over and come back to you." True to his word, he would then think it over silently, not wanting interruptions. Indeed, men mainly talk within their own heads: they are not good with interruptions, as mentioned before, they don't have the verbal capability that women have to use words, instantly, for communication. This is why it is only when he has the answer that he will speak loudly in order to communicate the solution. In his mind, this time of silence gives him two advantages: to think quietly without interruptions; and to find the needed words to express the solution.

When Olivia witnessed Peter doing this, she assumed he was bored or idle, or did not love her, or did not like talking to her; hence, she would try to talk to him or give him something to do to keep him busy, and to lift him from his boredom. However, this often angered Peter: men cannot do more than one thing at once.

This is noticeable in men's "quiet" hangout, or "quiet" drink after work, as these are exactly what these appear to be: quiet. Therefore, if a man is dealing with another man, talking inside his head is not a problem; they can stay silent for long periods without speaking a word, and feel no offense.

However, when Peter sat with Olivia, she thought he was distant, arrogant, and simply did not want to join in.

When Peter sat with his friends and had an urge to go finish personal things, he'd say, "I've got some things to do. See you later, guys; I have to go."

In this same situation, Olivia would most probably have verbalized all her tasks aloud in a random order, mentioning most of the options, possibilities, and things to do. "I have got to pick up the kids from school... I want to go to the dry-cleaning... I have to call my mum... I still have to cook... and Nicole's mother called me today and wanted me to tell her to call her back because she called her at five o'clock and she didn't answer..."

This was one of the reasons why Peter accused Olivia of talking too much. However, this ensuing tension aggravated Olivia, since she perceived such sharing to be friendly; however, Peter clearly saw it differently, thinking that Olivia was handing him a list of problems and tasks she expected him to fix, share, or find a solution for. Hence, over the course of her little monologue, he had become anxious, upset or tried to tell her what to do.

This is mainly why the woman who impresses men in business— and in life in general—is the woman who keeps her thoughts inside her head and only talks about conclusions, facts, and solutions.

Meanwhile, the building of relationships through talk is a priority for women; the British Medical Association reported that women are four times more likely to suffer with jaw problems than men, a woman speaking a daily average of 20,000 words to relate messages, whilst a man speaks around 7,000.

This speech difference became apparent at the end of the day when Peter and Olivia sit down together for dinner: when Peter had completed his daily average of 7,000 words during the day, he had no desire to communicate anymore—whereas for Olivia, this depended solely on what she had been doing during the day. If she had spent the day talking with people and chatting with friends, she may have exhausted her daily quota of words and thus had little desire to say much more; however, if she had been at home with the children, she would have been lucky to have used 3,000 words at the most—and so would still have up to 15,000 words to go with Peter.

Therefore, Peter felt as though he was being interrogated and became annoyed; he just wanted to be left in peace. Thus, in attempt to avoid arguments concerning why he was not talking, he would start to ask Olivia, "How was your day?" From that point, she would go on to tell him every detail of her day, feeling the urge to vocalize all her unspoken words. He wanted to be quiet and just stare at the wall, and this aggravated Olivia, who started to feel ignored and resentful.

This is why when Peter remained silent, it was easy for Olivia to start feeling unloved; it is also why Olivia felt relieved and happy when she finished speaking. She most probably was not looking for solutions to what she'd said, but just didn't want to be interrupted until she finished her balance of unspoken words.

Talking about day-to-day problems is a common way for modern women cope with stress. The past generations of women, however, never felt this problem—probably because they always had lots of children and other women for conversation and support. On the other hand, the modern woman, who stays at home, is likely to feel isolated and lonely, their female neighbors at work. Working women, however, have less problems with their male partners who are not talking, since they have also been speaking to others during the day.

Generally speaking, men's sentences are shorter and more structured than women's, selecting words that are more specific and clearer to indicate what they mean. When Olivia discussed several subjects with Peter, he easily got lost: whilst men can only deal with one subject/idea at a time, women have a multi-tracking ability, possessing a greater flow of information between the left and right hemispheres, as well as specific brain locations for speech—these being the reasons behind why they can talk about several subjects simultaneously without being easily lost, like men. However, whilst this was an advantage for Olivia, it was frustrating for Peter, since his brain can only handle one subject at a time.

To be clearer about the multi-trackng ability of women, it is better to simplify it in this way: a woman may start talking about one subject, switch mid-sentence to another subject, and then, without any warning, revert back to the first subject with a little bit of something different in this same first subject. It is here that the man gets lost, for whilst he may well be in following her during her first switch between topics, he gets lost in the second switch back to the first topic.

Therefore, it is no surprise to find that the majority of secretaries are women. Indeed, in one study conducted in the UK, from the 716,148 secretaries surveyed, 99.1% were women—only 5,913 being men. Further, even in other fields (e.g., community work; counselling; talk-show programs), women are the majority. Hence, it becomes clear that wherever communication skills, multitasking, verbal prowess are required, women reign.

When a woman is speaking, her brain scan showcase that her front-left and right brain centers (which control speech) are both operating simultaneously with her hearing ability, and it is such a powerful multi-tracking capability that allows the woman to speak and listen simultaneously—and even to do both on several unrelated topics. On the other hand, men can either speak or listen—they cannot do both at once—, which is why men usually only interrupt one another if they are becoming competitive or aggressive.

"Stop interrupting me"—does that seem familiar to you? This sentence was always shouted by Peter at Olivia. A man's sentence is usually solution-oriented, and he needs to get to the point and to the end of the sentence very quickly; otherwise, the conversation would seem pointless and boring to him. Hence, if a man is trying to make a strong or forceful point, he usually uses the language itself(i.e., definitions; concepts; short words) in order to succinctly indicate what he wants to say.

It is well-known in the science of relationships between men and women that if a woman likes a man, agrees with what he is saying, or wants to get closer to him, she will talk to him a lot. Indeed, the opposite is also true for the opposing situation: if she wants to punish him or let him know that she does not like him, she won't talk. "I will never talk to you again" is a sentence many men will have heard many times before from women. Meanwhile, "Get to the point, please," is something more usually directed to women.

It would have been easier for Peter to overcome this point with Olivia if he had understood that indirect talk is part of Olivia's brain's wiring—as well as the fact that to build a healthy relationship with his wife, he needed to listen effectively. He did not need to volunteer solutions unless asked—or, if he wanted, he could have asked directly if she needed solutions.

On the other hand, Olivia needed to understand that Peter's brain was wired for logical conversation, and so that it was important to give him space and time before asking him to listen to her. This is so he could organize his mind—silence and shut down all the other problems he had on his mind—and make it available for her speech, rather than talking to him or asking him something while he was already busy, talking to someone else, or focusing on something important. Direct speech is typically employed by men in business, or in their work in general, and this is why he finds it difficult to follow or understand indirect speech.

It is important to reiterate that none of this is anyone's fault; unfortunately, this is just how modern life is. Old generations had fewer problems to do with things like thee, as each one played a clear role in their relationship dynamic; nowadays, however, we don't have role models for successful relationships. The new generation has the same problems, only now with no clue on how to overcome them—because, again, they don't have role models.

EXAGGERATIONS AND EMOTIONAL WORDS

F OR THE VAST MAJORITY of women, the precise definition of words is irrelevant during a conversation—and so because of this, they may use some emotional—or sometimes exaggerated—words, not meaning for the recipient to take what they say literally.

In Peter's diary, he indicated how angry he had been at Olivia's exaggerated comments:

- You never agree with anything I say;
- You always disagree with me;
- You rarely buy me flowers for our anniversary;
- You do the same act every day without consulting me;
- You only touch me when you want sex;
- Ever since I have known you, you haven't washed your dish after eating.

However, the frequency of such statements only grew—particularly when he had rows with Olivia.

For Peter, he interpreted Olivia's words to their actual meaning, and responded accordingly—and, when responding to such emotional, exaggerated words, Peter had always been defensive; while she would continue arguing with the same emotional words to fight him back, he would keep defining her words, leading to the argument escalating to the point of no return.

By the same token, Olivia should have learnt that she should argue logically with Peter, without any emotional or exaggerated words, if she wanted to continue a healthy and constructive conversation.

Females read the meaning of what is being said through vocal intonation and the speaker's body language; the female's face will mirror the emotions being expressed by the speaker. On the contrary, males remain impassive whilst listening. Brain scans reveal that men feel emotion just as strongly as women, but avoid showing it; the emotionless mask that men use while listening allows them to feel in control of the situation.

Studies have consistently shown that, in business, a female with a deeper voice is considered to be more intelligent, authoritative, and credible within the workplace. However, in an attempt to gain authority, some women mistakenly raise their voices, giving the impression that they are aggressive. Studies frequently show two interesting observations in this arena: that some women use the "girlie" voice to counteract the power of their male acquaintances' large body sizes, and others use it to encourage protective behavior in the men they like.

PART V: DIVORCE IS
THE BEGINNING OF ANOTHER
STORY

Divorce is about exchanging an old set of problems with a new, more complicated set of problems.

OLIVIA

"**D**AD, DAD! WE MISS you!"

"We won at soccer!"

"I got a medal in judo in summer camp!"

Peter picked Mark up and swung him around rapidly, releasing him suddenly into a giggling heap on the drive before hugging Glenda.

I left them to it; they didn't need me. It wasn't right to think of the children as my private property—but then again, that's what I'd been doing. I had to face the fact that they didn't belong to either me or Peter: they were our children, not our possessions.

I walked into the kitchen, flicked the kettle on automatically, and opened the washing machine door.

"How are you?"

Peter leaned against the jamb of the kitchen door, hands in his pockets, a relaxed expression on his pale face. He stared at me, blue eyes blank. Blast him. Here I was, hyped up and nervous over seeing him, and here he was, looking at me as if he didn't have a care in the world. The shirt he was wearing was definitely new—and obviously expensive. He hadn't been sitting home trawling through his wardrobe, looking for suitable things to wear: he'd been shopping with that bitch he hung out with.

"Fine," I answered curtly.

"You're looking well, anyway," he pressed on amiably. "Have you lost some weight?"

I allowed myself to smile at him. "I don't know; I've just been so busy. Maybe I have."

"It suits you."

His voice was admiring. What was he up to? Flattery wasn't going to get him anywhere.

"I hope you've figured out what to tell the children," I said, determined to burst his bubble.

"I have," he responded wryly. "I'm sorry you've had to deal with everything... I didn't want it to work out this way. You must understand that, Olivia."

Oh God, I was going to cry. I'd been fine until now.

"I don't want to talk about it, Peter," I said quickly, turning away and bending down to drag the washing out of the machine. "Make sure nobody gives them Coke before they go to bed, all right?" I couldn't bring myself to say Jennifer. "When will you bring them back?"

"Is six okay?"

"Fine."

I didn't turn around; I couldn't. I just wished he'd go out to the car and let me say goodbye to the children on my own.

"We have to talk sometime, Olivia," he said suddenly, bursting into my thoughts.

"I know, I know. Just not now."

He paused for a moment. "See you tomorrow, then. I'll leave my new cellphone number on the pad in case you need to contact me." I heard him rifling through the jam jar where I kept odds and ends, looking for a pen that worked. "I'll wait outside, Olivia. Bye."

I slammed the door of the washing machine viciously and straightened, turning to find the children waving at me from the back seat, not a shred of sadness on their happy, laughing faces. I waved just as happily, a grin superglued onto my face.

When they were gone, I felt my entire body sag miserably. Whatever would I do until Sunday at six?

"Have dinner with us!" Nicole was begging on the phone five minutes later.

"I'd love to," I said tearfully, glad Nicole hadn't dropped in to find me sobbing into a tea towel. I couldn't imagine being even vaguely hungry; plus, the last time I'd had dinner with friends, Peter had been by my side. Then again, anything was better than an evening on my own—an evening of remembering.

That night, I slept fitfully, awaking in a cold sweat at five past seven. I knew I'd never get back to sleep; punching the pillows didn't help. What this did mean was plenty of time to clean, polish, and hoover—

meaning the house would be spotless when the doorbell rang a little after six that evening.

At six—sharp—, I opened the door gratefully, and, as promised, the children exploded into the house, dragging their luggage after them like corpses.

Peter didn't come in, simply waving at me from the car.

"Darlings, I missed you so much," I said tearfully, hugging them both tightly. "How did you get on?" I asked as brightly as I could.

Please say she was a hideous old cow, a bitch, and that the house is a pit, I thought bitterly.

"Jennifer is really nice," announced Mark, with all the tact of a traffic warden. "She's got this great car—a Mercedes Benz S series!" He could hardly contain his excitement. "Black. And she's brilliant at fashion."

I felt about two feet tall—two feet tall, stupid, and ugly. Clearly not content enough with taking my husband, this bloody woman had managed to charm my children as well. What a pity I hadn't taught them to hate the cow!

"She can't cook, Mum," Glenda interjected loyally.

"Yeah, we're hungry." Mark threw open the fridge door and peered inside anxiously.

"I'll make you something," I said gently. "Tell me," I added, hesitating slightly as I tasted my words, "what is she like? What's the house like?"

The how-to-split-up-nicely books probably didn't recommend pumping your children for information on their father's new wife, but I just had to find out something. I at least won in cooking.

"She's got this great garage door that opens when you press this thing in the car," Mark said enthusiastically.

Yeah, it's called somebody else's husband, I thought sourly. "But is the house nice?"

"It's okay," he shrugged indifferently. "She's got a big telly."

Great. What do you expect from children who wouldn't notice dry rot if they saw it? I wanted hard facts: modernist or romantic? All muslin curtains and brass headboards or icy white sofas?

"How's Daddy?"

"He brought us to that fancy casual dinner restaurant and got us new video games. I said I missed him, but he won't come home," volunteered Mark.

Unconsciously, I stopped stirring my spoon. "What did you ask him?"

"I said we wanted him back, and he said you and him had rowed and decided to get divorced," Glenda said quickly, obviously repeating what she'd been told verbatim. "He said you didn't love each other anymore."

Mark looked up at me, big, blue eyes welling up with tears. I cursed Peter and his honesty; how the hell had he expected his children to understand what I couldn't?

I pulled Mark to me and held him tightly. His green sweatshirt smelled of Peter's aftershave, as well as another scent I couldn't identify—something heavy and cloying. Her perfume. The bitch's perfume.

"Why can't he come home, Mum?" Mark asked.

I had no answer to that one, but I tried anyway. "Daddy needs to be away for a while; not away from you, kids," I added hastily. "Away from me. Mums and dads who've been married a long time sometimes need to have a break, you know. Lots of people do it. It can be good for everyone." My voice caught; I couldn't help it. "People get very bored when they're stuck together forever. You wouldn't want to be friends with just Greg and no one else now, would you?"

"No, but that's different."

"Why is it?"

"We're boys. Boys don't stay with boys. They're just friends. Not like girls and boys."

"It's not that simple, Mark."

Mark gave me a hard, inquisitive stare—so like Peter's that I felt my jaw drop. "Why not?"

Ask your bloody father and his bitch! I wanted to yell.

"This isn't easy for any of us," I said instead. "But your dad and I have split up for a while. It's very difficult for me; I miss Dad, too. But he's gone for a while, and we're just going to have to live with that. It's not your fault; he loves you both just as much as ever. So do I."

They flashed me a look that sent an odd chill up my spine; something was definitely on their minds.

"This is a grown-up thing, and we've got to get on with life," I pressed on. "I don't want you getting miserable thinking he's never coming back, or that he doesn't want to see you. Of course he does. That's why he brought you to see Jennifer today." Even saying her name hurt. "Besides, for the moment, you've got two homes. Isn't that great?"

"Yeah," Mark said cheerfully, "and three cars! I want Jennifer to pick me up from camp in her Mercedes Benz!"

I sloped a puddle of beans onto Mark's plate and wondered whether it too late to stick my head in the oven. A cheating husband, two irritable children, and a glamorous rival turning up with a size-eight bum and a sports car to pick my son was just too much for one woman to bear.

PETER

I WAS READING THE paper when the phone rang. "Hi."

"Peter?"

"Olivia?" I sat bolt upright. "Is anything the matter?"

"No, nothing at all." Her voice was shaking slightly. "Nothing's the matter, Peter."

"So why are you ringing me? You only ever ring if something's the matter."

"No, I don't. I ring to organize things."

"Or to change our arrangements," I added.

"Not unless I have to. Peter, this is stupid," she said suddenly. "This sounds like one of our old conversations."

"I know. I'm sorry." A heavy pause. "What did you call for?"

"I wanted to ask you something."

"Ask away."

"I was wondering if you could lend me some money."

Her question caught me off-guard. "Money? What for?"

"A new TV, a new washing machine, and some new clothes for the kids. You know Christmas is approaching, and we really need this stuff."

"What the heck are you saying, Olivia? A TV and a washing machine?"

"Yes."

"What's wrong with the ones you have?"

"They're broken."

Her tone sounded off. "Broken! Both at the same time?"

"It sounds bizarre, I know," Olivia conceded. "But, of course, for Mark, it's a complete disaster; he's missing all his favorite TV programs."

"Well, it would do him good not to sit glued in front of it all the time."

"I know, but you can't tell him that—and of course there's the PlayStation thing. He can't play games, either."

"Playing those games is just as bad—"

"You always used to enjoy them," Olivia interrupted me angrily. "As I recall, it was you who wanted it in the first place. Please don't start your lectures now, okay?"

"Okay." I exhaled. "Why can't you just buy a new TV yourself? It's not as though you're destitute, Olivia; you can't keep running to me every time you have a financial problem, you know. I've been generous enough as it is."

"I know you have, and I really appreciate how good you've been." Her tone sounded sincere. "I'm just a bit short of ready cash at the moment."

"Use your credit card, then."

"I can't; I'm up to my limit."

"What the hell have you been spending that kind of money on?"

"It's none of your business, Peter," she snapped. "All you need to know is that I'm up to my limit."

"Well, what about an overdraft?" I could hear my voice was growing more and more exasperated.

"Peter, if I could get an increase in my overdraft, then I wouldn't be calling you, would I?"

"You mean you're up to your overdraft limit too?" I echoed incredulously.

"You're doing it again! you're making me feel like a child. You're going to start lecturing me any minute now and I just can't bear it!"

I was running out of patience. "Really and truly, you'll have to get a grip on how you manage your money. I've always been ready to help you out in the past; don't you remember the gambling debts? But I can't now; I have other responsibilities. I can't be your lender all the time. If you come running to me every time you have a little financial problem, you'll never manage to sort it out for yourself, will you?"

"Fuck off, you pompous bastard!" she screeched. "And how can you call the flame-haired bimbo bitch you sleep with a responsibility? Doesn't she have a job of her own?"

I was rendered silent for a moment, shocked by her language. I could picture the tightening of her jaw, the narrowing of her eyes, the tension that would wrack her whole body. The jealousy was clearly killing her. "What the h—"

"So you won't give me anything, then," Olivia interrupted.

"It's not a question of can't or won't; it's what good for you. You have to manage your own finances."

"It's good for your kids to be without a TV, a proper washing machine, and new clothes for the winter? All their friends have!"

"Well, they'll have to learn, won't they?" I snapped. "They can't have what everyone else has."

"Well, they know that already," she shot back. "They don't have a father at home, do they?"

This pushed me over the edge. "You were the one, Olivia! You were the one that decided the marriage was over! You were the one who said it was better for the children to have no father than me as a father! You decided that you were keeping them! You brought solicitors into our private lives and, you tried to screw me for every penny you could! So, no; don't give me any shit about the children not having a father at home!"

"I just mean—"

"Oh, I know what you meant, Olivia!" I cut in. "You want to be perceived as some poor, abandoned ex-wife who struggles to keep home and family together under all the circumstances."

"I—"

"You're a strong, independent woman, aren't you? You don't need a man in your life. Men are useless, aren't they? Don't you remember? And you're able to run easily—alone—your life and the childrens' lives. Isn't that what you've kept bombarding me with?" My voice caught in my throat. "Well, your circumstances aren't that bloody difficult, Olivia; you make things difficult for yourself! And you can't decide now that it was a mistake to get divorced. You're a strong, independent woman now; manage your life alone!"

"It certainly wasn't a mistake," she said quietly. "It was the best thing I ever did, Peter. Go fuck your bitch."

"Likewise, Olivia." I threw the phone across the chair before me.

I pictured Olivia standing in the hallway, leaning her head against the wall, eyes glazing with the tears she could no longer control. Clearly, this wasn't how she'd planned for the conversation to go.

I T'S PROBABLY FAIR TO assume that divorce is a harsh reality for pretty much everyone who experiences it; however, a less frequent assumption is that the divorce process often includes elements of make-believe. It rarely occurs to anyone to look for the fictional elements of divorce, as fiction is still more commonly associated with happy endings—whilst the fiction/myth surrounding divorce is more reminiscent of a horror story. The divorce myth is the underlying cultural belief that divorce has the inherent power to make people unhappy—and, in some cases, it really does. This myth is the flipped version of the more exposed myth that marriage has the inherent power to make people happy.

It is also likely that the marriage myth has, in fact, given birth to the divorce myth: it is only if a society is romantically enamored with marriage that the same society can be made vulnerable to the most dramatic aspects of divorce. In other words, those who were taught to believe that marriage can create permanent happiness are prime candidates for believing that divorce will be either a disaster or a complete happy ending. We will examine the interrelation of the marriage and divorce myths by discussing the traditional rules of divorce as they correspond to the marriage rules:

1. Since we don't love each other anymore, nothing will work out. Spouses like Peter and Olivia who have been committed to a mythical marriage become painfully aware, when facing divorce, of how much they have relied on a sixth-sense in their communications. To them, it is clear that things weren't working out because they stopped loving each other. By believing this, the couple made no action to enhance the communication and problem-solving skills that would allow their relationship to survive the rough spots: now that divorce was imminent, they were still trusting fantasy (this time a lack of love) to dictate what will happen. The inordinate power attributed to love (i.e., something that can save and nurture their marriage) has now been transferred to the negative feelings surrounding divorce. There is very little awareness of the power of the individual to be proactive in responsible ways.

2. Always consider oneself first. Ask those who know, and they will tell you that this is the first and most important rule of

divorce. The legal process is based on the adversary relationship between spouses, and, thus, a couple are always quickly made aware of the foolish and dangerous things they have done within the relationship— even when one or both spouses have genuinely intended to be reasonable, or to at least put the children's needs first. The irony of this rule is that it most typically applies to divorcing couples with children— couples for whom a continuing relationship is inevitable (that is, if both parents wish to continue parenting in some form or another). This rule is often so profoundly reinforced during the divorce proceedings that it becomes an assumption for later negotiations.

3. Criticize everything; focus on the negative. If the rule in marriage is to swallow everything, the gross analogy in divorce is to vomit all the hurts, wrongdoings, and inequities of those years together. Cherished rules of fair play become inconsequential as one person's angry behavior soon becomes justification for the other to act in such a manner.

4. If things aren't going well, focus on the past. The mythical marriage thrives on the fantasy that the future holds fulfillment that the present isn't producing. The mythical divorce thrives on the fantasy that past wrongdoings, faults, and negative experiences reveal motives and hatefulness that were not apparent at the time. Here, the rationalization on both sides is unidirectional and uncompromising, insulating either one or both parties from the unpleasant possibility of being responsible and responsive to present circumstances.

5. See yourself as an individual first, and as part of a couple second. This divorce tenet is probably more useful for couples who have no children; in fact, some counselors would argue that this is one of the strong bases for a healthy marriage. When children are involved in a divorce, however, this rule promotes a fictional desire that the children have possess one functioning parent. When unilateral decisions are made that impact the children and the noncustodial parent, with no consideration of the consequences, the entire system is

aggravated—and, thus, when ex-spouses act as individuals only, it is the children who are left to negotiate, compromise, and experience the resulting confusion. As goes without saying, some children are not equipped for such complicated, subtle dynamics, and so these children adjust by some mental gymnastics—a lessening of commitment to one or both parents—, or by considerable agitation.

6.   What's yours is mine. This rule is probably the most self-explanatory, and alludes to the "grabbiness" that characterizes the hurtful, myth-laden divorce. It requires no elaboration.

7.   Divorce makes people significantly unhappy. It is as unpopular to say that your divorce was a good moment in your life as it is to say that you married your spouse because you liked him/her better than the rest; rather, the topics of marriage and divorce are better described in absolutes, hyperboles, and other poetic language. It is equally brazen to present a rational motive for divorce. Hence, the implicit emotional rule here is that divorce is beyond logical capabilities: if you can reason your way through your divorce, you are out of touch, insensitive, and generally somewhat inhuman. The only mythical disposition for divorce is to be severely distraught, and to remain so for a respectable amount of time (two years generally being tossed around as the appropriate recovery time for divorce).

8.   What is best for us must be devastating for the children. This rule is saved until last, considering its weight. If a couple can successfully combat all of the above rules, this last one will usually conquer their good intentions in the end. Regardless, there is an overriding conviction—one that has received a great deal of attention from the media, helping professionals, and religious figures—that stipulates divorce as being inherently harmful for children; statements like "divorce is neither more or less beneficial to children than an unhappy marriage" leave parents feeling powerless regarding the future of their children. Articles accompanied by pictures of children torn in half are a flagrant reminder of the emotional power of such well-documented myths, and frightening statistics are

used within professional reports based on weak, unreliable research designs. This rule also triggers another cycle of the divorce myth: "If I am going to do something terrible to my children by pursuing a divorce, I must prove to myself and everyone else that I am so desperately unhappy and am married to such a wicked person that it is my only sane recourse. I must become a better victim than my children appear to be by their very strategic positions."

GLENDA

I LOOKED AT MY radio alarm clock at around eight. The sun was streaming in the window; it was going to be a hot day. Part of me wanted to get up, but I had no intention of getting out of bed early in the summer holidays; thus, instead, I laid there, surveying the crack in the ceiling and thinking of my father and Jennifer, on vacation on a cruise ship.

I'd tried not to think about them, but it was impossible to keep them out of my mind: they'd been the last thing I thought about before I'd fallen asleep, and the first thing that had burst into my mind as soon as I had woken up. My father and Jennifer. I felt sick when I thought about them together. Had he seduced her? Or had she seduced him? How had he fallen onto his knees before her? The whole idea was disgusting.

Tears trickled down my cheeks. It was all very well for Mum to say we were better off without Dad, but I wasn't so sure; I liked knowing that Dad was there in the mornings when I woke up, even if he wasn't always there when I went to bed. I liked the way he looked sternly at me whenever I asked for something before laughing and saying, "Of course." I missed him already. Other people seemed to think that because he was living somewhere else, I'd be able to just forget about him—but they didn't know anything about it. How could they? He was still my father, and I was missing him.

Mum pushed the door open. "Are you awake?" she called softly.

" am now." I sat up in bed.

"I'm off to work; Mark's spending the day with Greg. Make sure that's where he goes, won't you?"

"Don't I always?"

"Of course you do." She smiled absently. "But I have to say it, all the same. That's the way it works with mothers; we nag. I think you're the best daughter anyone could ever have."

I felt the sting of tears behind my eyes. I stared unblinkingly at Mum.

"I'll be home by eight," she carried on. "My last appointment is for seven." And with that, she rose and walked to the door. "I'll see you later."

"Mum, will they have babies?"

Mum froze in the doorway. "Who do you mean?"

"Dad and Jennifer."

She paused and subconsciously starting chewing on her bottom lip. "I don't know." A mischievous glint sparkled in her eye. "She won't look so pretty, then, with a huge fat bump in front of her."

"Maybe they won't," I shrugged, brushing off her remark.

"Maybe." She didn't sound convinced.

As much as it angered me, I couldn't stop thinking of Dad making love to and enjoying his time with Jennifer on a cruise ship.

JENNIFER

IT WAS HOT THAT day. I sat beneath the shade of a palm tree and waited for Peter to come back, stretching my legs in front of me and surveying them for signs of sunburn. Nothing so far, thanks to the copious amounts of heavy-duty cream I was using. Even though I loved the warmth of the sun, I always sought out the shelter of the shade.

I leaned back against the tree and closed my eyes. We'd almost been back at the ship when Peter had cleared his throat and looked at me, his face struck with shame.

"What?" I asked, alarmed.

"I have to go back to the shops," he said quietly. :I need to pick up some things for the kids."

I looked at him, astonished. "Why didn't you do that earlier, while we were at the market?" I asked. "There were plenty of things there that I'm sure they would have liked."

"I know... It's just that I didn't like buying them in front of you."

"Oh, Peter!" I threw my arms round him and kissed him gently on the lips. "How bloody stupid!"

Peter smiled. "I know. I just felt that... Well, it's our time together, isn't it? It seemed a bit crass to say I wanted to buy gifts for the kids."

"Peter, I expect you to buy gifts for the kids," I assured him, "and I'll happily buy them with you—but not now. I haven't got the strength to walk along that road again. I'll wait for you here, in the shade."

"Thanks." Peter ruffled my hair. "I know I was being silly, but I couldn't help it."

I closed my eyes again. It was typical of Peter to avoid reminding me of his two children—typical, but stupid: his children were part of him. I had no intention of pretending that they didn't exist, as much as a large part of me admittedly wished they didn't.

I still hadn't got my head around the fact that I was a stepmother to a thirteen-year-old girl and a ten-year-old boy; I didn't feel like anyone's stepmother. The idea that I had some kind of authority, however tenuous, over a girl who could just as easily be my sister, was ludicrous.

I had no problem with giving orders to people who worked with me—they knew their place in the hierarchy, and so did I—, but I balked at the idea of ever telling Glenda what to do. I didn't think there was any love lost between Glenda and I, and I could understand that: I'd already assumed Glenda would find it difficult to come to terms with Peter ever marrying again, so I could accept Glenda's point of view— if, indeed, that was Glenda's point of view. So far, my conversations with Glenda had been practically monosyllabic.

I shuddered as I remembered the day I'd first met Glenda. It had been Peter's idea for me to meet her; it would help to break the ice, he'd said. I had, of course, reluctantly agreed.

Glenda had looked at me from dark-blue eyes beneath a long black fringe and said hello in the classic bored tone teenagers use when talking to an adult they are not exactly thrilled to see. In all honestly, she'd looked pretty disgusted, and, when we sat down to have lunch, Glenda hardly spoke at all.

The other times we'd met had hardly been any more successful. This had worried Peter, but we both agreed it would just take time; it wasn't a problem.

Like heck it wasn't. That girl didn't like me—and, much as I loved Peter, I wasn't mad keen on his daughter, either—even if she did have a lot to come to terms with.

I wondered how Glenda really felt about her father's marriage. Did it truly bother her? Or had the fact he'd already been out of the house for so long made it any easier? Was she simply wary of me because she didn't know me very well? Or did she see me as a danger to her concept of what her family should have been?

I had half-expected the children to be at my birthday. I'd told Peter that I'd be glad to have them, and, to be honest, I wouldn't have minded Mark too much; he was a straightforward type of kid, and he thought his dad could do no wrong. However, when Peter had told me they wouldn't be there, I'd felt relived; the idea of Glenda watching me and reporting everything back to Olivia was too chilling—and yes, I was fairly certain Glenda debriefed Olivia every time she returned from a visit to Peter.

I sighed. I didn't want to think about Peter's wife. Not today; not while everything was so perfect. I yawned. The warmth of the sun was making me sleepy.

"I'm here, darling," Peter's voice called from behind me. "We have to be on the ship in five minutes."

With that, we walked up the gangplank, placing our hands under the ultraviolet lamp that revealed the stamp that had been marked on them before we'd disembarked.

"Makes me feel like a spy," I muttered as I followed Peter to our cabin. I flopped down onto the bed. "What did you buy for the kids?"

"Oh, nothing much." Peter opened the wardrobe door and stashed the plastic bags inside.

"Don't be a spoilsport," I said, sitting up again. "Show me."

I reached into the wardrobe and pulled out a pink plastic bag.

"T-shirts," said Peter. "And shells. Things like that."

I unfolded a T-shirt with Jamaica Mon scrawled on the front.

"We're not actually in Jamaica," I pointed out.

"Mark won't care," shrugged Peter.

"And what did you get Glenda?" I deftly unwrapped a flat package and looked at it in surprise. "A photograph frame?" The frame was about four-by-four, and was made of silver.

"That's not for Glenda," said Peter, shuffling his feet uncomfortably. He cleared his throat. "It's for Olivia."

"Olivia," I echoed. My heart had felt like it had stopped. I stared at him blankly. "You bought a present for Olivia?"

"I thought she might like something. She likes photographs, so I thought a frame..." His voice tapered off sheepishly as he met my eyes.

"You bought Olivia a present?" My voice dripped with disbelief.

"Well, why not?" he shrugged. "I thought it would be a nice gesture."

I dropped the frame onto the bed. "Why not," I repeated. I pushed my fingers through my hair, the beads clattered.

"It's nothing special," he went on, "but it just felt odd to bring back loads of stuff for the kids and nothing for her. Besides, she's been pretty good about everything lately, and ..." Peter shrugged helplessly.

"You're separated," I said quietly. "There's no other way she could be."

"But she could have kicked up a fuss about the kids—anything like that."

I sighed. "Being with me doesn't mean she can deny you access to the kids. Olivia's only ever done what she's supposed to do."

"But it's the way she's done it," he insisted. "She's made things easier for me, Jennifer, and I appreciate that."

I bit my bottom lip, and then smiled at him. It was time to swallow my pride. "You're a nicer person than I'll ever be, Peter Nelson."

"Not at all." Peter wrapped his arms around me. "You can practice being nice to me now. I'm sure you have your little ways."

"I'm sure I do," I said, grinning as I kicked off my sandals. "Just let me show them to you."

PETER

I CAN RECALL THE moment I first ever saw Jennifer. I'd known, even then, that she was going to be important to me—but then again, I'd thought it would be a work thing. That was the way I was used to thinking: people I met during the day were either rivals, or clients—and, from the second Jennifer had walked into the room, I'd marked her down as a rival. I'd been giving the lecture on financial products' sales techniques; I had given it every time the company brought in a batch of new salespeople. I'd been introduced as the top financial salesman for the past five years, and I was there to tell them how to close a financial sales deal, as well as to disclose how much money they could make if they did.

I'd started the talk by stating, as usual, that the top ten salesmen all loved their jobs—and Jennifer had interrupted me almost immediately.

"Are there any women in the top ten?"

I'd stared at her. She was wearing a charcoal-grey trouser suit, a white silk top, gold earrings, and a gold chain. Her long red hair was tied back behind her head.

"Pardon?" I said.

"Women," she repeated. "Are there any women in the top ten?"

I cleared my throat, slightly embarrassed at being caught off-guard. "No, not last year," I clarified. "Last year, in fact, the top fifteen salespeople were all men."

"Why?" pushed Jennifer.

I raised my eyebrows in silent query.

"Why?" she repeated. "Is this technique more suited to men? Do women feel uncomfortable with it?"

"They shouldn't," I frowned, "and if they do, then that's their problem, don't you think? After all, this is the technique that has allowed me to have an all-expenses-paid two-week vacation in Cape Town for me and my family—as well as an all-expenses-paid holiday to Madrid. It's also allowed me to drive a two-liter car and to buy decent mansion."

"Yves Saint Laurent," was all she said.

"Pardon?"

"Your suit. Yves Saint Laurent. It's nice." Her lips twitched in a half-smile.

"Thank you. Now, if we can continue?"

I spoke for about an hour, bringing them right up to the point where they should be closing the sale.

"And that's it," I smiled at them. "Peace of mind for your customer leads to business for the company— and money in the bank for you."

I'd thought Jennifer would ask me more questions. I'd put her down as the pushy type; the one who wanted to score points off you all the time. I loved them as trainees.

But she didn't; instead, she stood in the corner of the room, sipping her coffee and leafing through one of the company's brochures.

"Will you be able to handle the pace?" I said to her, leaning against a wall beside her.

She looked up from the brochure, frowning at the interruption. "What?"

"Can you do it?" I asked. "Close a sale?"

"I don't know." She grinned at me. "It's a challenge, though."

"Lots of people don't like it," I said. "You have to make them say yes. Lots of people are no good at making people say yes."

"Why are there so few women?" she asked, cocking her head to the side.

"Because they don't like selling financial products," I responded. "Or because they sell less valuable products. They look at the family's outgoings, and they think they should keep them as low as possible— so they sell something cheaper."

"Next year, I'll be number one salesperson." She was smiling, but I could tell she was serious.

"No, you won't. But I hope you make a damned good attempt at it." I winked at her.

She didn't take the number one the following year; I did. Then again, she was hot on my trail at number four.

"Didn't quite make it," I said. "But you sure put in a brilliant year."

"I did my best," said Jennifer. "Beaten by a better man."

"By three better men," I reminded her.

"Oh, I'm not sure about that." She smiled.

I wanted to take her to bed. I was astonished at how strong the desire in me was.

The second marriage is the triumph of hope over experience.

GLENDA

I COULDN'T QUITE BELIEVE that Dad had moved out with somebody else—that this woman, Jennifer, was now part of our family. Well, not exactly, I supposed; after all, Mum would have a fit if I she thought I thought of Jennifer as part of the family. But how else was I to think of the woman who'd married my father? Some kind of distant friend?

It hadn't been comfortable, finding out about Jennifer; Dad had told me one Sunday as we had lunch together.

"You'll like her," he was saying. "She's a great person. I want you to meet her."

I had looked at Jennifer, with her mass of curly red hair, twinkling eyes, and ultra-fashionable clothes, and couldn't believe she wanted to marry my dad; he was positively ancient compared to the girl standing beside him, who looked young and vibrant and fun.

I couldn't help but compare her to Mum, who would walk around with a perpetual frown; who wouldn't dream of wearing a skirt that revealed more than a centimeter above her knee. It wasn't as though Mum couldn't be stylish—I knew that a lot of Mum's clothes were very stylish—, but they had an indelible mark of maturity about them—one that the sky-blue miniskirt Jennifer was wearing that day certainly didn't.

I didn't want to compare Jennifer and Mum; there was nothing about them that I should have compared. Dad hadn't made it easy for us, had he? He'd left us to fend for ourselves, and now, he was going out with someone who could had been my older sister—my prettier, more stylish older sister. My sexier older sister. There was something uncomfortable about it—something unreal about it.

Jennifer wouldn't have wanted me at her birthday party; Dad had said she was perfectly happy to have me along, but I knew that, in Jennifer's place, I wouldn't have wanted my new husband's daughter there to remind me that he'd been married already. Didn't she worry that Dad was over forty? Did it bother her? Did she ask Dad questions about what life had been like when he was still with Mum? When he'd lived with them in the five-bedroomed house, when I'd had a huge bedroom, with plenty of room for my stuff?

"Can I come in?" Mum tapped at the door, and I sat up.

"Hi." Mum sat on the edge of the bed, surveying me thoughtfully. I looked tired, my eyes solemn and my hair falling in disarray around my sunburned shoulders. "Did you have a good lunch with your dad?" she asked tactfully.

"It was okay."

"How were Jennifer and Peter?"

I felt a sudden surge of pity for Mum—one that I couldn't dismiss. I didn't want to tell her that Dad was enjoying Jennifer more than her. I had never seen my father smile as wide as he had that day.

There was a sudden silence. I was reluctant to answer, and so I changed the subject. "What did you do?" I asked.

"Oh, bits and pieces. I bought a few things."

"I thought we didn't have enough money?" I said slowly.

Mum made a face. "We don't."

"So how could you buy a few things?"

"We don't have lots of money," Mum amended, "but we're not destitute, Glenda."

"We didn't have enough money for me to buy a leather jacket; you told me we had better things to do with our money than waste it on an overpriced jacket. And it had cost less than the bag you'd bought."

An awkward silence elapsed. After a few moments, Mum smiled awkwardly and left the room.

I lay back on the bed and closed my eyes. It had been such a weird day—and it was equally weird hearing Mum saying that Dad never shown her how much he loved her. That was ridiculous. He'd bought her loads of things, including this big house we were living in—anything she'd ever wanted.

I rubbed my eyes. I'd always secretly harbored the hope that one day, Dad would come back; that Mum would realize how much he loved her; that they could live together as a family again. But there was no point in hoping that anymore; he wasn't ever coming home again. Jennifer had changed everything.

That bitch.

NICOLE

OLIVIA AND I WERE sitting together in front of the TV.

"Why should you feel jealous?" I asked. My legs were curled up beneath me, and I plucked a chocolate from the box before me, lying open on the coffee table.

"Because they're on a cruise together," she responded stiffly. "Because she's young and pretty—prettier than me. Because she's so different to me."

"She's older than you were when you first met Peter."

Olivia grimaced. "But she looks much, much younger."

"And what's stopping you from going on a cruise with some desirable young man?" I demanded.

"Oh, come on." Olivia ran her fingers through her hair. "Don't be bloody ridiculous. I wouldn't know a desirable young man if he was standing in front of me—not to mention the fact that I'm far from being able to afford it."

"Borrow the money," I said simply. "You deserve a break."

"And what about the children?" she sighed. "If I suddenly took off, what exactly would they be doing in my absence?"

"You could always let Peter look after them…"

"Peter? I couldn't."

"Why not? Now that he's settled down with Jennifer, he can take some time off from work."

"You mean they could go and stay with both of them for longer periods than the weekend?"

"Sure."

"No. I don't want them to stay with that bitch."

"Don't be silly, Olivia," I chided.

"I'm not!" she shot back. "I don't want her getting to know my kids."

"She's bound to get to know them, Olivia," I sighed. "She'll hardly be out of the home whenever they're there."

"Fine, but I don't want her to be friendly with them," she grumbled. "And I don't want them to be friendly with her. And I definitely don't want them staying with him while she's there."

"I think you're being a little unreasonable," I said calmly.

"No, I bloody am not!"

I remained silent for a few moments. Olivia sighed and rubbed the base of her neck. "I don't know why I feel like this," she said quietly. "It's not as though I care about Peter anymore; truly, it isn't. And yet I just can't accept that someone like that bitch would marry him. And I absolutely cannot accept that my children should get to know her more. I guess I never thought about him getting married at all; I thought things would carry on for some time, and that he would then leave her—you know, after fulfilling his sexual desire, or whatever." She paled.

"You decided it was over. You decided to get a divorce—not him. Remember?"

"He made me decide," she argued. "It was me or her."

"What's happening about money now?" I sighed, changing the topic slightly.

"He's still providing for the children until they leave school. And if they go to college, he'll stump up the fees for that, too."

"But what about you?"

Olivia shook her head. "He cut back on what he gave me once I went back to work; he doesn't see why I should get paid by him at all, even though I keep telling him that raising two kids is bloody hard work—and bloody expensive, too!"

"I'm sure it is—though I wonder how the new Mrs. Nelson will feel when she realizes how much he has to pay towards his kids." I grimaced.

"I don't give a shit how she feels," Olivia snapped. "It's our money, and we're entitled to it. Besides, she earns a fortune, too—the bloody red-headed bitch!"

"Maybe they won't be happy in the long-term," I mused.

"Oh, come on, Nicole! Why wouldn't they be? Peter's over the moon, and what does she have to care about that would give her grey hairs or worry lines?"

"Who knows?" I said indifferently.

"Skinny cow." She took a swig of wine.

"But maybe she'll spread a bit as she gets older," I shrugged.

Olivia looked at me. "Why?"

"Well, if they have kids, she'll hardly—" I broke off as I saw Olivia's expression.

"What?"

"What did I say?"

"He doesn't want any more children," Olivia said quietly. "He told me that. When Mark was five, I asked him what he thought, and he said he didn't want any more."

"But she might."

"I don't think so." She swilled the wine around in her glass. "She seems to be as caught up in her career as he does—although God knows why; it's a rotten job. To be honest, I don't know when they have time to even see each other."

"All the same, she's young; she can't have made up her mind already," I pointed out.

"Apparently she has."

"I bet she changes it."

Olivia picked up her glass and took another gulp. "I don't want her to."

"Why not?" I asked. "That way, at least he gets to see her in her unglamorous role as baby-feeder and nappy-changer."

"I'd prefer it if she didn't," Olivia insisted. "I don't like the idea of them having kids."

"Why?"

Olivia shrugged. Her anger had suddenly disappeared, a tremor instead resounding through her voice. "I... Well, the way things are, I'm the mother to his kids. It's unique to me. If she has kids, then maybe Peter will love her kids more than Glenda and Mark."

"Oh, Olivia, no." I leaned over and wrapped my arm around my friend. "He wouldn't think like that; you know he wouldn't. He adores those kids."

Olivia blinked to keep back the tears. "Now he does—but if Jennifer has children of her own, that might change. You can see that, can't you?"

"He wouldn't love them more," I said firmly. "He'd love them, but not more."

Olivia pulled a tissue from the pocket of her jeans and blew her nose.

"I'm sorry, Olivia. I'm sorry it didn't work out the way you thought it would."

"So am I," said Olivia ruefully. "If we'd still been married, maybe it would have been me on that cruise!"

"You got some great holidays, though," I reminded her.

"Madrid and Cape Town," she said wistfully. "I loved Cape Town. I miss that, Nicole; I bloody miss the money. I hate having to budget all the time. I'm useless at it, anyway; I see things and I want them, so I buy them. Besides, I can't always tell the kids we can't afford things; they're entitled to whatever he can provide for them. It's me who should be walking around in sackcloth!"

I laughed loudly. "It could be worse. You could still be married to him."

"Or worse than that again—I could still want to be," she seconded with forced gaiety.

PETER

"**I** MARRIED YOU FOR the wrong reasons," said Olivia.

"What?" I looked up sharply in surprise.

"I married you because I wanted to be married." Her eyes were slightly glazed. "Especially to someone like you—someone who'd been around the world and had fun. I wanted to have a house of my own, and I wanted my mother to envy me. And those were the reasons."

"Olivia!"

"I loved you too, Peter." Tears glimmered in her eyes. "But I was too young and silly to marry you."

I was shocked, and it showed.

"Don't think it makes me happy to realize that I was as much of a fool as you," she pushed on, "and don't think I'm proud of the fact that I resented you marrying Jennifer."

"You resented it?"

"Of course! For heaven's sake, Peter, you married a gorgeous, young, clever woman; how the hell did you think that would make me feel?"

"I suppose I knew how it would make you feel," I admitted. "I suppose that was part of it."

"Peter!"

"Well, not all of it," I said hastily. "But when I was thinking about marrying her—and I married her for so many reasons, Olivia, honestly—, I also thought that it would hurt you—and I wanted to hurt you like you hurt me."

Oliva remained silent.

"I wanted to hurt you because you were the one who asked me for a divorce, and I was shattered by that." I was having to force the words out; it felt like my throat was closing up. "It was you, Olivia. You ended it."

"I had to." Olivia's voice was almost a whisper. "And now? What about you and Jennifer?"

I sighed. "I've had a row with her, but I still care about her a lot; I love her independence and her way of doing things, and the fact that she never asks me about anything; she just gets stuck in and does it herself."

"The complete opposite of me when we were married." Olivia looked so sad. So hopelessly, painfully sad.

"Well, yes," I admitted. "And then she changed jobs. Without asking for my advice."

"So she did the things you wanted: she was independent and gutsy, and you got annoyed with her."

I said nothing.

"Why is it such a big deal?" she pressed.

"Because I realized I wanted her to ask me about things, to rely on my opinion... To defer to me, I guess."

"Oh, Peter!"

"In fact, I wanted her to be more like you, Olivia."

"Even though you married her because she was different," she reminded me, resentment creeping into her tone.

"I know." I sighed deeply. "You know, I think I really need professional help."

"Maybe you do."

"The kids said I spend too much time with you and not enough time with her lately."

"You do."

"I don't know why."

Olivia looked me straight in the eye. "Of course you know why. You wanted to make her jealous. And I wanted to let you."

"I didn't. You didn't."

"You're lying to yourself," she said firmly. "You did. And I'm just as much to blame. I feel pretty rotten, to be honest."

"Am I that bad?" I asked despairingly. "I mean, am I utterly useless? Is it just me? Is any of it her fault?"

"I don't know!" Olivia burst out. She wiped her eyes roughly and sighed. "I'm sorry, Peter. I'm tired and not thinking straight anymore." She bit her lip. "Why don't you ring her? Apologize to her. Get on with it."

"I'm not sure I want to."

"Why?" Her eyes roamed over mine thoughtfully. "Is it really over between you, Peter? Already?"

"I'm not sure we can salvage it."

"Stop being so melodramatic," she scolded. "If you've fallen out of love with Jennifer, then you need to talk to her about it. It's her you should be talking to now—not me."

"You don't love me anymore, do you?

Her eyebrows furrowed. "Why do you think I divorced you?"

"You can still love someone and not be able to live with them."

"No, you can't."

I looked at her ruefully. "What is it about me, then? What am I doing wrong?"

To my surprise, Olivia smiled at me. "You're just a man, Peter. You do everything wrong."

"Very funny." I allowed the corners of my lips to tug upwards. "You're an angel, Olivia, aren't you?"

"Nope, I certainly am not," she said breezily, "but you think too much of yourself—how things affect you; how you feel. It all goes back to the job with Jennifer, doesn't it? How you got mad at her because she didn't tell you about changing her job. I bet you froze her out; wouldn't talk to her; gave her the silent treatment."

I stared at her, speechless.

"Peter, every single time we argued, that's what you did—and after a while, I couldn't stand it anymore. If something was wrong, it was always on me to try and put it right; to apologize; to appease; to cheer you up. I got fed up with it—and it seems that Jennifer, has too. Only it hasn't taken her very long."

"I'm not like that," I protested, defensive.

"Peter, I'm tired," she sighed. "I really don't want to sit up all night talking to you about your damn bitch and your marriage. I have things to do."

With that, she rose and took the mugs back into the kitchen.

"Peter, if you can't talk to Jennifer, then I'm truly sorry," she called behind her, "but you have to try. I think we maybe didn't try enough, and we should have. You don't want to make the same mistake again. Think about it. I'm going to have a shower and get dressed for work."

I sat at the counter long after Olivia had left the room. I wished I'd been a better husband to her—and a better father. And now, I wished I'd been a better husband to Jennifer. Had I simply been bowled over by the way Olivia and Jennifer looked? Was that all it was, in the end? Were they good wives, anyway? It was impossible to think this mess could only be because of me... It couldn't have been. They were manipulative; all females are. Why should I always blame just myself? They were my partners, anyway: we had fun together; we liked the same things; we went to places they enjoyed; I tried my best to fulfill their endless needs. I shouldn't take all the blame, all the time. They wanted me to feel miserable and useless; wives always do that with their husbands.

I closed my eyes. Thinking was making my head hurt even more.

The Confabulation Concept: The filling in of details missing from either perception or memory. Olivia, Glenda, Jennifer, and Peter started to invent the missing details to construct a consistent narrative of what they had been going through—each according to their own perspective on the situation.

MOST PARENTS LOVE THEIR children, and want to be responsible parents—yet many divorcing couples find themselves acting out aspects of the divorce myth, despite the fact that it hampers their ability to parent their children effectively. In the majority of such cases, this is not a conscious choice; rather, it is an understandable response to the tremendous social pressures supporting the divorce myth. The following is a few of the major social forces:

The Legal System:

Although the legal system may do a good job in representing the financial interests of a divorced couple (which may also be challenged), the makeup of the procedures themselves eliminate any possibility of doing justice to the delicate intricacies and relationship variables of parenting; in fact, the future parenting relationship between divorcing couples is rarely a concern of the court.

The role of the attorney is also adversary to parenting, since it is to focus on all that is right with their clients and all that is wrong with the opponent. Attorneys are trained to focus on the unusual and ignore the usual; the game is to win or lose, and, unfortunately, divorcing families rarely leave the courtroom feeling like winners. In terms of integrity, emotional honesty, and compassion, everyone loses, the power of the court oftentimes bringing out the worst in us.

Many couples who begin divorce proceedings find themselves in the midst of a battle they find they were emotionally unprepared to fight; in fact, divorcing individuals who sound too understanding of their spouse's point of view are usually advised to "toughen up" if there are any contestable issues.

Focus on the Way of the Divorce:

In addition to the win/lose dichotomy, there is an illusion created that the day of the divorce is the end of negotiation and relationship. Since the majority of divorces involve children, this is a disservice to the parents who, in most cases, will have to negotiate parenting issues in the near future. In addition to this, the negative predisposition required in order to prepare oneself for the legal battle with one's spouse makes it extremely difficult to reverse such a position, once established. This is an all-or-nothing situation—or at least it seems to be—well before the court date is set. Unfortunately, the couple is not given counsel regarding what to do after the divorce.

The Fear of Poverty:

For women especially, a very real fear of poverty places them in a position to believe that divorce will wield devastating effects for them. Women with few work skills and enormous financial responsibilities are quick to realize that even with consistent child support, they are at a distinct disadvantage in the economic arena. Meanwhile, men who are losing their home in a divorce are hit with the inflationary costs of replacing possessions bought years earlier, paying child support, and possibly being given the custody of one or more children, thus also finding themselves in somewhat of a financial panic; certainly, the sizable financial cost of divorce when children are involved tempts parents to overlook the emotional costs during legal negotiations.

Emotionalism:

Emotions are an integral part of divorce, and so it is essential for divorcing adults to recognize their own emotions, face them, and encourage their children to do the same. However, emotionalism—the act of feeding emotions to keep them alive—is often substituted for emotional release—and, although many counselors indeed believe that catharsis is actually important in an inherently emotional situation, an avoidance of which leading to a later inability to move forward. Further, when the people in question are parents and responsible for the lives of others, it becomes even more important to avoid emotionalism. In some cases, the hurt may be so deep that a true catharsis will be required in order to "unblock" the person. Saying this, In many cases, being "stuck" in emotions is a way to buy time; to keep from having to brave a new way of life that isn't currently perceived as being as rewarding as the old. Meanwhile, at other times, emotionalism is a very efficient way to keep social support coming, as well as to punish the ex-spouse passively. Of course, this type of activity supports the divorce myth tremendously, making it more real every day.

Divorce Studies:

One of the most active concerns of divorce studies concerns the impact of divorce on children. Hosts of studies have attempted to pair divorce with the future dysfunctional behavior of the child in question. However, the major methodological problem concerning such studies surrounds the fact that they begin with a dysfunctional group (e.g., alcoholics; delinquents; the emotionally unstable), then investigating the member's family backgrounds for patterns. Unfortunately, this kind of study says nothing about the large segment of the population that are left unrepresented by these groups—and, even with this in mind, the results of these studies generally have not supported the assumption that divorce causes behavioral problems, anyway. The occurrence of divorce is consistently less important than the predivorce atmosphere, adult reactions to divorce, socioeconomic factors, or the child's personality, etc.

There is evidence signaling that parental divorce provides children with a better than average chance of being divorced themselves—which, of course, provokes even more questions and assumptions: do children of divorced parents become desensitized to divorce after surviving the one in their family? Do children of divorce learn faulty criteria for partner selection? These are only a couple of the many unanswered questions regarding the occurrence of divorce for adults whose parents were also divorced.

In this regard, there have been attempts by researchers to discern the attitudes of children of divorce toward marriage, family members, or divorce itself—and, as may be expected, such studies show that children of divorce are somewhat wary when it comes to the prospect of marriage and family life in general. However, here, experimenter bias is, again, obvious.

There is no question that divorce has the power to shatter childhood innocence and leave a child more suspicious of the myth of marital bliss than they otherwise would have been—but there is no evidence that this is bad for children. It is equally possible that this phenomenon leaves children more realistic in terms of their expectations of marriage, or less vulnerable to the tremendous pain of disillusionment, should their own marriages end in divorce.

The Marriage Myth:

Since the roots of the divorce myth are grounded in the marriage myth, the latter will always possess the most power to influence and perpetuate societal expectations. Further, as long as people believe, at any level, that marriage will save them and will make them happier, some are grossly vulnerable to the belief that divorce will destroy them, and others that divorce will make them happy. The two go, perhaps counterintuitively, hand-in-hand.

OLIVIA

I LOOKED AT MY watch. Peter should be here shortly to pick up the kids. Glenda usually loved going out with her father, but as of late, she had begun objecting to it more and more after her realization that there was no way back between Peter and me. Today, her excuse had been that she had homework to do. I found myself in a quandary about Glenda's unusual interest in doing homework; as much as I wanted to encourage her in her studies, I couldn't help but feel Glenda would simply wait for Peter and Mark to go out before disappearing to meet Shauna, her friend.

I went upstairs and tapped on Glenda's door.

"Come in," she chimed from within.

I pushed the door open and went inside. Glenda was sitting at her desk, her Math book open in front of her.

"How are you getting on?" I asked casually.

"Oh, all right," she sighed. "Math is not my thing."

"It wasn't mine either," I smiled, perching at the end of her bed.

"I like languages. I'm okay at French, German, and Spanish; I stumble around at Geography, but I get reasonable marks for it; but Math... I'll never be any good at Math."

"My best subject was home economics," I said, "though it was the cooking and food science part I was good at. Not the household management."

Glenda smiled at me. "But now Dad has sorted that out and made a financial plan."

"If I can stick to his plan."

"I like having him here. It was nice."

"I know."

Glenda frowned. "Do you ever think you shouldn't have gotten a divorce?"

I considered my words carefully. "No. Sometimes I miss having your dad around, but that's just because it's hard being on your own. At first, I thought I'd made a mistake divorcing him, considering it's so difficult to go through with it—but it was the right thing to do, Glenda. Even though it might not always seem like that." And the fact that he got along with another woman and I still hadn't moved on also didn't mean it had been a mistake—even if I sometimes felt that way.

"I thought that one day, he'd just come back," Glenda confided quietly. "That he'd realize he missed us."

I shook my head. "That'll never happen, Glenda. I don't want it to happen."

"I know, but it's nice to imagine it, sometimes."

"Are you going to go out with Dad this afternoon?" I ask, trying to tactfully steer the conversation.

Glenda sighed. "Do I have to?"

"It's part of the custody agreement."

"But surely I should be able to say what I want to do."

"I'll talk to your dad about it, but I'd like it if you go out with him today. Unless you really have loads of homework."

"Why? What exciting things have you planned for our absence?" she huffed.

"Washing your clothes; cleaning the bathroom; vacuuming the house... Wonderful, domestic sort of things." I smiled.

Glenda grinned and closed her books. "Oh, okay. I've finished this, anyway. I'll be a dutiful daughter."

"That'll be a first."

Peter was late; it was way after one o'clock before he arrived.

"Sorry," he said hastily as I answered the door. "I couldn't help it."

I was certain that it was that bitch, Jennifer, that was the cause of him being late. Maybe she was complaining about him being obliged to spend the weekend with his kids, and not with her... Maybe they had been making love, and their intense pleasure had put them behind schedule. Maybe they were having a late breakfast at one of the fancy restaurants Peter took her to while he was cheating on me, and when they were done, he had just remembered he needed to pick his kids up. Hundreds of black thoughts crossed my mind in just few seconds. That cow Jennifer.

"Olivia! Did you hear me?"

"Sorry," I said, flushing. "What did you say?"

He followed me into the kitchen. "There's something I wanted to ask you."

My heart dropped. "What is it?"

"It's my parent's golden wedding anniversary next month, and they'd like you and the children to come to their celebration."

"Oh. Do they still celebrate it?"

Peter looked at me with shock.

"Sorry," I said quickly. "I didn't know that they still celebrated it."

"Olivia, you've always got on with them," he sighed. "They adore the kids, and they'd really like all of you to be there."

"Will Jennifer be there?"

"What do you think? Of course she'll be there, Olivia. And I understand if you don't want to come, but I know that Mum and Dad want you to—and so do I."

"Why didn't Emily and Steve ask me themselves if they want me to come?"

"They were afraid you might say no. I told Mum I might be able to persuade you."

"And how did you think you could do that? Tie my hands behind my back and march me there?"

"No, of course not."

I sighed. "It's difficult, being there with your... I mean, Jennifer. I know I should be able to cope with it, but..."

"You don't have to talk to her, Olivia." His eyes were pleading.

"I know. And I won't."

"She's more likely to be intimidated by you than you are by her."

"What on earth makes you think that?"

"Oh, come on, Olivia. You're older than her; more mature. You can cope better."

"I beg your pardon?" I stared at him, utterly dumbfounded.. "I'm the person who had to call you in to look over her finances, remember? Coping is not exactly my thing."

"Olivia, you cope really well. I know I've always been dismissive of how you deal with money, but there's more to life than that: you bring up the kids; you work now; you look after the house... There's a lot of coping going on there, Olivia."

"Not really," I murmured.

He took my hand and held it between both of his. "Honestly. I never used to appreciate you. That's all."

"You're being silly." But I was smiling. I couldn't bear him touching my hand with his warm hands, in exactly the same way he had done so many times in the past.

"So, will you come?"

I sighed. "When?"

"On the twenty-ninth, on Friday."

"Oh, okay—only I want a proper invite. I don't want to arrive and for people not to know that we're coming."

"They're not sending out invites." Peter laughed at me. "It's informal, Olivia. Just family and friends."

"And ex-wives," I said dryly.

JENNIFER

I COULDN'T REMEMBER THE name of the woman who'd spent the last fifteen minutes telling me what a wonderful woman Olivia was; all I knew was that she was one of Peter's relatives attending the party. If Olivia's that fucking wonderful, I thought savagely, Peter would never have left her. Why was it they all seemed to like her so much? She hadn't been able to make him happy, had she?

I watched her laughing and joking with some of Peter's relatives. Stupid bitch. I bet none of them really liked her; they were just being polite.

"Why are you all by yourself?" Glenda asked, standing beside me.

I blinked at her a couple of times. "I don't know many people."

"Dad should introduce you. He's not great at the social niceties, though."

I grimaced. "You think?"

"Nope; Mum was always saying that. Dad does his own thing, she used to say—and he does."

"You might be right, Glenda." Glenda was more tuned-in than I'd realized—and she was being amazingly friendly. I wondered why.

"Don't you visit Gran and Grandad often?" asked the young girl. "We used to come here a lot when Mum and Dad were together."

"I haven't been here since before your dad and I got together," I answered truthfully. "I don't think they like me very much."

"Why?"

"Well, because they may be thinking that I took your Dad from his family. And maybe they think there's a chance he'll still get back with your mum."

Glenda sighed deeply. "I thought that, too."

"And is that what you want?" I wasn't sure I wanted to hear the answer, but I asked anyway.

"I don't know, really. Sometimes. But sometimes not." Glenda looked at me quizzically. "Do you love him?"

"Pardon?"

"My dad. Do you love him?"

"We're married." In retrospect, I don't think I shouldn't had talked to Glenda like that; she was Peter's daughter, and she was only a kid. "I suppose I must love him, if I married him."

"But Dad is old, and you're so pretty." Glenda smiled at me. "I know I wasn't nice to you at first, Jennifer, but I honestly couldn't believe that you are going out with Dad. It seemed... Well, disgusting, I suppose."

"And do you still think it's disgusting?"

Glenda frowned. "Sometimes, I admit. But if you love each other, maybe it doesn't matter."

"That's an interesting way of putting it, Glenda."

"Mum doesn't love him anymore."

I looked across the room to where I'd last seen Peter. He wasn't there, and neither was Olivia. "Perhaps," I said. "But perhaps your Dad still loves her."

OLIVIA

I FELT MY THROAT constricting as I watched Peter and Jennifer talking to Emily and Steve. Jennifer was leaning against Peter, using his body as support. She's had too much to drink, I thought, recognizing the pose. It was probably quite hard for Jennifer to be here tonight, amongst people she didn't really know very well. I felt a sudden surge of pity before quickly dismissing it: Jennifer had everything she wanted.

I walked past the four of them, holding my stomach in and my shoulders high. Jennifer was married to Peter, and I had no interest in him anymore—yet I still wanted to look as desirable and attractive as I could, just so he'd know I wasn't ready for the scrap heap yet—and so Jennifer would know it, too.

I walked out into the relatively quiet space of the back garden. The sky was black, and yet it was impossible to see the stars through the white and yellow glow of the city lights. I remembered when I'd first come out here with Peter: we'd stood in this garden and looked up at the star-studded sky. He'd pointed out constellations to me—Orion, with his three-starred belt, and Cassiopeia, the beautifully named W-shaped collection of stars. Now, I craned my neck backwards, but couldn't make any of them out tonight. I'd loved him then—I really, truly had. I'd believed all would work out; that I'd be with him forever.

I shivered and rubbed my shoulders; it was cold, but I needed some time on my own. It wasn't easy to watch Jennifer with Peter, no matter how my feelings for him had changed; it was a territorial thing. Even though I no longer wanted to be with him, it was always going to be hard seeing someone else stepping into my shoes.

I wished Nick was there that night, with me, so he could wrap his arms around me and tell me he loved me. Registering this thought, I laughed at myself for being naïve: Nick wasn't going to make declarations of undying love—that's for teenagers, not adults. Even still, I wanted him to. I wasn't anything less than Jennifer—was I? Since I'd gone out with Nick, it was as though my whole life had changed. I tried to tell myself that it was childish to feel like this, but if it was childish to feel fizzing excitement about life again, then it was a damn nice way to feel. It was the way Peter had always made me feel—well, before things had gone south.

JENNIFER

I WAS LEANING AGAINST the wall, watching Glenda and Peter dancing together. I was shocked at how grown-up Glenda looked that night; how attractive she was with her black hair, dark eyes, and sallow skin, contrasting strikingly with her red dress.

Sure, she was my stepdaughter of sorts—but if we'd gone into a pub together, people would have thought we were sisters. Had Olivia looked like that once? Mind you, Olivia was a lot fairer—a lot less dramatic in appearance. Olivia was a comfortable-looking woman; attractive without being threatening. Saying that, she was more attractive tonight than I had ever seen her. I couldn't understand how Peter had fallen for a younger Olivia, with firmer breasts, finer features, and—as he'd once told me—a body like a rake.

"Hello, Jennifer." Olivia had decided, it seemed, that she couldn't put this off forever: she had to speak to me at some point. I was conscious from the corner of my eye that almost everybody in the party was watching us, undoubtedly wondering what we'd say to each other.

I stood a little straighter. "Hello, Olivia."

"Enjoying the party?"

"Sure," I shrugged. "It's not exactly my thing, but it's okay."

"What would be your thing?" I'm sure it wasn't intentional, but her tone sounded challenging. "All-night raves?"

"Pardon?"

Olivia laughed loudly, as if trying to persuade me it was just a joke. I half-smiled back at her, somewhat bitterly, and turned around, blankly watching people dancing.

"Emily looks great tonight, doesn't she?" Olivia chirped, changing the subject swiftly.

"She's a good-looking woman," I conceded.

"Maybe that's where Peter gets it from."

My eyebrows shot up.

"I always thought he was very good-looking—especially when I first met him." Olivia smiled. "Long hair, good body... I couldn't help myself at the time."

I noted Olivia's sudden hesitation. She still loved him, and she'd like to get him back—and maybe Peter wanted to go back. Or maybe Olivia wanted to tell me, implicitly, that Peter no longer looked good like he had in the old days, and was trying to annoy me by saying I'd married an old, deteriorating man. Either way, I felt sick.

"Excuse me; I need to go to the bathroom," I breathed, pushing past Olivia and hurrying from the room.

This bitch of a woman wanted to be friendly! No; she wanted to make me feel inferior to her.

I looked around the crowded room, everyone actively avoiding my gaze. Well, sod them all; I didn't need to know them anymore. I didn't need to care.

MARK

I GOT OUT OF bed and pulled on a sweatshirt over my pajamas, trotting downstairs and into the kitchen to make myself some breakfast. It was then that I saw Dad lying on the sofa.

"Dad! Dad, wake up!"

Eventually, Dad opened his eyes, blinking in surprise to see me standing in front of him.

"Morning, Mark," he said gruffly, reaching up to tousle my already-tousled hair.

I plonked myself on the sofa beside him. "What are you doing here, Dad?"

"I stayed here last night."

"Well, I can see that," I sighed. "I mean, that's obvious. But why, Dad?"

He sighed. I believe he didn't know how to answer my question.

"Did you have a row?" I pushed. "Fought with Jennifer?"

Whatever it was, Dad didn't want to admit to it—at least, not to his ten-year-old son. Perhaps he was embarrassed to tell me he had been thrown out of his house for the second time—and this time from a different partner altogether.

"We had a bit of an argument," he admitted eventually.

"Gosh. So you came home to us?"

"Only for last night," he said quickly. "That's all; only for last night."

We both remained silent, glancing at the gold carriage clock on the mantelpiece. It read that it was five to nine. It had been a Christmas present from Dad to Mum.

"Should I tell Mum you're awake?" I said after a few moments of silence. "She'll probably want to say good morning."

"I doubt it." Dad winced as he swung his legs over the edge of the sofa. "I'm sure she isn't too pleased with me for turning up at all."

"Mum says you're hopeless," I grinned. "A great worker, but absolutely hopeless."

"Charming," murmured Dad grimly.

"We were talking about you on holiday."

"Oh? What did she say?"

"She said you were good to us." I cuddled up beside Dad. "That you'd paid for our holiday to Portugal, and that she'd only had to suggest it to you and you'd agreed. She said that you'd bought the TV—well, actually, you bought me a TV; Granddad bought that one, here."

"Did he?"

"Only you're not supposed to know that." I grinned. "Mum didn't want to tell you; she was afraid you'd get narky with her. Maybe she thought if you knew it, you won't agree to give her money again, if she ever asked for help again."

"Why? Do you think I would do that?"

"I dunno."

"Okay." He exhaled heavily. "So, what else did she say about me?"

"That you're happy with Jennifer," I shrugged, "and that you won't come back to us. And that Jennifer doesn't like us much, and doesn't want us to stay with you. She doesn't like kids. Does she, Dad?"

"Jennifer is a good person, Mark. She does like you and Glenda, very much."

"She calls Jennifer the bitch, and sometimes the cow."

"Mark! This is inappropriate. You shouldn't talk this way about Jennifer."

"Sorry Dad, but it's not me," I insisted. "Mum said so."

"Whatever. You shouldn't repeat it."

I felt the hot sting of tears in Dad's eyes before they even spilled. Now I thought of it, I couldn't remember Mum ever telling him he was a good father; as far as I could remember, she'd always yell that he was a useless father. I have to remind you about their birthdays days ahead, she used to shout. I always heard her yelling at him that he wanted all the comforts of a family and none of the responsibilities. Not once had she told him, to his face, that he was a good father. There was always something he didn't do, or something he forgot to do, that made him undeserving of the "good father" title—that's how Mum perceived it. He hadn't been a good husband, though—that I could agree with.

"Is Jennifer mad at you, Dad?"

"I rather think she is. Silly things," Dad shrugged.

"She looked lovely last night at the party," I said. "I liked the spangly things on her tights."

"Mark!"

"They were great."

"You're not meant to fancy your Dad's partner!" He was laughing, hard—full, belly laughs.

"I don't fancy her!" When the smile faded from his face, so did mine. "How long do you expect to stay here?"

"Not long."

"But why didn't you stay with her?" I burst out. You love her. Did she throw you out—even though it's your home?"

Dad's head snapped up at this, his face contorted in a frown. "Give me a break, Mark."

"You can't run back here every time you have a row with her, can you?"

"I know. And I won't."

"It'd be different if you and Mum were getting back together again," I pushed. "That's something else altogether."

"Would you like that?" he asked, an odd expression on his face. "Would it make you happy?"

I bit the corner of my nail and looked at Dad. I'd wished so much that he'd come back; that he and Mum would live together again. But Mum had told me so many times that it just wasn't possible. And yet here he was, spending the night here—although not with Mum. Dad had spent the night on the sofa with the old blankets for warmth. I'd often imagined him staying with us, but I hadn't expected it to be like this. Mum had grown apart from Dad; they'd both made new lives for themselves, and I knew things could never be the way I had once wanted them to be.

"Mark?" Dad pushed, interrupting my stream of thoughts. "Do you want me to come home?"

"It isn't your home," I said, hardly believing the words coming out of my own mouth. "It was different before. This is our place. Me, Mum, and Glenda."

"I see." He dropped his gaze to the ground.

"It's not that I don't love you, Dad," I said quickly, putting my arm round his shoulder. "I do. And I've wanted you to come back more than anything. But it's all changed, hasn't it? You've got Jennifer, and things are different." He remained mute. "What did you row about? I saw she wasn't very happy at the party. Was it about you and Mum?"

"Why would we row about that?"

"Oh, Dad!" I sighed, exasperated. "She got jealous, certainly. Mum was gorgeous."

"And so was Jennifer, wasn't she?"

"Yes, they both were, but you were following Mum around all night."

"No, I wasn't."

"Come on, Dad." I rose from the sofa. "You were. Now, would you like a cup of coffee or anything?"

"No thanks, Mark."

JENNIFER

I DIDN'T KNOW HOW I'd arrived at Olivia's house. I hadn't meant to come here—at least, I didn't think I'd meant to come here—, but I'd wanted to find Peter, and I'd told him to go to Olivia last night. I was pretty sure that was what he'd done.

You're a real sucker for punishment, I thought as I pressed the doorbell. It was only when I heard footsteps inside the house that I realized Peter's car wasn't parked outside.

There was no time to run, however—even if the thought had rushed through my head.

After a few seconds, the door swung open, and there was Olivia, standing in front of me, a shocked expression on her face.

"Hi," I said, somewhat sheepishly.

Olivia stared at me. "Hello."

"Can I come in?"

"Sure." She opened the door wider and I stepped inside. "Come into the kitchen. Mark's in the living room. Glenda has gone out." She led me into the kitchen, pulling out a stool for me. "Sit down. Would you like something to drink? Juice? Or tea? Something stronger?"

I shook my head. "No, thanks."

I sat down opposite to Olivia, unsure what to say.

Then, I did exactly what I never, ever would have wanted to do in my husband's ex-wife's presence: I exploded into floods of tears.

"Where is he?" I finally managed to force out.

Olivia's eyes were wide and sympathetic. "I don't know."

"Wasn't he here? Last night?" My voice was shaking uncontrollably.

Olivia was silent, seeming unsure whether it was better to say yes or no. "Yes," she said eventually.

She realized there was no point in lying; I would discover it sooner or later.

"Why did you come to the party?" I asked briskly, attempting to pull myself together. "Why did you come and make him feel that you were really the one?"

"He doesn't think I'm the one." Her tone was sincere. "I was once, but I'm not anymore."

"He still loves you." I looked up. My eyes were red; my face blotchy. "He still loves you, and it's destroying our marriage."

"He doesn't love me," she said, shaking her head. "He probably never did."

"Oh, come on!" I couldn't help but feel angry. What was the point in denying Peter's blatant feelings for her? "What was last night all about? Laughing together? Dancing together? Talking together?"

Olivia bit her lip.

"You're so perfect in his eyes," I carried on. "'Olivia kept the house so well'; 'Olivia was a great cook'; 'Olivia was great with the children.'" My tone was bitter, but I couldn't help it.

"Oh, don't be ridiculous," she chided. "I was good at all those things, but that didn't make him come home to me at night, did it? It wasn't enough. It might have been if we'd worked at it harder, but in the end, it wasn't."

I said nothing.

"He came here last night and stayed the night—but on the sofa, Jennifer."

"You danced with him. I had to do something about it." My voice shook again. "You humiliated me."

"I know," said Olivia. "I'm sorry. I shouldn't have. I was being stupid myself, Jennifer—trying to prove that I could be just as sexy as you."

"You looked great, and you know you did. You made things worse between Peter and I. You wanted to make things worse between us, didn't you?"

"Jennifer, I... Maybe temporarily. But believe me, Peter loves you. I know he does. He told me himself."

If anyone had told me a few months ago Olivia would be telling me not to worry that he loved me, I'd have told them where to go.

"No, he doesn't," I said.

Olivia sighed. "I think you're wrong."

"Why should you care?"

"Because I want him to be happy." With that, she got up and took a carton of apple juice from the fridge. She poured us two glasses. "I do want him to be happy," she said, sitting back down. "I really do. And I want you to be happy too, Jennifer. I don't care that he married you; I'm just glad Peter found someone."

I was silent, unsure whether Olivia was telling the truth or just making fun of me. What she'd done last night at the party was the opposite to what she was saying now, after all. This bitch must be hiding the truth.

"And what exactly did he say to you?" I said, my tone cold.

Olivia grinned. "That you'd thrown his stuff from the apartment window."

I smiled faintly. He deserved it, the bastard.

"I liked that, Jennifer. I thought it was great." She was chuckling softly to herself.

"It was stupid. I'm not that type of childish person, you know."

"Oh, I don't know; I bet you got great satisfaction out of it, Jennifer."

"At the time," I admitted, "but not now."

"He's not a bad person," Olivia hedged. "He's just... He likes to be in charge, Jennifer. He thinks he doesn't, but he does; he likes showing off and generally being top dog. I suppose you could always trace that back to his childhood, or something—or maybe it's just that that's the kind of person he is."

"I thought we had so much in common," I said quietly. "But later, I thought he just wanted you all over again."

"It's not easy," Olivia admitted. "You think you know someone, but you only ever know part of them—and you think you'll die when someone leaves you, but you put the pieces back together again." She paused. "And you think you can't talk about things, but you can."

"With Peter, yes!" A flash of spirit returned to my eyes. "It's like talking to a brick wall!"

"I know, Jennifer. God knows I tried often enough."

"It's like the way his face kind of shuts down." I could feel my face flushing. "As if he's filtering you out of his mind."

"And he stares at a spot past your head," Olivia laughed.

"And then his eyes narrow."

"And then his nostrils flare a little."

"And he looks at you as though you were about six years old!"

We smiled at each other.

"He spent the night on the sofa, Jennifer," Olivia said softly. "Nothing happened."

"But he didn't come home." My voice trembled.

"He will."

I sighed. "I hated you, Olivia, you know."

"Why?"

"Because you married him first." My throat felt like it was closing to be saying the words aloud. "Because you were always there."

"I hated you too, Jennifer."

I blinked. "Me?"

"Come on, Jennifer!" She shook her head incredulously. "You're younger than me; you're thinner than me; you can wear something that resembles a black silk hanky at a party and still look great."

"I wanted to stab you last night, Olivia, because I thought you looked sophisticated, and I looked like a kid."

"We don't have to like each other, Jennifer," she said. "We don't have to get on. But there's no need to hate each other and make our own lives miserable."

"I know."

Right on cue, the doorbell rang. It was Olivia's friend, Nick.

"Is he...?" I countered.

"A friend," said Olivia hastily. "A good friend."

"Peter never told me you had a—"

"Peter didn't know," she said, somewhat coldly. "He does now."

"You really don't want Peter back?"

"I really don't." She offered a small smile. "And, Jennifer: it's not a case of what I want; he really doesn't want to come back. He might moan and groan and talk about old times, but it's all a load of rubbish; we lived apart for a long time before he met you. It's not a question of you or me."

"Maybe not," I said.

"Absolutely not."

"I don't know whether I love him or not anymore myself. Sometimes I do, and then sometimes I... Well, it's just not cut and dried, is it?"

"I wish it were," Olivia sighed.

"And it's not cut and dried with you and Nick, is it?"

"I don't want it to be. Not yet." Olivia smiled. "I rushed into things with Peter, and though part of me is still rushing, I'm going to take it easy with Nick."

I nodded. "I'd better go; leave you to it. Thank you, Olivia; for having such sincere words with me."

Olivia smiled at me. "Good luck with Peter. I want you both to be happy together."

"Thanks." I exhaled slowly. "I think I'm going to need it."

OLIVIA

THE SMELL OF FURNITURE polish hit me the moment I opened the front door. I gritted my teeth; every single time that Mum came over, she did something around the house—whether that was cleaning the windows, washing every piece of crockery, or polished our meagre pieces of silver, despite the fact that I did all these things regularly myself. No matter how many times I told her not to bother, she ignored me. Mum was obsessed with cleaning. I couldn't remember a single time in my childhood when every surface in the house wasn't dusted; when every floor wasn't washed; when anything left lying around wasn't put away. It had driven us crazy as children, but it had rubbed off on us in some ways, too. I knew she was a good housekeeper, which made her behavior even more irritating.

I pushed open the living room door to find Mum sitting in the armchair nearest to the TV—Glenda's armchair. I dropped my bags on to the sofa.

"Hi," I greeted. "How did you get on today?"

"I polished the hall floor. Honestly, Olivia, you should look after it better; it didn't look as though it had seen a cloth in months," she scolded.

"That's because of Mark," I said, as calmly as I could. "He walks muck and dirt into it, and no matter what I do, it ends up scruffy."

"He's in his room at the moment. His friend is with him."

"And Glenda?"

"She's in her room too." Mum pursed her lips—a sign, I knew, that meant there was more Mum wanted to say, but was holding back. Well, I thought, I'm not going to give Mum the opportunity to complain about Glenda. I shrugged of my jacket and deliberately threw it on to the sofa, over the bags.

"Why don't you put things away properly?" Mum huffed. "You're going to have to put them away sooner or later, so why don't you do it now?"

"Because I'm tired," I snapped. "It was a hard day at work, Mum, and it's nice to come home and just sit down."

"If you'd stayed married to Peter..."

"Please, Mum, don't start all that again," I cut in. "I'm fed up of listening to it. Peter is now with another woman. Let's drop it, shall we?"

"That's the way you'd like it, isn't it?" There were two pink spots on Mum's cheeks. "If you don't talk about it, then it doesn't matter, and you can always go shopping to make yourself feel better anyway."

"Rubbish!" I sat up straight in my seat, visibly annoyed. "And even if I do think like that, where do you suppose I learned it from?"

"What do you mean?"

"Oh, come on," I said, exasperated. "I was brought up by you, wasn't I? You were never a great one for talking, were you? I don't remember any heart-to-heart conversations when I was younger—well, not with me, anyway. You had quite a few with Mia."

"Don't talk nonsense, Olivia."

"I'm not; I'm just saying you never gave a toss about me. The only person you bloody cared about was Mia, and you're happy that my marriage fell apart; it justifies your belief that I'm useless and incompetent. But good old Mia and her perfect bloody family are living proof that you did something right." I heard the quiver in my voice at the end of the sentence. I bit the inside of my lip, not wanting Mum to realize how upset I was.

"I never believed you were stupid until today," she said under her breath. "But I was wrong. You know perfectly well that I love you both equally."

"Bullshit!" I retorted.

"There's no need to descend to that level," she shot back. "If you can't argue with me without swearing, then you're less educated than I thought."

"Oh, for God's sake, Mum! I'm sorry if I struggle to wrap my head around the fact that my own mother thinks I'm a stupid, incompetent woman who couldn't keep her husband and or manage her home!"

Mum said nothing, and she began to blur before me as tears filled my eyes filled with unshed tears. I was not—not—going to cry in front of Mum; I hadn't cried in front of Mum since I was twelve years old, and even then, I'd been told that girls my age shouldn't cry—which I hadn't believed then, and didn't believe now. There were plenty of things to cry about in life, and a lot of the time I felt much, much better for it. But not in front of Mum.

I took a large mouthful of water. "Look," I said, my voice still trembling, "I married the wrong man, and it didn't work out. You didn't like him when I married him, but ever since I divorced him, you've gone on and on about him, as if he were God's bloody gift to man. Well, he wasn't; you were right about him at the start, which should make you feel good. But he's with another woman now, and he's not coming back, and, believe it or not, I don't care. I'm glad. I don't love him anymore; I haven't for a long time, and I'm doing a hell of a lot better without him—even though that means sometimes I don't put my clothes away immediately, or polish my floors. As if it matters whether they smell of pine trees or not!"

"Olivia! I told you there was not need to swear," was my mother's response.

There was a hint of hysteria in my laugh. "That's all that matters to you, isn't it? How things look, rather than how they actually are. You'd have been perfectly happy for me to be utterly miserable with Peter once we'd stayed together."

"That's not true, Olivia."

"Isn't it?"

"Of course not." Mum rose from the armchair. "And if you think that, then I'm going home. I won't stay where I'm not wanted—or, at least, where I'm not wanted now. I was wanted earlier, of course, when you were working. It's okay for me to be here when you need me, isn't it? But once I've outstayed my usefulness, I've outstayed my welcome!"

I rubbed my temples, trying to erode the pounding headache creeping into my skull. "I'm sorry... I didn't mean to—"

"You did mean to," she spat. "You meant every word."

"It's just..." I swallowed. "You always criticize me. I don't need you to tell me where I'm going wrong; I just need you to love me all the same. But you don't."

"How dare you say that?" she burst out. "You know perfectly well that I love you; you and Mia."

"But you love Mia the most."

"Oh, grow up, Olivia." Mum draped her silk scarf around her neck. "I love you both equally."

"Well, it sure doesn't seem like it."

"I can't believe I'm hearing this—after all I've done for you!"

"Oh, all what?" My voice was shaking again. "All the times you told me I shouldn't have married Peter? All the times you told me I should have stayed with him? All the times you've cleaned out my cupboards and told me that they were hygienic now? All the times you've waved around my house when I haven't asked you to?"

"You ungrateful little wretch!" Her words had more fury than I had ever heard before.

I winced. We both watched each other silently, like two lions, waiting for the perfect moment to attack one another.

Finally, she broke the silence. "I'll go."

"Don't, Mum." If she walked out the door now, we may never set foot in each other's houses again.

"You want me to stay so that you can insult me some more?" she challenged.

"No, I don't—but I don't think you should drive home when you're mad at me."

"I'm not mad at you; I'm disappointed in you."

"You were always disappointed in me," I said quietly. "And maybe you've a right to be: I messed up my life, after all. And I guess I am grateful. You came here today and looked after Glenda and Mark, and I should be grateful to you. I'm sorry."

"I'm disappointed that things weren't better for you," she responded indifferently. "I'm not really disappointed in you, Olivia; that was the wrong thing to say. And I don't want you to feel obliged to be grateful, either; I want to feel as though you're not simply putting up with me, wishing I was someone else looking after your children."

"I don't wish that."

"Don't you?"

"No! I trust you with them. I know that they'll be okay with you."

"And you know that I love them?"

"Of course." Mum did love them, although I suspected Mum loved Mia's daughter more. "I don't love anyone more than anyone else," she added, as though reading my thoughts. "They're all my grandchildren, and I love them all equally. As I love my children equally."

I grimaced.

"I'm sorry if you don't believe me."

"I thought I knew what I wanted from life, and I thought it was Peter."

"I knew it wasn't Peter, Olivia," she sighed. "Don't lie to yourself." She paused. "Saying that, once you'd married him, I did think you should have tried harder."

"I did try! You don't know how hard I tried."

"I suppose I don't," she admitted. "It just seemed to me that you were so crazy about him that it couldn't have all changed. I remember it, you know—the day you came home and talked and talked about him. How good-looking he was." Mum made a face.

"I didn't want it to end in divorce," I sniffled. "I really didn't—but I was going crazy, and I knew that things weren't going to get better."

"I wanted to help you. I wanted to tell you that it would be okay. But you wouldn't let me."

"You told me—"

"Goodbye, Olivia."

When Mum was gone, I hung my coat and brought my bath oils and face mask upstairs. It was the biggest row I'd had with her in ages— and the deepest conversation, at that. We'd actually dealt with issues. Despite the shouting, it had been really quite grown-up.

Usually, dealing with my mother made me feel as though I was about sixteen again. I always felt that, with Mum, criticism was only just below the surface—and I'd always supposed that the criticism had been because Mum didn't love me—or at least not as much as Mia. Not because she did. Yet I hadn't felt that way this evening; I'd seen Mum as another adult, possibly for the first time in my life. It was pretty odd to think that it was only now that I considered myself to be an adult in the company of my mother.

But that wasn't Mum's fault, because despite sometimes getting depressed about being forty, sometimes thinking that my life was over before it had even started, and having had meetings with divorce lawyers, I'd never actually managed to feel properly grown-up.

I was the divorced mother of two children, and yet I sometimes didn't feel any more qualified for life than I had when I actually was sixteen. The world is full of people doing their grown-up things, and ii was only now that I was beginning to feel that I may actually be part of it.

GLENDA

"I DON'T WANT TO go." I was staring defiantly at Mum, who was stacking the breakfast things in the dishwasher.

"Look, Glenda, it's the only time he gets to see you," Mum sighed pleadingly. "How do you think he'll feel when you say you don't want to go out?" She scraped a dish and stashed it next to another in the machine. "Glenda, are we really going to have this ridiculous conversation every weekend?"

"Why should he care?" I carried on. "He's probably just as bored as us traipsing around."

"That's not fair. I thought you understood, Glenda."

"I'm fed up of understanding!" I snapped. "Why don't you understand me for once? I don't want to be dragged to another restaurant, or bowling alley, or art gallery, or whatever he thinks might be a worthwhile excursion just because he has access. I'm not a commodity, you know, and yet that's what you both deal with me as! Just orders, all the time."

"How about if he simply brings you back to the apartment? That's not being dragged around."

"No."

"Why not?" Mum was becoming exasperated. "What else are you planning to do with the day? And don't say study," she added, holding a finger up, "because I won't believe it."

"I want to go out with Bobby," I shrugged, diverting my gaze to the floor.

"Oh, I see. That's it." Mum scratched the side of her head; she now understood perfectly why I didn't want to go out with Dad. My boyfriend was now a priority. As a small smile flashed on her face, I felt I'd made myself too clear. I should have kept quiet; in the matter of dads versus boyfriends, dads were always going to lose.

"Your dad will be disappointed," was her response after a few moments.

"Well, he can't always have everything the way he wants."

"He doesn't always have everything he wants."

"Yes, he does," I retorted. "He has us, and Jennifer, and the money."

"What?"

"It's funny with Jennifer."

"In what way?"

I paused as I thought. "I don't know how, exactly; it's an odd kind of relationship."

Mum rinsed the teapot and turned to look at me. "What on earth makes you say that?"

"They hardly spend any time together," I shrugged. "I ask Dad about his day, and it's always that he was at work all day, and so was Jennifer—and he takes us out on Sundays. The only day they can possibly be together is Saturday."

"People live their lives in different ways. They're probably happy that way." Even with the nonchalance with which she spoke, I could tell Mum was intrigued by my insight into Dad's life.

"I wouldn't be."

"You never know, Glenda," she said. "Sometimes, you don't want the other person to be around all the time."

"Speaking of relationships," I countered, deflecting the topic somewhat, "how's Nick?"

Mum blushed. "Nick?"

"Yes, Nick." I grinned. "Did you ring him back?" I'd told Mum Nick had phoned late last night, and she'd thanked me for telling her, barely looking up from her magazine. I'd wanted to ask more about him, but Mum's face warned me not to—that, and the fact that she'd kept herself busy with the magazine, eliminating any chance for further discussion.

"Yes, I phoned him," she said now, curtly.

It seemed she'd called him at nearly midnight, wanting to wait until I was asleep.

"And what did he want from you?" I pushed.

"To see me sometime."

It felt terrible when Mum kept things from me; she'd even had lunch with Nick before without telling me—something she still didn't know I knew about.

"I don't like him," I said firmly. "He's not Dad."

"Of course not!" Mum hugged me. "Of course not."

"So are you going to go out with him?"

She considered her words. "How would you feel about that, Glenda?"

"Odd," I admitted. I smiled slightly at Mum. "Is he in love with you?"

"Don't be silly."

"But do you love him?"

"No, but I like him."

"So do I."

"I know. I thought, maybe, you kind of loved him yourself."

"Mum!" I exclaimed. "That's gross. He's loads older than me."

"You said yourself that it's the same difference between Peter and Jennifer," she pointed out.

"Yeah, and I think their relationship is on the rocks."

"Well, it isn't, Glenda."

"Wanna bet?" I shot back. "What is it with grown-ups? You'd think you'd manage to sort it all out by now, wouldn't you? But you're just as bad as any of us."

Mum laughed. "That's what makes life so interesting; you never learn it all—and I only decided that last night."

I smiled. "I don't know if I want you to go out with Nick. I like him, but I don't know if..."

"Glenda, don't worry."

"How can I help worrying? You have my heart scalded," I laughed, clutching my chest.

PARENTAL DIVORCE CONSTITUTES A moment of emotional shock and high anxiety for the majority of children—something that is likely to be the case, irrespective of whether the final sequence of events is anticipated or not. Certainly, Mark and Glenda had become aware that something was seriously wrong in their parents' relationship long before their separation occurred; they knew something wrong was happening. It is important to recognize that there are patterns and commonalities in children's experiences and emotions regarding the separation of their parents. Saying this, children are no more a homogeneous category than any other, and their reactions cannot be predicted to the point of certainty in all cases.

There can be great variations in the responses of children to divorce; depending on the interaction of individual characteristics of the child and pre-and post-divorce experiences, new problems may emerge, old ones may be exacerbated or attenuated, and children's adjustment may be enhanced by their parent's marital dissolution. Regardless of what occurs here, children often still have to deal with ongoing conflict between their parents, as well as their own emotional reactions to the separation.

Mark and Glenda became sad, angry, and fearful when regularly exposed to the conflict that was handled tactlessly and counterproductively. Indeed, children are usually more aware of what is going on between their parents than the in question adults may think, and the fact that children can be harmed by the way in which their parents handle disagreements has led to many of them concluding that they would be better off if their parents did split up. Even still, many children are still hurt by how their parents fight— regardless of whether or not they stay together—, and, because their parents still have not learned the skills necessary so as to handle conflict in a healthy way, these children don't really do that much better if their parents do divorce. Indeed, if parents are to also make regular negative comments about one another's motivations and behavior, their children learn to do the same in relation to their peers' behavior. Further, for some couples, an escalation in emotions takes them closer to the line between nasty emotional patterns and physical aggression—and this heightens the tension for everyone in the home.

By the time of their parents' separation, Mark and Glenda knew, at least, that all wasn't well between their parents, and began to feel that their parents' separation had been inevitable; as a matter of fact, children and adults tend to recall this process differently. Divorce is a new, uncharted, and stressful experience for everyone involved, and parents and children alike face uncertainty concerning what to say or how to say it. In line with this, Olivia and Peter often did not know what was happening themselves, and so didn't know what to tell their children. This, in turn, leads to the children feeling that they don't know how to ask for the information they feel they need—and, with all of the above combined, both parents and children ultimately tend to shy away from talking about the divorce, each feeling the need to protect the other. Generally speaking, the majority of children are told exclusively by their mothers about their parents' separation, girls being more likely than the boys to be told about their parents' separation by their mothers. Further, most children seem to face particular difficulties in talking to their fathers about sensitive and emotive issues, feeling it to be easier to talk to their mothers. Therefore, most children downright refuse to talk to their fathers about the divorce, feeling that their fathers know nothing—or very little— about their feelings concerning the divorce, whilst their mothers know everything. In fact, this reluctance is apparently shared by many fathers, who may try to avoid talking to their children about the marriage breakdown.

Hence, there are very few cases in which children are told about the separation by both parents together; unfortunately, when both parents choose to talk to their children, it is more common that they will do so separately (as in Olivia and Peter's case). What they fail to realize is that a key consequence of telling children separately is that children end up with completely different accounts of what was happening and why during the divorce due to the parents' different perspectives.

Olivia explained to Glenda her reasons for ending the marriage with Peter a few weeks before leaving, without Peter's knowledge—and, when Peter came to explain the situation to Glenda, he gave her a range of different reasons to those of Olivia, leaving Glenda confused and questioning her father's honesty. Meanwhile, when Olivia had gone out, Peter had explained to Mark that his Mum and himself don't love one another anymore—whilst Olivia, a few weeks before, had claimed this to be a lie, stating the main reason of divorce had been that Peter had cheated on her; she also said she still loved Peter, and that Peter was telling a lie. Hence, for Glenda and Mark, when their parents said something, they grew clueless as to whether they were telling the truth or not—and, as we have seen for Glenda and Mark, this confusion and doubt would eventually impact how they came to relate to their father and Jennifer.

Some parents may neglect to tell their children about the separation and its true reasons so as to shield their children; however, for the children, this is perceived as a breach of trust, and, predictably, the situation worsens significantly when one parent leaves suddenly. In this situation, it often falls to the remaining parent to pick up the pieces. Like many children, Glenda and Mark had always assumed that their parents would stay together forever, and so they remained in disbelief for a while after their finding out that their parents were going to split up. This emotional shock is particularly evident when the separation is unexpected—as is the case when children are told of the separation of their parents in an informative, matter-of-fact way, with little discussion about their feelings or the potential consequences of the breakdown. Whilst Glenda happened to feel upset initially, others feel a massive anger that is usually directed towards the parent the child feels is responsible for the family's breakdown.

Despite all of the above, the emotional shock experienced by children may still be overlooked—even when parents attempt to talk directly to their children about the separation (rather than simply presenting the separation in a rather matter-of-fact way, as some parents do). However, in some (minority) cases, children feel relieved when they first find out. Here, the children usually feel the family circumstances have become intolerable, and so are glad that things are finally going to change—hopefully for the better. However, they still remain upset; regardless of children's initial feelings towards a breakup, confusion and uncertainty remain common after the initial shock.

Mark and Glenda's initial feeling was a sense of injustice at the situation, feeling that it was simply "not fair" that this should be happening to them. However, once the initial shock begins to subside, a range of feelings start to emerge as the children begin to come to terms with their parents' separation; Glenda felt a mixture of relief, anger, loss, sadness, and uncertainty about the future—all at the same time. In such a period, the majority of children feel unsettled, and sometimes suffer from disturbed sleep patterns. During this time, Glenda was trying to come to terms with the changes happening in her family, new living and contact agreements, ongoing feelings of uncertainty about the future, and her continued confusion and worry surrounding the breakdown, all at the same time. During this period of readjustment, some children express concerns for their parents' happiness, and worry about them being lonely in the future; whilst others, like Glenda, try to deal with strong feelings of loss. She missed her absent parent, and, unfortunately, for some children who find such readjustments difficult, feelings of upset, anger, confusion, and loss last longer. Some children continue to feel isolated, and can see only the negative side of what has happened for a considerable period. Children additionally tend to find it very hard to accept that their parents really have separated, and continue to experience "magical" hopes of reconciliation—like Glenda and Mark. These children feel that the whole experience is a dream from which they will wake up, and then it will all be over.

Therefore, it is necessary to highlight the importance both of being told what is happening, and of being given an explanation of why the changes are necessary. At the height of emotional crisis of divorce—as well as afterwards, for most children—a sufficient degree of emotional support needs to be identified, and children need to be told what is happening. Furthermore, in order to restore some kind of balance, a degree of cognitive control over events is needed; being left out of the explanations could feel very like being left out altogether.

By not explaining and giving reasons to their children about the separation, Peter and Olivia failed to see that they were compounding their children's confusion and uncertainty about the future. Instead, the children needed to be told about the changes before they had happened— like when Peter left home without telling his children. What was particularly difficult for Glenda and Mark here was that they had not been given the opportunity to say goodbye to Peter.

Glenda and Mark simply did not know how to approach asking their parents questions when they wanted to know something about the breakdown; perhaps they didn't want to ask for fear of the consequences of doing so—or maybe they just intuitively thought it best just to "keep quiet".

In the absence of adequate information and explanation, some children glean what they can from a variety of sources: some rely on their friends' first-hand experiences of family breakdown, whilst others learn about separations and divorces at school. Meanwhile, some read books about divorce—and, certainly, television is the most common source of information about divorce and family breakdowns, including the repercussions they can have on the whole family dynamic.

After the divorce, Glenda harboured a parental relationship with both Peter and Olivia, characterized by a negative affective content, a degree of unresolved conflict, less satisfactory interparental relationships, and a distortion of parent-child relationships. These less-satisfactory relationships with her parents were primarily dominated by expressions of anger, this oftentimes being located in herself—whilst at other times, the origins of the anger were more clearly articulated ("Hell; I hate him! Couldn't stand her.") Children experiencing unhappy or strained relationships with one or both of their parents frequently attribute the source of their anger to be the breakdown of the trust that had previously existed between them. For Mark, the consequences of the "lies" he felt he had been told seemed likely to wield long-term impacts on the nature of his relationship with his father. Mark lost faith in his father, whom he felt had broken a "promise" not to leave him—something highly notable, since the language of "promises" and "lies" remains important to children. Therefore, children's anger at their "blameworthy" parent also takes into account the perceived effects of their actions on the other parent—often the one with whom the kid is living. Sometimes, Glenda felt unable to forgive Peter for leaving the family home, even though, for her, the overt conflict had ended. Further, even though it had been Olivia who had thrown Peter out of the home, Glenda's relationship with her father seemed shaky and to have altered. Children also sometimes resent the demands made by their absent parent, particularly when this leaves the residential parent with additional burdens—and, sometimes, such resentment is felt even more directly. Glenda's rejection of her father would seem to have grown from her perception that he had already rejected her when he left the family home. Her comments to Olivia captured such anger and sense of betrayal, as well as her sympathy for the resident parent and her resentment of Peter's new wife, Jennifer. All of this combined gave way to a deep, personal hurt and confusion. However, other children may express their feelings towards their absent parent in terms of regret and loss, rather than in terms of anger.

Because the conflict continued between Peter and Olivia long after their divorce, the children were made to carry what felt like very uncomfortable emotional burdens—and, in such circumstances, Olivia used her children as conduits for information and as a mean of communication between herself and Peter—ultimately a stressful role they hated to play that produced even greater anxiety. These children undertook an emotional "maintenance work" in support of their parents, feeling confused about which side they are to back up and whether they are required to be fair to both parents, when they really feel anger at one (or both) of them. They feel obliged to absorb their parents' regrets about the past, as well as how they allegedly sacrificed their own happiness to make the family survive and not break down. Therefore, they consider themselves to have a specific role in maintaining communications between their parents, sometimes even assuming the responsibility for supporting a parent financially—at least indirectly—by not being an extra burden by asking for money, as they normally would have done when their parents were living together.

The time of the parents' separation is a major and often quite rapid change: at this stage, Glenda and Mark felt a great deal of uncertainty about the future, and were preoccupied with concerns about what would happen to them and their mother. The most clearly discernible changes to their lives appeared in terms of their new "time maps", as well as having to accommodate to belonging to two households, both of which being "new" in the sense that each had rules, domestic arrangements, and patterns of expectation that were unfamiliar. However, such practical aspects of family change became absorbed into everyday life; alternatively, having to deal with these changes posed a great challenge.

Perhaps one of the most difficult situations children have to manage is when they experience divided loyalties, which occurs most prominently in relation to contact visits between children and their absent parent.

One of the most striking ways in which Glenda and Mark spoke of their relationships with their parents following the separation was through the lexical field of "time" and "doing things": expressions of loss were often mediated through a metaphor of time and/or activities like, "He always used to sit with me when he came in from work," and " He used to take me to places I liked to go; the, cinema or to watch football matches." Now, it was, "Now, we don't see more of him." The time spent together was prized, and appeared to be important in sustaining a positive view of the relationship a child had with their parent—even when other indicators suggested the relationship with a particular parent was not all that the child may have wished it to be. Glenda and Mark used time/activities to convey much more about their relationship with Peter than simply listing a detailed record of events, whilst Glenda, still angry with her father, allocated time to him to reflect her feeling of anger towards him.

The time spent together seemed to stand as a metaphor/symbol for the relationship between a child and parent—particularly the child's absent parent in the context of a perceived breach of trust on the part of one parent or both (broken promises). To extend this metaphor, here, children do not easily accept excuses for being "late" for an arranged meeting, the child's first thought usually being that their parent is not interested in them anymore and no longer loves them like before; similarly, they may assume that their work is now more important than them, or that their new partner is more important than his children. For children and adults lacking a complex emotional vocabulary, the "facts" of time spent together is a very visible way of sustaining and managing their relationship—even if it may be a little forced sometimes. Some relationship maintenance tasks performed by parents may be understood as—usually appreciated—attempts to compensate for what has happened through the divorce. Children describe this as "I now gets on better with my mother/father."

As well as sustaining, managing, and caring for their relationships with their parents, some children have to negotiate a range of new step-relationships. These are rarely introduced tactfully to children; indeed, it would seem that many parents simply don't know how to tell their children they have a new partner—and, when the parent in question is not living with their children and their relationship with them is poor, some will simply keep it secret—even to the extent of not revealing they had remarried. Resident parents sometimes try to integrate the new partner into the household, but children soon notice when furniture and fittings begin to change! In other instances, children discover for themselves that their parents have new relationships—largely through overheared conversations, or through their own observations. For others—like Glenda and Mark—, such a discovery comes as a shock, as when Peter introduced Jennifer in his life after meeting them "accidently-on-purpose" while out with the children. In such a situation, Glenda and Mark felt extremely awkward and embarrassed. Much depends on the skill of all concerned in smoothing this over and enabling the new relationship between the child and new partner to begin positively; in general, children appear to be most comfortable when the introduction is gradual and they are able to familiarize themselves with the new partner over a period of time. The single biggest influence on whether the children and their parent's new partner "get on" with each other concerns the degree to which the new partner attempted to act like another "mum" or "dad"; when the children feel this to be the case, they become overwhelmingly hostile, regarding this as an attempt to replace their own parent and to assume a role the person is not entitled to play.

Children who feel that their parents' new partners are like adult "friends" express the most positive feelings about them. This may change over time, of course; it is possible that the "friendship phase" represents a stage that such relationships go through before they move into a more overt, quasi-parental model—or vice versa. In other instances (like that of Glenda's), where not only were the divorce's circumstances acrimonious, but where the ensuing emotions were raised, leading to children remaining implacably hostile toward their parent's new partner. The majority of children in this situation reflect on the advent of the new partner either wistfully or with sadness. In a similar vein, a similar but more intense expression of such feelings could arise concerning the presence of new stepsiblings; in this instance, children use the familiar metaphor of time to describe their relationship with their parent and their parent's new child. Children directly think the stepsibling had taken all the interest and attention of the parent, and that the parent no longer cares about them anymore. However, additions to the household are not always seen negatively; there have been numerous instances of positive feelings whereby the children again use the metaphors of time and activities as a way to describe this developing new relationship with their step-siblings.

Whether such changes are welcomed or not, children feel obliged to learn to negotiate the new ways of engaging with their parents as a result of the advent of their new partners; in this regard, Glenda expressed her frustrations at having to find new ways of relating to her father on her visits to him and Jennifer. She sometimes felt Peter to be annoying, and quickly stopped enjoying going to his house—especially when Jennifer was been present, during which times Glenda would feel uncomfortable. She felt as though she was being monitored, all her movements and actions not only under surveillance, but also being scrutinized by Jennifer. Therefore, she found herself watching her own actions all the time, ultimately feeling chained in fear of embarrassing her dad and causing him problems if Jennifer got embarrassed herself.

Whilst children as being more prepared to talk to their mothers is widely reported in the literature, it is apparent that the circumstances of divorce greatly influence children's willingness and/or capacity to talk to their parents. Because it is mostly fathers who leave, children's opportunities to talk to them automatically reduce, oftentimes leading to the fathers being "blamed"; meanwhile, in most cases. it is mothers who stay and who actually have to care for the child on a day-to-day basis. Therefore, children usually talk more readily to their mothers.

The quality of children's relationships with their parents after divorce is largely related to the relationship that existed before the divorce: good, open, and communicative relationships between parents and children seem to be able to withstand a great deal of internal and external stress. Indeed, once any divorce-contingent conflict subsides, relationships can even improve—and so in situations where relationships between children and parents have grown to be less equitable and mutual than desired, the stress of divorce creates an even larger negative impact.

A factor that is absolutely critical to the potential of relationships between children and parents during—and immediately after—parental separation is the arrangements they have for contact, the making of which having proved to be one of the most difficult aspects of the whole process of separation and divorce. Even when, on the surface, the family relationships appear to have reached an equilibrium, contact arrangements retain a disruptive potential to reopen old wounds and tensions. Indeed, there is clearly no prescription for successful contact arrangements—and, even to date, there is little evidence on which to base an evaluation of the different types or frequencies of contact that should be employed. In fact, the existing evidence outlines the many difficulties involved in establishing workable arrangements with which all parties are happy. Maintaining contact arrangements requires a considerable amount of negotiation between parents who may already be experiencing communication difficulties—and, to make matters more difficult, there are no clear roles/norms for post-divorce parenting. It is therefore unsurprising that, in spite of parents' wishes for ongoing contact, up to a third of children lose contact with their non-resident parent within the first couple of years of divorce.

With all of the above in mind, it is also unsurprising to know that more than half of the children in such situations are not consulted over the question of residence; here, it seems that children and young people are perhaps not consulted as widely as you one may expect, or, indeed, as much as the children in question would have preferred. Glenda and Mark felt excluded from this decision, feeling obliged to say yes to every instance of seeing Peter and staying in touch with him. The most common pattern for consultation with a child is for parents to make decisions and then ask their children what they think about the proposed arrangements—a practice that usually makes the children feel excluded from the decision-making, and, in turn, like they are no more than a "personal belonging" that the parents are negotiating about as part of the divorce deal. Indeed, most children feel they should have more say in decisions about contact, and that they feel they should be able to alter contact arrangements if they are unhappy with them.

However, in the majority of cases (like Glenda and Mark), children usually accept that the final decision is not theirs—particularly those who are afraid of the burden of making the final decision. When it comes to residence in particular, children experience difficulties when deciding who they wanted to live with, usually feeling torn between wanting to have their say and not wanting to hurt their parents' feelings. Most of all, it is important to children that they are at least given the opportunity to prevent themselves from being forced into arrangements with which they are unhappy with.

Glenda and Mark's attempts at continuing a meaningful relationship with each parent after their separation were mediated by a number of other practical issues besides the simple availability of time: whilst their parents were attempting to disengage from the marital relationship and began to build a new life for themselves, the children were trying to develop individual relationships with each of their parents in a changing environment—and often in a new location. Hence, the immediate aftermath of the separation was a time of great uncertainty. Children require a great deal of reassurance concerning the fact that they will be able to continue to see and spend time with their non-resident parent—and yet even with such reassurance, temporary living arrangements, parents moving long distances away from the family home, or feelings of upset, guilt, or blame surrounding the separation, mean that such visits often take some time to establish—leaving a number of children having to live through an initial period of not seeing their non-resident parent.

The children's descriptions of such feelings surrounding contact highlighted the emotional highs and lows that characterized spending part of their lives with Olivia and part with Peter and Jennifer. Indeed, whilst many children may look forward to and enjoy contact with their non-resident parent, they often still miss their resident parent, as well as other elements of "normal home life". Likewise, when at home with Olivia, Glenda and Mark missed Peter, and looked forward to their next visit greatly. Children usually consider their resident parent as being the best one at providing them with support, and many regret the limited access they have to their non-resident parent; however, not all children choose to go to their resident parent for help, feeling that they do not understand what they are experiencing and, therefore, cannot help. Thus, in this situation, they choose not to talk about anything at all with them. Meanwhile, other children recognize their resident parent is too upset themselves about what is happening to be able to provide help, as they are themselves in need of help—and these children are thus primarily concerned with not upsetting their parents further. At the other end of the picture are some children who feel that their parents have "moved on" and thus don't want to remind them of what happened in the past—even though the children still feel a need to talk about it themselves.

Children's ways of adapting to the repeated waves of emotion associated with contact vary; whilst some manage to adjust to their feelings quickly, the anticipated highs and lows becoming part of their accepted new routine, others find managing the highs and lows to be more difficult. For some children, dealing with contact visits also means having to manage their parents' feelings, meaning children often come to be aware of the difficulties their parents are experiencing in trying to adjust to being essentially "part-time" parents.

Mark and Glenda found themselves becoming directly involved in the issues related to their parents' continuing relationship, often witnessing their parents arguing—particularly at the beginning and end of their visits to Peter, when the parents would be picking up or dropping off the children. Olivia and Peter's behavior ultimately left their children feeling as if they were fighting to hold together positive parent–child relationships—something that often proved difficult to manage.

Regardless, Glenda and Mark felt able to talk with Olivia about the time they spent with Peter and Jennifer, and, upon returning home from contact visits, they began by talking through their visits and how they had spent time with Peter and Jennifer. However, this easy exchange is not always possible for other children; Glenda, for example, felt that talking to Olivia about what she had done with Jennifer specifically may cause her to feel jealous. This led to Glenda trying to avoid going to visit her father while Jennifer was around at all costs—and, indeed, children whose parents are unable to communicate reasonably often feel a similar way, taking it upon themselves to deliver messages between their parents—usually concerning practical details about contact arrangements. When such messages involve simply passing information between parents, children are usually happy to do so—particularly when they feel they are helping their parents.

A common feeling amongst children is that they should be prepared to deliver messages between their parents so as to avoid any conflict they think would occur if their parents were to communicate directly with one another; however, the occasional instance of parents wanting their children to pass on "bad" messages is a very upsetting experience for the children involved—although despite their finding their parents' negative comments about each other to be upsetting, some older children are still able to reason through why their parents act in such a way.

Glenda and Mark also found themselves having to cope with Olivia asking questions about Peter's new life—and when such questions concerned practical issues, they felt they could be of help by answering, and were happy to do so. However, Glenda experienced Olivia asking for more personal information about the relationship between Peter and Jennifer—something Glenda usually found to be uncomfortable and difficult to manage.

Finally, in some cases, one parent does not want the other to know certain details about their new life, and ask their children to keep secrets; and at other times, the children themselves feel a parent may come to be upset if they know of certain things about the other, thus deciding to keep certain details secret themselves. Whatever the situation, keeping secrets is practically and emotionally difficult for most children.

Dear spouses: you can disagree, with one another, but don't fight nasty. If you have a disagreement in your children's presence, use a time-out to bring things to a better place as quickly as possible, and let them see you coming back together; they often can't see how you do that, because many couples make up behind closed doors. As far as your children's wellbeing is concerned, coming back to some point of emotional harmony is more important than resolving whatever it was you were fighting about—so do your children a favor and work together to manage your conflicts well and with respect.

An awareness of the extent to which children are going about to recover a "balance" in their lives should also influence the pace and timing of any formal interventions during the critical phase in which children begin to absorb the fact that their parents are separating/divorcing. I am not pretending that understanding and respecting children's own emotional pace is easy, but what I am presenting here is just a reminder that we have to recognize the difficulty that children have in expressing their emotions. They are also inclined to express their sensitivities through their use of metaphor, etc. This is also a reminder that children are able to demonstrate a sympathy for and understanding of their parents, even in the midst of their own upset.

Parents are the most obvious actual/potential providers of support to children throughout the divorce process, and so when parents remain on reasonable terms with one another—or where the children feel able to sustain separate and positive relationships with both parents—, children often consider their parents to be an accessible, useful source of emotional support, information, and advice.

It is additionally useful to mention here that the majority of children possess little to no knowledge, understanding, and experience concerning the legal process of divorce; hence, it is crucial to mention that the degree to which children are kept informed (or aren't) of the major events and decisions that are to significantly impact their emotions, reactions, relationships with their parents, and coping mechanisms, concerning their parents' divorce, is pivotal. Although they may not be informed directly, it may so happen that some children overhear the adults conversations and telephone calls between their parents, through which children pick up some legal terminology that they don't really understand and may interpret them wrongly—especially when they are offered no explanation. This leads to even more resentful feelings towards one (or both) of their parents, and, in most of these cases, children feel obliged to "work things out for themselves", seeking the relevant information from different sources (e.g., the media; internet; friends; books). Two major problems arise from seeking information from sources other than their parents: first, the "law", according to such children, often focuses on criminal cases that bear little relevance to the civil proceedings in which their parents are engaged; and secondly, the legal system portrayed in such mediums is often not related to the country of residence of the children. Hence, somewhat unsurprisingly, whilst children may indeed reach conclusions that are realistic, it is more often that they are completely wrong.

What parents should be aware of before making the decision to divorce:
- The emotional crisis of the children accompanying their parent's separation;

- Meeting the children's informational needs;
- Meeting the children's support needs;
- Managing the ensuing critical family transitions and their aftermath;
- Children's use of social support systems;
- Children's coping mechanisms.

Sheldon Kopp (1978), in his poignant little book titled An End to Innocence, contrasts innocence and pseudo-innocence—the former being that real stage in our young lives dictated by fairytales and maxims (e.g., "if you work hard and always try to do your best, people will respect you."), when trust is a nonissue and things are as they see; and the latter being a caricature of innocence, being both like and unlike that original state. The pseudo-innocent is the adult who is unable to give up those childhood securities of believing that life is predictable and follows certain known rules, and are always vulnerable, since they have no protection from life's irregularities, cruelties, and simple realities.

We are a society that values childhood for its own sake; we take great pride in protecting innocence, and we worry about children whose innocence is shattered too early. Meanwhile, there are other societies that emphasize being an adult, carefully planning experiences that will lead children to adulthood as soon as possible. Given our values, it is no wonder that our approach to marriage and divorce is often immature. Perhaps the divorce myth is a creation of crumbling pseudo-innocence— or, worse, a refusal to abandon pseudo-innocence in the face of a hard reality. The petulance, naivete, and fear that are often exhibited during divorce recalls a childlike disillusionment; after all, divorce is no time to grow up. It is more disturbing, however, if parents do not grow up during their divorces and move beyond their pseudo-innocence.

We must point out mythical positions and confront them—not to minimize the experience of divorce, as of course, with all myths, there is a strong element of truth that must be accepted, examined, and lived out, but rather to stop integrating fantasy into reality.

Although we are accustomed to thinking of grown-ups as more mature than their children, what if some children come into the world and are more emotionally mature than their parents, who have been around for decades? What happens when these immature parents lack the emotional responsiveness necessary to meet their children's emotional needs? The result is the mentally and emotionally distorted generations of youth that we see nowadays.

ABOUT BELIEVING
YOU ARE LOVED

From Glenda's Diary:

WE LEARN ABOUT LOVE in early childhood, and—whether our homes are happy or troubled, or our parents are functional or dysfunctional—home is the original school of love. I cannot remember ever wanting to ask my parents to define love; in my mind, love is the good feeling I get when parents treat me like I matter, and I treat them like they matter. For me, love is always and only about good feelings. Thus, when Mark and I would be reprimanded and told that our punishments were "for our own good" or that they were "doing this because they loved you," I was confused; how could harsh punishments be a gesture of love? However, as all other children do, I pretended to accept this as a piece of grown-up logic I didn't yet understand—although I knew in my heart it was not right. Really, I knew it was a lie—like the lie my parents tell me now, when they explain after a harsh punishment that "It hurts me more than it hurts you." There is nothing that creates more confusion about love in my mind and heart than unkind or cruel punishments from the people who have taught us about love and respect. I learnt early on to question the meaning of love; I yearned for it, even as I doubted its very existence.

On the flip side of my story, there are masses of children who grow up confident that love is a good feeling, who are never punished and are allowed to believe that love is only about getting their needs met and desires satisfied. In their minds, love is not about what they have to give; love is mostly something given to them. When children like these are overindulged—either materially or by being allowed to act out—, this is a form of neglect; they, though not in any way abused or uncared for, are usually unclear about love's meaning, thus being emotionally abandoned. Both groups learn to think about love primarily in relation to good feelings, in the context of reward and punishment.

From early childhood onwards, I remember being told I was loved when I did things that pleased my parents—and, in turn, I learned to give them affirmations of love when they pleased me. Whilst growing up, I associated love more with acts of attention, affection, and caring, and even now, I still see love as being when my parents attempt to satisfy my desires.

When asked to define love, my friends told me, "Like when I have something to eat that I really like, especially if it's my favorite." They will say, "My mommy loves me 'cause she takes care of me and helps me do everything right." When asked how they love someone, they talk about giving hugs and kisses, or being sweet and cuddly.

The notion that love is about getting what one wants—whether it's a hug, a new sweater, a trip to Disneyland, or a favorite cooked food— makes it difficult for us to acquire a deeper emotional understanding when we grow up.

Parents like to imagine that most children will be born into homes where they will be loved, but love will never be present if the parents don't know how to love.

Not too many years from now, it will not matter what sort of house I lived in, what was in my bank account, or the kind of car I drove—but the world may be different because I was important in the life of my parents.

DO WE EVER CHANGE?

Just when you think you have learned the way to live,
life changes.

OLIVIA

"TELL ME ABOUT NICK. Is he drop-dead gorgeous? And does he have any brothers?"

Nicole surprised me with the question during our daily venting session.

I hadn't expected her to be particularly curious over Nick—at least, not to the point of wanting details. I had avoided any previous discussions with her involving Nick; it wasn't a serious relationship yet—at least, not from my side—, and yet she wouldn't give it up.

"Not that I know of," I countered. "But then, there are lots of things I don't know about him."

This was true: since the first—and only—date we'd been on, I'd spoken to him on the phone twice, both conversations being funny, jokey, and devoid of any information or substance. It was so blissfully unlike all those stilted boy/girl conversations I'd had years ago, when I'd started going out with boys: you talked about what school you'd gone to, or what courses you were doing in college, and where your parents came from—all so you could "place" the person and figure out if it was safe to bring him home.

I'd been married for so long that I could barely remember life before Peter, when I had gone on dates with a variety of men—always unsuitable ones, in my father's opinion. Dating as a grown-up was much more fun; no one had to approve of my choice, except myself.

"No," I said thoughtfully, "I'm pretty sure Nick has a couple of sisters, but no brothers."

"That's perfect," she grinned. "If he has sisters, he'll understand women—not like those who've grown up with an adoring mammie and no female company to educate them about the ways of the world."

I laughed. "Peter has a sister, and he still doesn't know shit about women."

"You look great, recently, Olivia," Nicole said suddenly, with sincerity.

"The slightly plump, out-of-shape Olivia was a thing of the past." I burst into laughter.

As much as I had started to make more of a physical effort as of late, it wasn't even how I looked that made the difference: I'd changed from the inside out. The nervous, miserable woman of six months ago—someone constantly on the verge of tears—had now been replaced by an attractive woman who had learned to live life on her own terms. The life I had led before was a house of cards, bound to tumble down sooner or later—and, as much as it had been agony when it all fell apart, let's be honest, there's no easy way to break up a marriage; there are always waves of troubles that follow.

"Are you all right?" Nicole asked gently.

"Yes." I cleared the lump that had raised in my front. "I was thinking whether I should have accepted Nick's dinner invite today. Should I?"

"Definitely. You should go, girl; let this little beautiful heart overflow with love again."

Apprehension had nagged at me all night—maybe because I'm not sure of my feelings toward Nick—hence my need for Nicole's approval.

My marriage with Peter and everything that it entailed still crept like a shadow in the back of my mind at all times; even shoving it to the back of my mind, or to deny it entirely, was next to impossible.

Nothing would ever come close to the intensity of my first true love—kind of like fantastic sex: nothing is ever be able to top one's first time having sex, the, "Holy crap, what the hell was that?" type of first time. That was what first true love felt like to me. Peter was my first real everything, and, if he hadn't walked out on me, I would have remained the most faithful, wonderful, respectful wife to him for the rest of my life. It was all his fault, not mine.

However, looking back now, I couldn't be more grateful that we separated. During those months of crying in bed, stuck in a somewhat catatonic state, something shifted inside me: the perfect, obedient, sweet lady named Olivia Meadow grew the beginning of a backbone while lay dying in her bed. I don't know how, but the shift had slowly begun.

I had suffered through very few bad relationships before Peter—and, after my marriage ended, I came to the conclusion that true love wasn't real... And then I thought back to my time with Peter, and realized that had been real—the most real love anyone could possibly experience in a single given lifetime. Certainly, I would find true love again—and so here I was, still wondering about Nick. I had tried to look him up on Facebook and Twitter in attempt to glean more information, with no luck.

The phone rang and broke into my thoughts. I turned to answer it, but was beaten by Glenda, who'd jumped up at the first ring; certainly, she thought it to be her boyfriend calling her.

"Oh, hi," she said somewhat disappointedly, pressing the receiver to her ear. "Yes, she's here. Do you want to talk to her?" She held it out to me. "it's for you. Nick."

I took the phone, and Glenda winked at me.

"Hello," I greeted. "How are you, Nick?"

"I'm fine. How are you? And how are the kids?"

"All is fine, thanks."

"Do you want to go out today?"

The question caught me off-guard—not because he was asking it, but because of the certainty of my own immediate reaction: I wanted to see Nick again. I was surprised at how strong the desire was.

"Okay," I said swiftly. "What time?"

"Now?"

"Not just yet; I've things to sort out. What about four o'clock?"

"Okay." I felt the warmth of his voice radiate down the phone. "Four o'clock. See you later, Liv."

The thought of Nick penetrated my mind—another long-haired, athletic person. I bit my lip. Was I really going to walk down that road again? I wished I could stop thinking about Nick, as though he was a real fixture in my life—as though he was someone I could even contemplate marrying. I'd made a mess of one marriage by thinking of Peter in exactly the same way before I'd really got to know him. The thing about life is that you only think you've learned from your mistakes, when in fact, we all make the same ones over and over again, but with different people and in different ways.

"Hello again, Liv. How are you, honey?"

Nick's voice hadn't lost its attractiveness, a subtle warmth dripping from it that made the endearment "honey" sound deliciously sexy.

"Still on for today?" he was saying.

"Of course; it's not every night I get brought to a dinner and concert, so I'm not going to miss it." I smiled despite myself.

"Are you finally going to tell me what you're wearing, or is it still a big secret?"

I stifled my irritation: ever since Nick had asked me to accompany him to the concert, he had been wheedling away to find out what I will be going to wear.

"It's a surprise. I want to dazzle you."

"Dazzle?" echoed Nick, somewhat suspiciously.

"Yes, dazzle." I felt myself growing agitated.

What was the matter with this man? Every time he mentioned hanging out, he wanted to know what I was going to be wearing—even though I'd told him it was to be a surprise more times than I could count.

"I just want to know; that's all," he said dejectedly.

"Why?"

I couldn't help my voice from sounding irritated; I was annoyed by the implication that I couldn't pick something suitable for a concert without his help. I wasn't some hare-brained bimbo who couldn't tell a black-tie affair from a beery barbeque in somebody's back garden; I was a working woman—a successful working woman, at that. So why the hell was he treating me as if I was an imbecile with no fashion sense?

Damn him. He was so square when it came to clothes, never satisfied: after buying me a ludicrously childish dress the first time we went out shopping, he'd subsequently surprised me with another maidenly outfit—this time an expensive white ghost dress that made me look like a milkmaid. He was probably expecting me to wear that to the concert! Well, he could forget about that quick.

As if reading my thoughts, he said, "I'd love to see you wearing my dress, Liv. You look beautiful in it; so feminine and elegant." There was a pause. "I'm sorry," he added in a low voice. "It's childish to want you to wear my present."

I sighed. Don't be so hard on him, Liv; you're just out of sync with normal relationships, I lectured myself. Most men probably want their girlfriends to wear feminine outfits instead of knock-them-dead sexy dresses. Perfectly normal, isn't it?

"I love the white dress you bought me." It was only a half-lie; I did like it, but it still wasn't the sort of thing I wanted to wear to the office—and it was far too impractical to inspire confidence in my clients. "But I've bought a lovely dress for this concert specifically, and I want to wear it. You'll like it when you see it, I just know it."

"Okay, darling," he said. "As you wish. I'll come to pick you up soon."

He'll hate it, I thought as I hung up. It was very sexy—the complete opposite of the white dress he'd bought. A year ago, I wouldn't have dreamed of wearing anything like it—but then again, a year ago, I wouldn't have fitted into a long, oyster-colored halter-neck dress—especially not one that molded my body like surgical gloves. Even still, I wouldn't surpass this chance; looking sexy is an unbeatable joy.

The only problem I faced was that Nick would surely go ballistic when I told him I had to work late nights for the next coming week—and potentially a lot more in the future. Nick didn't seem to understand that I was now a different person, having changed completely from the inside out. Besides, I was now a skilful, successful working woman; he'd known what I wanted to do when we first met, but now, he really seemed to hate me working at night and wearing revealing dresses. I don't know why.

I was afraid that this was a typical male reaction, when independence is wonderful—an attractive quality, in fact—, like wearing sexy clothes—that is, until you become an item. Then, it's "don't go out wearing that dress; cover up your boobs; cover up your legs", or whatever else, and then you become Little Miss Stay-At-Home.

Nicole had told me this was because Nick wasn't confident and secure in himself—but could that really be? Nick loved the fact that I'd made my own way in the world after my divorce—he'd praised me all the way long—, so what had changed? And why did I always get stuck with the ones who wanted to turn me into the bloody housewife from hell?

Relax, Liv, I thought to myself now. Breathe. Come on, give him a chance. He's probably trying to protect you. He can see that you're stretching yourself by doing two jobs inside and outside home.

I was beginning to feel claustrophobic—yes, that was it. It had been rattling around in my head for the past two weeks. In the three months since I'd dated Nick, I'd had a marvellous time, nearly all the time. He was a handsome, attentive lover, and this had doubled my confidence, making me feel happy, relaxed, and as secure as a recently separated woman could be.

Nick stayed at my house on the nights when the kids were with Peter, and we made passionate love before falling asleep wrapped in each other's arms; then, on Sunday mornings, we'd sit in bed, watching the TV and having breakfast, before making love again—usually with toast crumbs sticking to our bodies.

In fact, I was amazed at how quickly I'd gotten used to his presence in my life—and my bed. When Peter had left, I'd genuinely thought I'd never want another man ever again—and yet here I was, in a serious relationship with Nick.

Nick had certainly improved my life and made me feel better about myself in every way—but there was something not quite right about our relationship lately. I'd first noticed it when he rang me from his office a few days before to tell me his trip to California the following day had been cancelled. Instead, he'd invited me to have a romantic dinner for two—and I'd turned him down. I told him I had to stay with the kids during the weekdays, and that I wasn't really able to do late nights in the middle of the week; I'd fall asleep at my desk if I didn't get a decent seven hours' sleep. Essentially, I rejected him, and hoped he understood my reasons—but, as became clear later, he didn't.

Well, the kids were more important than a night out; they needed me, and there had been enough troubles and uncertainty in their lives recently. They needed a stable home life, and I was out often enough as it was because of my work. They needed to know I was there when they wanted me.

Nick had slowly but surely grown even more annoyed the following weekend, when I couldn't spend Saturday afternoon with him; I felt it more important to cook for the kids, since they'd had to find something to eat the whole week when they come back from school.

"You can't work all the time," he'd snapped. "You've got to stop working so hard. This bloody business and your kids will mean I'll never get to see you."

Ahh; that was more like it. He wasn't upset at the idea of me working too hard to build a future for me and the kids; he was just cross because it meant he couldn't get what he wanted. Typical man. He'd been so cold towards me during our recent meet-ups that I'd found myself apologizing for Saturday, as well as my staying with the kids during the week. I told him I'd consult him in the future so my cooking wouldn't impede on our time together, and that I'd try to check with him in the future, in case he already had anything nice planned, before committing to late nights at work.

It was as soon as I said these things that I realized I'd made a huge mistake: I'd made a rod for my own back, and had basically signed myself up for a bad patch.

Was I sickeningly in love? Was I so seduced by the way he made me feel that I'd really just put my kids second? Or had I just wanted to get my own back at Peter by having such a sexy, handsome boyfriend? Had I let that, and his amazing ability in bed, blind me to his faults?

I hated myself; I hated love; I hated my heart—but for God's sake, I wouldn't do anything he wanted so long as he kept behaving childishly. My future and my kids were my priorities—and my red lines. He had to understand that; otherwise, it will be time to say goodbye. I wouldn't make the same mistake twice.

"Hi, Nick," I said now after dialling his number. "Sorry, but I actually won't be able to make it today; Mark caught a cold, and he has a fever. I have to stay in to take care of him. Sorry for the short notice, but it's out of my hands, you know?"

"It's all right. I understand," Nick said sharply. "But I'm leaving for California in two days, and will only be back in three weeks. I have a lot of work there."

"Hold on," I cut in, my heart dropping. "Three weeks? I hadn't known that; can we have our dinner tomorrow, just after work? I can't bear to not see you for a whole three weeks!"

Typical male; typical female.

PLEASE, TELL ME MORE SWEET LITTLE LIES

From Olivia's Diary:

SOMEWHERE ALONG THE WAY, I must have deemed myself worthy of happiness, because here I am, in the center of emotional reincarnation. I'm changing—and I'm terrified of it. I'm losing touch with the world I have always known; I'm being challenged to look beyond my illnesses, and I'm scared of what I'll find. Am I looking toward love, happiness, and stability? Do I even know what that means? I'm stepping out of my homely darkness into the light—and it is blinding. That is where I am now: sleeves rolled up, immersed in the work of my soul. The pain I spent a lifetime building up must now be dissected in a matter of time; it is only the demolition of my emotional walls and the destruction of what I have known as safety that will provide that for me. I am tortured by my thoughts and plagued by my feelings, and all my escape routes have been disposed of. This process is known as getting better. I am building the life I never knew I could have.

Olivia and Mia had dreams that were shattered and worn down with age: they found themselves disappointed by their husbands, people, events, and realities that didn't (and couldn't) match their ideals. Nick and Ross were their ideal lovers, but people who thrive on their broken dreams spend their lives dwelling on fantasies, longing for romance, adventure, and lofty spiritual connections. Nick and Ross reflected their fantasies; they were artists in creating the illusion they required, idealizing their portraits. In a world full of disenchantment and baseness, there is limitless seductive power in following the path of the ideal lover.

Nick and Ross's method was simple: they studied Olivia and Mia, went along with their moods, established what was missing from their lives, and provided it. They made themselves the ideal lovers, fulfilling Olivia and Mia's cravings for adventure, romance, and someone who would sacrifice time and comfort to have them. Playing the ideal lover role, Nick and Ross successfully seduced Olivia and Mia, constantly adapting himself to the woman's ideals and effectively bringing her fantasy to life. Once she had fallen under his spell, a little ruse and calculation sealed the romance. The ideal lover is rare in the modern world—they knew that—, and so they focused intensely on the other person, fathoming what she was missing and what she was disappointed by. Mia and Olivia revealed this in subtle ways—through gestures, tone of voice, and looks in the eye. By appearing to embody what Olivia and Mia lacked, Nick and Ross became their ideals—and, to create this effect, they had been patient and gave special attention to detail. Olivia and Mia couldn't resist the temptation of following their ideal lovers, who seemed so attuned to their desires that they could bring their fantasies to life.

Mia and Olivia carried inside them an ideal—either of what they would like to become, or of what they wanted another person to be for them. This ideal goes back to what they once felt was missing in their lives—either what others did not give to them, or what they could not give to themselves.

Their ideals were buried in disappointment and yet continued to lurk beneath, waiting to be sparked—and, thus, when Ross and Nick seemed to have that ideal quality and the ability to bring it out in them, they fell in love.

The key to following the path of the ideal lover was their ability to observe: they focused on the tone of their voice, a blush here, a look there—and all of these compounded into signs that betrayed what their words could never say. They made Mia and Olivia feel nobler, and made the sensual and sexual seem spiritual. Like all seducers, they played with power, always disguising their manipulations behind the façade of an ideal. Nothing is more seductive than patient attentiveness; it makes the affair seem lofty and aesthetic, and not really about sex.

The opposite sex is a strange entity we can never fully know—and this excites us, in turn creating the proper sexual tension. However, this is also a source of annoyance and frustration as men do not understand how women think, and vice versa, each still trying to make the other act more like a member of their own sex. Dandies may never try to please, but in this one area, they have a pleasing effect: by adopting the psychological traits of the opposite sex, they appeal to our inherent narcissism.

Overt strength and power are rarely seductive; it makes us afraid, or envious. Rather, the royal road to seduction is to play up your vulnerability and

helplessness. You cannot, however, make this obvious; to seem to be begging for sympathy is to seem to be needy, which is a blatantly unattractive trait. Do not proclaim yourself to be a victim or underdog, but reveal it in your manner—in your confusion. A display of "natural" weakness will make you instantly lovable, both lowering people's defenses and making them feel delightfully superior to you. Put yourself in situations that make you seem weak, in which someone else has the advantage; they are the bully, and you are the innocent lamb. Without any effort on your part, people will feel sympathy for you. Once people's eyes cloud over with sentimental mist, they will not see how you are manipulating them.

AND WHEN THE STORY IS OVER, NOTHING IS LEFT BUT REGRET AND BLAME

From Olivia's Diary:

ONCE UPON A TIME, you were the wildest of my dreams that had come true. We were too young when we fell in love, not even knowing what it was, but I still had every faith in what I was seeing; faith in me, and in you. Your love was like a knife that cut through my soul, but it was the sweetest pain. How naïve I was when I'd believe that if I did everything perfectly, nothing unexpected would ever happen to me... But now that I'm falling apart and the light that once dawned on me is becoming nothing but darkness, and now that I find myself obliged to run away, searching for the light again, I know that not to be the case. It is a tough choice, but one must learn how to kill before one can feel safe—and I am choosing to kill my old self. The truth is, it is not until we are lost that we can begin to understand ourselves; all I remember now is your back, walking towards the door, leaving me in your past. I begged you to want me, to stay, but you didn't want to—and I got tired of listening to the sound of my own tears, desperate that the best years had already gone by. But if you have held me tight, we would have been holding on forever, and we would have only been making it bearable for the time being.

Not knowing when the dawn will come again, I opened every door. He came when I was afraid of the world, and picked me up from the ground. He came to fill the holes that you burned in me; he took care of me and loved me. He restored my faith that a man could be kind and caring. I made something of myself, and he let me feel worthy. Back then, I didn't have anything you needed, so I was deemed worthless. He promised he will never leave me like you did, because unlike you, he was going to put me first, and would always love my flaws before praising my strengths. He will never break my heart. He will be fighting against all the odds; I know it will be alright this time.

From Peter's Diary:

I am editing the memories of you, pretending you thought more of me than you actually did—and I'm much happier. Maybe I was foolish and made mistakes, but the blame isn't entirely mine; you made me scared to confess my flaws, since they would make you jump to conclusions and incoherent judgments. Take a look in the mirror and tell me what you see: do you see yourself clearly, or are you still deceived? You were terrified of feeling incomplete; you had a fear of becoming nobody, and so you wanted to break me down, too. Your favorite position was beside yourself, thinking only about your needs and incompleteness—and so I took all my expectations and buried them all at the bottom of the ocean, because I alone was never brave enough to dive that deep. I took my pain—all my anguish—and turned it into power; that's what men do. I found more of myself in the loneliest of hours; I used my tears to create rivers for my boat, and I floated. And even when I begged for forgiveness, your ego was too high to confess your flaws.

I took your refusal as a sign to move on—and I found a woman, one that is stronger than anyone I know. I found a love to carry more than just my secrets—one that knows I am human after all, not prophet or a Messiah.

Now, the melody has changed and I sing a new song.

References

- Akestam, N., Rosengren, S., & Dahlen, M. (2017): Advertising "Like a Girl": Toward a Better Understanding of "Femverstising" and its Effects. Psychol Mark (34, pp.795-806).
- Ann, M. G. (1998): The Basal Ganglia and Chunking of Action Repertoires. Neurobiology of Learning and Memory (70, pp.119-36).
- Ann, M. G. (2008): Overview at Habits, Rituals, and the Evaluative Brain. Annual Review of Neuroscience (31, pp.359-87).
- Ariely, D. (2008): Predictably Irrational: The Hidden Forces That Shape Our Decisions. An imprint of HarperCollins Publishers, New York.
- Baudrillard, J. (1990): Seduction, Trans. Brian Singer. New York; St. Martin's Press.
- Bennett-Goleman, T. (2001): Emotional Alchemy: How the Mind Can Heal the Heart. Harmony Books.
- Brilliant, A. (1979): I may not be perfect but parts of me are excellent. Santa Barbara, California, Woodbridge Press.
- Butler, I.; Scanlan, L.; Robinson, M.; Douglas, G. & Murch. M. (2003): Divorcing Children: Children's Experience of Their Parents' Divorce.
- Catherine, A. T. et al., (2010): Differential Dynamics of Activity Changes in Dorsomedial Striatal Loops During Learning. Neuron (66, pp.781-95).
- Chalon, J. (1940): Portrait of a Seductress: The World of Natalie Barney, Trans. Carol Barko. New York: Crown Publishers, Inc.
- Charles D. (2013): The Power of Habit: Why We do What We do and How to Change. Random House Books.
- Chase, H.; Clark, L., (2010): Gambling Severity Predicts Midbrain Response to Near-Miss Outcomes. Journal of Neuroscience (30; 18, pp. 6180-87).
- Chomsky, N. (2002): Understanding Power.
- Chrisler, J.C.; Johnston-Robledo, I. (2018): Woman's Embodied Self: Feminist Perspectives on Identity and Image. American Psychological Association.
- Cottler, L.; Leung, K. (2009): Treatment of Pathological Gambling. Current Opinion in Psychiatry, (22; 1, pp. 69-74).
- De Angelis, B. (2005): How Did I Get Here? Finding your way to renewed hope and happiness when life and love take unexpected turns. St. Martin's Griffin, New York.

- Dixon, M.; Habib, R. (2010): Neuro-behavioral Evidence for the 'Near-Miss' Effect in Pathological Gamblers. Journal of the Experimental Analysis of Behavior (93; 3, pp.313-28).
- Erin Gibbs Van Brunschot (2009): Gambling and Risk Behaviour: A Literature Review. University of Calgary.
- Farber, B.A.; Blanchard, M. & Love, M. (2019): Secrets and Lies in Psychotherapy. The American Psychological Association (pp.31-53).
- Feldman, C. (2004): The Buddhist Path to Simplicity: Spiritual Practice for Everyday Life.
- Freud, S. (1995): Psychological Writings and Letters, Ed. Sander L. Gilman. New York: The Continuum Publishing Company.
- Germer, C. (2009): The Mindful Path to Self-Compassion: Freeing Yourself from Destructive Thoughts and Emotions. Guilford Press.
- Goldman, J.; Coane, J. (1977): Family therapy after the divorce: Developing a strategy. Family Process (16, pp357-362).
- Goldstein, J.; Kornfiled, J. (2001): Seeking the Heart of Wisdom. Shambhala.
- Greenberger, D.; Padesky, C. (1995): Mind Over Mood. Guilford Press.
- Greene, R. (2001): The Art of Seduction. A Joost Elffers Book, Penguin Books, New York.
- Hanh, T. N. (1999): The Miracle of Mindfulness: A Manual on Meditation. Beacon Press.
- Hayes, S. (2005): Get Out of Your Head and into Your Life: The New acceptance and Commitment Therapy. New Harbinger.
- Heath, C.; Heath, D. (2013): Decisive: How To Make Better Choices in Life and Work. An imprint of the Crown Publishing Group, New York.
- Hojoon, C.; Kyunga, Y.; Reichert, T.; Michael S. (2016): Do feminists still respond negatively to female nudity in advertising? Investigating the influence of feminist attitudes on reactions to sexual appeals. International journal of advertising (Vol. 35; No. 5, pp.823-845).
- Janine, M. B. (1981): The divorce myth (pp.67-71).
- Kabat-Zinn, J. (2005): Coming to Our Senses: Healing Ourselves and the World Through Mindfulness, Hyperion.
- Kaus, G. C. (1935): The Portrait of an Empress, Trans. June Head. New York: Viking.
- Kopp, S. A., (1978): End to innocence. New York: Macmillan.

- Lawrence, A. J. et al. (2009): Problem Gamblers Share Deficits in Impulsive Decision-Making with Alcohol-Dependent Individuals. Addiction (104; no.6, pp. 1006-15).
- Lesieur, H.; Blume, S. (1987): The South Oaks Gambling Screen (SOGS): A New Instrument for the Identification of Pathological Gamblers. American Journal of Psychiatry (144; 9, pp. 1184-88).
- Linehan, M. (1993): Skills Training Manual for Treating Borderline Personality Disorder. Guilford Press.
- Luke, C. (2010): Decision-Making During Gambling: An Integration of Cognitive and Psychobiological Approaches. Philosophical Transactions of the Royal Society of London (Series B: Biological Sciences 365; 1538, pp.319-30).
- Monique, L. W.; Harrison, K. (2005): The impact of media use on girl's beliefs about gender roles, their bodies, and sexual relationships: A research synthesis. American psychological association.
- Nolen-Hoeksema, (2002): Overthinking: Women Who Think Too Much. Henry Holt.
- Philpot, C.L.; Brooks, G.R.; Lusterman, D.D. & Nutt, R.L. (1997): Why men and women Clash and How Therapists Can Bring Them Together. American Psychological Association (pp. 253-296).
- Ruth, B. (2005): Mindfulness-Based Treatment Approaches: Clinician's Guide to Evidence Base and Applications. Academic Press.
- Schwartz, J.; Begley, S. (2003): Mind and Brain: Neuroplasticity and the Power of Mental Force. Regan.
- Scott, B. S., et al. (2007): Positive Transfer of Adaptive Battlefield Thinking Skills. U.S. Army Research Institute for the Behavioral and Social Sciences Research Report 1873.
- Segal, Z.; Williams, M. & Teasdale, J. (2002): Mindfulness-Based Cognitive Therapy for Depression. Guilford Press.
- Siegel, D. (2007): The Mindful Brain: Reflections and Attunement in the Cultivation of Well-being. Norton.
- Smith, D.A. & Bolam. P.J. (1990): The Neural Network of the Basal Ganglia as Revealed by the Study of Synaptic Connections of Identified Neurones. Trends in Neurosciences (13, pp. 259-65).
- Steinzor, B. (1969): When Parents Divorce: A New Approach to New Relationship. New York: Pantheon Books, Random House.

- Thompson, J.K.; Heinberg, L.J.; Altabe, M. & Tangleff-Dunn, S. (1999): Exacting Beauty: Theory, Assessment, and Treatment of Body Image Disturbance. American Psychological Association.
- Williams, M.; John Teasdale, Z. S. & John, Kabat-Zinn (2002): The Mindful Way through Depression: Freeing Yourself from Chronic Unhappiness. The Guilford Press.